ABOUT THE AUTHOR

CHRIS WEST has written widely in a variety of genres. His titles include *A History of Britain in Thirty-six Postage Stamps,* a bestselling business guide, and a quartet of crime novels. He inherited a love of history from his father and an Edwardian "Lincoln" stamp album from his great-uncle as a child. His love for stamps was revived when he found that same dust-covered album in his attic as an adult. He lives in Cambridgeshire.

A HISTORY OF AMERICA IN THIRTY-SIX POSTAGE STAMPS

Also by Chris West

A History of Britain in Thirty-six Postage Stamps

Chris West

A HISTORY OF AMERICA IN THIRTY-SIX POSTAGE STAMPS

PICADOR

NEW YORK

www.picadorusa.com
www.twitter.com/picadorusa • www.facebook.com/picadorusa
picadorbookroom.tumblr.com

Picador® is a U.S. registered trademark and is used by St. Martin's Press under license from Pan Books Limited.

For book club information, please visit www.facebook.com/picadorbookclub or e-mail marketing@picadorusa.com.

Designed by Steven Seighman

The Library of Congress Cataloging-in-Publication Data is available upon request.

ISBN 978-1-250-04368-9 (hardcover)
ISBN 978-1-250-04369-6 (e-book)

Picador books may be purchased for educational, business, or promotional use. For information on bulk purchases, please contact Macmillan Corporate and Premium Sales Department at 1-800-221-7945, extension 5442, or write specialmarkets@macmillan.com.

First Edition: November 2014

10 9 8 7 6 5 4 3 2 1

To Rayna, with love

CONTENTS

AUTHOR'S NOTE

LIKE MANY MEN of my age—I've just hit sixty—I collected stamps as a boy. The adventure then was about geographical space. Stamps took me to all sorts of places I'd never been to: coral islands in the Pacific; mountainous European principalities; African plains where lions and giraffes roamed; space itself, with its sputniks and cosmonauts. When I became an adolescent, other aspects of life became more pressing, and the stamp album disappeared into the family attic. Many years later, it was rediscovered, and I fell for philately all over again, but now with a different focus: It was all to do with time. Each of these little pieces of paper, it seemed to me, was a time-travel machine that could whisk me back to another era. It could do so with its design, with the way it was made, with the political/national story it was intended to tell—and, of course, with the story of each individual stamp. Someone stuck this 2¢ stamp with George Washington on it on a letter in 1884. What was America like then? What was Americans' life like? Who was the letter sent to and why?

Hence this book. It has grown naturally out of a collection that I slowly filled with pages of notes on the history of the stamps themselves and on the eras that they took me back to. I hope you, as a reader, will enjoy making thirty-six of these journeys with me.

I should say a few words to nonphilatelists who might read this book, explaining some technical terms (though don't worry, I'm not going to get *too* technical). Stamps can be divided into two types, "definitives" and "commemoratives." Definitives are the ordinary stamps we buy at the post office and stick on letters. They are on sale all the time, or at least for a number of years until a new series replaces them. Commemoratives are special stamps, issued to commemorate a special event and only on sale for a short while. Years ago, commemoratives were rare: As you will see from the main text, the first U.S. one was issued in 1893, to commemorate (belatedly) the 400th anniversary of Columbus's arrival on San Salvador. Modern commemoratives don't necessarily commemorate anything—they just look nice, as the USPS has worked out that we'll buy a stamp simply because we like its appearance.

Stamps come in two conditions, "mint" and "used." A mint stamp has never been stuck on an envelope or put through the post—and is usually, though not always, worth more than a used one. Used, rather obviously, means postmarked. A special kind of postmark makes a "first day cover," or FDC: All stamps are formally issued on a specific day, and if the stamp is on an envelope and stamped with this day, that makes it an FDC. Such envelopes may often have special designs or "cachets" on them, hammering home the message that they were posted on the day the stamp or stamps first went on sale to the public.

Philatelists often talk about such-and-such an "issue," meaning a set of stamps issued at a particular time. The 1893 Columbus stamps are sometimes called "the Columbus issue" or "the Columbian issue." Stamps from the definitive set produced the following year, the first to be printed by the Bureau of Engraving and Printing, are called the "first Bureau issue." And so on.

Each stamp in this book is shown with its "Scott catalog" number. This catalog is *the* reference book for philatelists, in which each stamp is lovingly numbered (and its many varieties explicated).

I had a clear plan when writing this book, that each chapter would be about the era in which the stamp is issued. I found this difficult to keep to, however, as it is hard to write a book on American history that doesn't start in, or around, 1765. (The fact that the Revolution was effectively ignited by a law called the Stamp Act makes this even harder in my case.) So 1765 it is. However, the United States didn't issue stamps until 1847. I've cheated here: The first few chapters show stamps that feature the historical figure who inspired the chapter but that were actually issued later. What I have kept is historical sequence: The thirty-six stamps are all in temporal order (except one, as you will find out as you read this book).

I would like to thank some other people who have made the book a reality. My agent, Diane Banks, and my editor at Picador, Stephen Morrison, must come first, but others have contributed, too. Daniel Piazza at the Smithsonian was a mine of information, an excellent host when I visited the National Postal Museum, and also kindly provided images of the stamps for our use. Earl Toops shared both his enthusiasm for U.S. stamps and a wonderful set of albums and catalogs, as well as coming up with some great suggestions for subjects. LeeAnn Falciani produced this fine jacket. (Every time I look at it, I hear a Sousa march strike up.) Peter Horoszko did sterling work on getting permission to use the images, as well as other editorial jobs; India Cooper was an excellent copyeditor, respecting the text but ever-vigilant for errors; Casey Maloney has been an enthusiastic and assiduous publicist. Don Sundman of the Mystic Stamp Company and Denis Tucker gave me useful "steers" when looking for information. And, of course, back home, Rayna and Imogen gave unfailing support and encouragement. Thank you, and anyone else involved that I haven't been able to mention by name.

Finally, please get in touch if you have enjoyed the book—or if you disagree (or strongly agree) with anything I've said! I can be contacted via my Web site, www.chriswest .info.

That's enough intro. It's time to clamber into the first of these thirty-six little rectangular time-travel machines and get moving . . .

A HISTORY OF AMERICA IN THIRTY-SIX POSTAGE STAMPS

ONE

Smithsonian National Postal Museum

LIBERTY, PROPERTY, AND NO STAMPS!

George III of Great Britain
Revenue Stamp, 1765

THE UNITED STATES OF AMERICA began with a stamp. This one.

There had been, of course, other American beginnings. Nobody knows exactly when the country's first human inhabitants crossed the frozen Bering Strait from Siberia, or how many waves of such immigration took place: Three is the currently accepted figure, and 15,000 B.C. an estimated date for the first arrival—into a land of giant bears, mammoths, and saber-toothed tigers, most of which soon became extinct. We do know that around the year 1000, the Vikings crossed the Atlantic in 50-foot ships to trade for wood and furs. Their main ports of call were in Canada, but a Norse coin has been found in Maine.

Christopher Columbus landed on October 12, 1492—on an island he named San Salvador. He never actually set foot on mainland North America, but despite this, he became lauded as the "discoverer" of the continent, as a magnificent 1893 stamp issue, the nation's first commemorative set, attests. Amerigo Vespucci, after whom the continent was named in 1507, never visited mainland North America, either (and never even got to appear on a U.S. stamp).

In 1620, the *Mayflower* battled its way across the Atlantic to Cape Cod, its captain, passengers, and crew determined to build a free, godly "City on a Hill."

By 1692, there were more than 10 million Native Americans, comprising around five hundred tribes. To European eyes, North/Central America was part of three empires. The empire of Spain consisted of Mexico, the Southwest, and Florida. France ruled Louisiana and along the Mississippi. Britain controlled modern Canada and the thirteen colonies along the Eastern Seaboard. There was virtually no communication among these empires, and not a great deal among the thirteen British colonies, which were essentially ports on the edge of a vast, unexplored landmass. The year 1692, by the way, is significant because it marked the setting up of British America's first formal postal system—which soon collapsed, due to the difficulties of organizing regular transportation and exchanging payments between the colonies, which had their own monetary systems. (The fact that the man in charge of the new system, Thomas Neale, lived in England and had never crossed the Atlantic didn't help.) In 1711, another, more serious attempt at creating a "national" postal service was made. This one took root. Long-distance communication was beginning to improve, though it would still take a letter a month to get from the post office in Williamsburg, Virginia, to the one in Boston. There were also by this time more colonists to send letters. The population had surpassed 250,000 in 1700 and was growing fast. By 1750 it would be over 1 million, and by 1765, the date of the stamp that opens this chapter, nearly double that. The Spanish and French empires did not share this dramatic growth, nor did the Native Americans, who were beginning to suffer from deadly diseases—smallpox, measles, influenza—brought across the Atlantic by the colonists.

Between 1756 and 1763, Britain and France fought a vast war, arguably the first truly global conflict. Like most wars, it had left the combatants hugely in debt. In 1765, Britain wanted its colonies—which it considered itself to have "saved" from French domination—to pay some of that debt. On March 22, King George III's Parliament passed the Stamp Act, which required that his American subjects pay a new tax. All printing was to be carried out on paper embossed with a stamp like the one above, for which the printer had to pay a charge. The rate varied. A license to sell alcohol was to cost £4, while an employment contract or the grant of probate on a will would be charged 10 shillings. Also taxed would be almanacs, playing cards, and newspapers (taxed double if they featured writing in a foreign language). The penny stamp at the opening of this chapter would have been required on every example of a one-page pamphlet.

Previous taxation in the thirteen colonies had taken the indirect form of import tariffs, but the Stamp Act cut straight to the heart of daily colonial life: It was a tax on information and communication. The response was immediate. The governing body of Virginia, the House of Burgesses, met on May 29 in Williamsburg to discuss a set of "Resolves," the third of which argued that only "the taxation of the people by themselves, or by persons chosen by themselves to represent them" was legal. At the forefront of the debate was a young lawyer named Patrick Henry. During his speech, he declared: "Caesar had his Brutus; Charles the First his Cromwell; and George the Third"—at which point, he was interrupted by cries of "Treason!" Henry paused, reminding himself, perhaps, that he was speaking to get a motion passed, not to incite regicide, before continuing, "May he profit by their example!" The Resolve was passed.

Protests took place in the colonies' streets, too. Stamp commissioners had been appointed to oversee the new tax, which was to take effect on November 1, and these individuals became the targets of rioters. On the morning of August 14, Boston awoke to find an effigy of Andrew Oliver, the local commissioner, hanging from an elm tree by a main road. Attached was a couplet:

A goodlier sight who e'er did see?
A Stamp-Man hanging on a tree!

People gathered and mocked the effigy; in the afternoon, it was taken into the center of town in a procession, the crowd shouting a new slogan: "Liberty, Property, and No Stamps!" Their first port of call was the newly built Stamp Office, a small wooden building that proved easy to demolish. The procession then headed to Oliver's house, outside of which the effigy was beheaded. Oliver resigned the next day.

Similar "liberty trees" sprang up around the colonies. If no suitable tree could be found, a "liberty pole" sufficed, often topped with a red flag or a red conical Phrygian cap, a traditional symbol of revolt. These, naturally, served as meeting points for disaffected citizens. Often such meetings turned to violence: A few weeks after the Oliver incident, a crowd in Newport, Rhode Island, attacked the house of a man who had unwisely written a pamphlet called *A Colonist's Defense of Taxation*. These meetings were initially spontaneous, but they were soon being orchestrated by the Sons of Liberty—a group that became ever more "national" in its organization, at least partially thanks to the Stamp Act. Other, more constitutionally minded opponents of the tax met in October to petition London to repeal the act. The proceedings came to be known as the Stamp Act Congress, the first meeting of colonial representatives not officially sanctioned by the crown. It drafted a Declaration of Rights and Grievances, a precursor to the Constitution and the Bill of Rights.

By the time the Stamp Act was due to come into effect, there were hardly any commissioners left to enforce it. (The last one struggled on until November 16 before resigning.) The act limped along, ignored whenever possible, until a vote to repeal it was passed in the British Parliament on February 21, 1766. The Revenue Stamp that introduces this chapter was no more. But the mood that it had created—of rebellion, but also of unity between the previously disparate colonies— lived on.

In June 1767, Britain tried taxing its unruly American colonies again. It went back to the old idea of import tariffs, raising duties on glass, paper, and tea. However, America would no longer accept even these. Boycotts of British goods were organized. A vicious cycle of public protest and official overreaction developed, centered on Boston. In February 1770, a crowd surrounded the house of Ebenezer Richardson, a customs officer, and started throwing stones at it. Richardson responded by shooting at the crowd, and a ten-year-old boy,

Christopher Seider, was killed. A fortnight later, an argument outside the Customs House between a Bostonian and a British officer about an unpaid bill turned into a full-scale confrontation between Redcoats and colonists, ending up with the former firing on the latter and killing five people.

The British decided to back down again, in part at least. Most of the new duties were rescinded, but tea remained taxed, and an effective monopoly on its importation was given to the British East India Company, an attempt to bail out a corrupt conglomerate that had gotten into financial difficulty. Cue the famous Tea Party of 1773, when Sons of Liberty disguised as Mohawks boarded ships in Boston Harbor and threw 342 crates of tea into the water. In response the harbor was blockaded and Boston placed under martial law, with British soldiers billeted with local families. These measures, which became known as the Intolerable Acts, incensed Americans further: Even the previously moderate George Washington commented that "the Crisis has arrived."

The Continental Congress that convened in September of 1774 was divided between sending further petitions to the king and pushing for independence. In the end, a petition was sent—but a response from London would take months (two Atlantic voyages, seven weeks out and even longer coming back, on top of however long it took the British to make up their minds), and many people weren't prepared to wait that long. Radicals urged the formation and training of armed local militias. Patrick Henry, unsurprisingly, was among these, calling out in another debate, "Give me liberty, or give me death!"

On April 19, 1775, a group of British soldiers set out from Boston to Concord to search for hidden arms. Such sorties had become quite common: The army had been transforming into an occupying force since the reaction to the Stamp Act a decade earlier. Halfway there, on the green of the village of Lexington, they encountered the local militia, who had gathered, alerted by Paul Revere on his famous ride. Debate still rages about who fired the first shot—there are all sorts of theories, ranging from an outside provocateur to Redcoats trying to stop a prisoner escaping. An exchange of gunfire followed.

Lexington was more a skirmish than a battle. Eight militiamen were killed, and their compatriots quickly fled their numerically superior opposition and hastened to Concord, where a better defense could be mounted. Even there, the Americans were initially outnumbered. The British searched the town, finding armaments (though most had been spirited away) and damaging property. While they were doing this, the American force grew in size: The colonials' strategy was to use small, mobile forces that could be quickly augmented by "minutemen," local part-time volunteers. Battle was finally joined at Concord's North Bridge. The British were forced to retreat. After a final attempt at a face-saving arms search, they headed back to Boston, harried with ever-increasing violence, where they were then encircled. The city was under siege.

And all because of a stamp . . .

TWO

Smithsonian National Postal Museum

THE BRITISH ARE GOING

George Washington 10¢, 1847;
Scott catalog no. 2

GEORGE WASHINGTON HAS APPEARED on more U.S. postage stamps than any other individual—including this one, the first issued for nationwide use, in 1847. The actual date of issue was July 1, after which 10¢ allowed you to send a letter weighing up to half an ounce anywhere in the United States. Few people would deny Washington this honor—though the depiction of him on the stamp is not exactly flattering. A number of Washington portraits share this quality. Energetic and impatient, especially when young, he hated sitting around posing to be painted, and it usually shows. He also had bad teeth, some of which had been replaced with ivory replicas, which explains the puffiness around his mouth.

The X on the stamp tells us a lot about Washington, too. It is the Roman numeral ten. Washington, an eighteenth-century landowner, would have had an education in classics. Ancient Rome was part of his culture, as were Shakespeare, the European Enlightenment, and the ways of rural Virginia. One of his greatest heroes was Lucius Quinctius Cincinnatus, a fifth-century B.C. Roman consul who retired from politics to till his fields but was summoned back to power when his country was attacked by a confederation of unfriendly tribes. Cincinnatus saw the invaders off and was offered all kinds of inducements to stay in power, but he went back to his plow.

Washington's life had already begun to follow this trajectory. He had fought as a British officer in the 1756–63 war, acquiring a reputation for bravery by rallying troops under fire in the disastrous retreat from Fort Duquesne in 1757. After this, he returned to his farm, or rather to his estates, which expanded considerably after his marriage to Martha Custis, a wealthy widow, in 1759. Rather than plowing, he experimented with new agricultural methods (and, of course, used slave labor, as was standard on plantations at that time).

Washington's conversion to the cause of independence was slow but thorough. He had found the British regular officers alongside whom he had fought to be arrogant. The Stamp Act and the Intolerable Acts had convinced him that the rulers in London were as bad. By the time musket balls were flying in Lexington and Concord, he was convinced it was time for the colonists to take up arms. When the Second Continental Congress met in May 1775, it took upon itself core governmental tasks such as appointing ambassadors, borrowing money, and setting up a formal army, which, of course, needed a commander. When the debate was held on who should fill this position, Washington attended the proceedings in uniform. The other delegates took the hint.

The new commander in chief's first job was to continue

the siege of Boston. He reinforced the artillery around the city and bombarded the British into submission—though not surrender; in March 1776, they escaped by sea. Washington moved his headquarters to New York, but here things started to go wrong. In June, the British landed on Staten Island; Washington was outnumbered and had to retreat. He managed this with skill, slipping away rather than suffering formal defeat, but was then hounded across New Jersey. At the end of the year, his force escaped across the Delaware, after which both sides appeared to hunker down for the winter. Washington then led a guerrilla raid across the river on Christmas evening, capturing a force of German mercenaries at the Battle of Trenton, which restored honor. But overall, from a military point of view 1776 was not a year of American glory.

However, 1776 isn't about the military point of view but about ideas.

On January 10, a pamphlet called *Common Sense* appeared. In it, the author (initially an anonymous "Englishman," later revealed to be Thomas Paine) not only laid out arguments for independence but staked out a future for America: This was a chance to build a new nation, a republic based on rational, democratic principles. The pamphlet, in clear simple English, sold 100,000 copies and was read aloud in homes, at meetings, wherever people gathered. It convinced many colonists, previously uncertain where to place their loyalties, to join the fight against the crown.

On March 9, a book written by an eccentric Scottish academic was published in London. In *Wealth of Nations*, Adam Smith talked about the newly emerging system of industrial production and competitive markets, which he believed would bring prosperity to many, not just to the already rich. In 1776, this book did not attract much attention in America, but in years to come its message would be taken to heart by the new nation.

Then there was the Declaration of Independence. At the start of the year, Congress had been hesitant to formally make such a declaration, even though hostilities were open and irreversible. No state seemed to want to formally initiate the final break. On May 15, Virginia took the plunge. A committee of five sat down to draft a document, though in the end the writing was left to a thirty-three-year-old lawyer and landowner named Thomas Jefferson. The text was then edited (or "mangled," to use Jefferson's word) by various members of Congress, a process that included removing a long section accusing the British of foisting slavery onto unwilling plantation owners. The second sentence (the first explains why the Declaration is about to begin) is arguably the most famous in the English language:

> We hold these truths to be self-evident, that all men are created equal, that they are endowed by their Creator with certain unalienable Rights, that among these are Life, Liberty and the pursuit of Happiness.

It was the mission statement of a new nation.

The document was signed by the fifty-six members of Congress, although possibly not on July 4, the day it was presented in its final form to John Hancock, Congress's president (a formal role abandoned in 1788). Hancock contributed a particularly expansive signature, commenting as he did so that King George should be able to read it without his glasses. All signatories knew that in signing they were risking their lives, as the Declaration would be seen as treasonable across the Atlantic. The text was quickly distributed around the thirteen new states—using the newly established Congressional Post, whose area of operation extended from Falmouth, Maine, to Savannah in Georgia. Washington read it to his troops, still in New York at that time, on July 9. On the same day in that city, a large equestrian statue of George III was torn down.

By coincidence, as these events were unfolding, 3,000 miles to the West, seaborne Spanish explorer/missionaries were making their way up the coast of a land they had named Las Californias after a fictional island ruled by fierce but beautiful Amazons. (Values haven't changed much in Hollywood.) In March they found a particularly fine harbor and made a fort at its mouth. A mission was built nearby, and five days before the signing of the Declaration, Fathers Palou and Cambon delivered its first mass, an event that is regarded as the official founding of San Francisco.

Back east, the fighting continued. Despite the morale boost of his Christmas victory at Trenton, the new year did not turn out to be a good one for George Washington. He was defeated by the British general William Howe at the Battle of Brandywine Creek and lost Philadelphia. However, farther north, things were going better. The British tried to march down the Hudson from Canada, hoping to meet up with their forces in New York and cut American territory in half. But they were harried the whole way, and when they met General Horatio Gates in Saratoga, still 160 miles north of New York, they were soundly beaten. Saratoga effectively ended the war in the north and, even better, attracted the attention of the French, who were eager for revenge on the British for the defeats of 1756–63 but who had been unwilling to support the colonists, afraid of backing a losing side. Saratoga reassured them that the Americans were winners.

Despite this good news, farther south Washington could only retreat further and find a place to sit out the winter, with a sick, demoralized, ragged army. Murmurs began to run around Congress that he should be replaced as overall commander by Gates.

Washington's winter quarters were in Valley Forge, Pennsylvania, which has since become a symbol of American fortitude and resourcefulness—often inspiring later stamp designs. A 1928 150th anniversary red/brown 2¢ shows Washington beneath a tree at these quarters, praying for the well-being of his troops. By 1976, stamp issues had become more extravagant and a special sheet was issued, based on William T. Trego's 1883 painting of a Napoleonic-looking Washington, officers, and foot soldiers in the snow.

Washington used that winter to rebuild his army's health, morale, and professionalism. The first of these he accomplished with a program of vaccination against smallpox, a killer disease that was threatening to destroy his troops. The second he achieved with his personal leadership. Men were encouraged by this tall, purposeful figure striding around the camp. The moments of prayer celebrated in the 1928 stamp were private; in public, the commander in chief exemplified confidence. The army's professionalism was boosted by Friedrich Wilhelm von Steuben, a Prussian mercenary originally recommended to Washington by the French. Honesty was not Steuben's greatest virtue—he awarded himself a title and upgraded his original military rank, probably that of captain, to lieutenant general—but he was a man of genuine ability. He organized the layout of the camp, including preventing men from digging latrines right next to kitchens. He improved discipline through regular and repeated drills: no doubt unpopular with a force full of former guerrilla fighters, but essential if they were to win full-scale battles. He taught modern methods of fighting with bayonets. For all this, Steuben was made chief of staff and was honored on a stamp 152 years later. When Washington emerged from these quarters in the spring of 1778, it was with an army of revitalized professionals, while his opponents were just tired and far from home.

The war was not yet won, however. For the next two years fighting was intermittent, with no clear advantage accrued by either side. The British turned their attention to the far south and made early gains: Savannah and, in 1780, Charleston were captured. In the latter defeat, the Americans were not allowed the traditional surrender with honor, whereby they could march out with flags flying and muskets over their shoulders. Instead, they were made to furl their flags and march with muskets reversed (pointing downward). Horatio Gates, victor of Saratoga, was then trounced by the British at the Battle of Camden in South Carolina. By September 1780, the redcoats were marching north.

After Camden, Washington replaced Gates with Nathanael Greene, a former Quaker who had made his way up through the ranks and who favored guerrilla methods. His motto was "We fight, get beat, rise, and fight again." This proved too much for the immobile British; their commander, Charles Cornwallis, headed to what he thought was the safety of the Yorktown peninsula in southeast Virginia but was blockaded there by French ships. Washington marched south to do battle. He found his opponents well entrenched but slowly moved his lines closer, pushing the British into an ever-smaller space. On October 15, two strategic hills were captured, one by a force under the leadership of Colonel Alexander Hamilton. From these, the main British garrison could be bombarded. Four days later, Cornwallis surrendered—or got his second-in-command to surrender, pleading illness himself. Remembering what had happened at Charleston, Washington insisted the British troops march out with furled flags and muskets reversed. Their band played a tune called "The World Turned Upside Down."

Skirmishes continued for many months, and no formal treaty was signed until 1783. This took place in Paris, a location that must have delighted the French, who had essentially entered the war to exact revenge on the British. Apart from this pleasure, they gained little else, and in pursuing the war had amassed a large debt, which some historians argue triggered the 1789 French Revolution (during which Washington's ally Lafayette was forced to flee France and ended up in an Austrian jail, while his fellow commander at Yorktown, the Comte de Rochambeau, was imprisioned and was lucky not to be guillotined). Britain simply shrugged off the defeat and started thinking ahead to profitable trade with the new nation. The biggest losers from the war were the Native Americans, many of whom had sided with the British. In 1763, the western boundary of the colonies had been the crest of the Appalachians; in the Treaty of Paris, the United States received most the territories east of the Mississippi.

George Washington could have used his victory for all kinds of personal gain, monetary, political, or both. Instead, once the treaty was signed he emulated Lucius Quinctius Cincinnatus, resigning his commission and returning to working his estate at Mount Vernon.

However, like his hero, he was not able to stay a gentleman farmer for long . . .

THREE

Smithsonian National Postal Museum

WE, THE PEOPLE . . .

Ben Franklin 1¢, 1851;
Scott catalog no. 5

THE 1¢ FRANKLIN, issued in 1851 and in use for a decade, is a favorite with serious collectors because of the variety of forms in which it exists. It was issued both with and without perforations. At different times, twelve different templates were used to print it, and it takes an expert to tell which one an individual stamp is from; there's nothing so obvious as a plate number of the kind you would find on a contemporary British Penny Red, and the stamp's origin has to be established by looking at minute variations in the lettering or in the scrollwork around the edges. Beyond that, subvarieties abound: Stamp printing was in its infancy, and no two print runs were exactly the same. This 1¢ Franklin has even had books written about it: *The United States One Cent Stamp of 1851 to 1861* by Mortimer L. Neinken runs to 552 pages.

Unlike on George Washington's 10¢, there is no Roman numeral on this stamp, just ordinary writing—which suits its subject fine. Washington was patrician; Ben Franklin was a man of the people—his father had been a chandler, a maker of soap and candles. Washington had grown up on the family plantation, which it was (correctly) assumed he would later own and run; Franklin had been apprenticed to his elder brother, a printer, at twelve and left home at seventeen. Washington looked to the ancient world for values; Franklin strove for his in the here and now, ever eager to learn more and make himself a better person. One of the results of Franklin's striving was his list of twelve "virtues," which he drew up at the age of twenty-six and then endeavored to live by the rest of his life; for many years he kept charts on how well he had adhered to them. They were temperance, silence (by which he meant avoiding "trifling conversation"), order, resolution, frugality, industry, sincerity, justice, moderation, cleanliness, tranquillity, and chastity. A thirteenth virtue, humility, was enjoined on him by a friend but is often left off the list; Franklin admitted that he found it the hardest one to adhere to. He didn't observe the others perfectly, either—for example, he fathered an illegitimate son—but this makes him all the more intriguing. As well as developing himself, Franklin sought to help others grow and change. He is the founder of the self-help genre, with his bestselling *Poor Richard's Almanac,* a mixture of factual information and practical maxims such as "God helps him who helps himself," "There are no gains without pains," and "A friend in need is a friend indeed." One can't imagine George Washington setting aside Livy and Herodotus to read this publication.

Franklin was fascinated by the natural world. He was a student of demography, ocean currents, light, waterspouts, and, of course, electricity. He invented the lightning conductor, a stove that gave more heat and less smoke, a swimming flipper, a urinary catheter, an odometer, and bifocal glasses—and refused to patent any of them, arguing that "as we enjoy great advantages from the inventions of others, we should be glad of an opportunity to serve others by any invention of ours."

He was also a political reformer—especially of the postal system, which played a large part in his life. His postal career began in 1737, when he became postmaster of Philadelphia. The system at that time operated around such offices, hubs from which post was sent and to which post was delivered ("post" at that time consisted of about half correspondence and half newspapers and pamphlets). The public had to come to their local office to collect their post—there were no mailmen walking the streets in 1737. Deliveries between offices were made by postriders, couriers on horseback. This system was open to abuse. Many newspaper publishers sought to become local postmasters, after which they would ban rival publications from the mail. Franklin allowed all press equal access to the system. He also ran his office with great efficiency, and in 1753 he became deputy postmaster of North America. He carried out his new duties with the same energy and conscientiousness, extending the fast-growing network of "post roads" (the expansion of the post was the main impetus for road construction in Franklin's era), improving accounting methods, insisting on mail traveling by night as well as day on key routes, and preventing dishonest postriders from running private delivery businesses on the side. He developed ways of clearing the blockages of uncollected letters and newspapers that built up at post offices. He made the system pay off, too: In 1762, it returned its first-ever profit of £1,438 9d. Franklin retained this job till January 3, 1774, when his increasing revolutionary activities—including opening mail addressed to the British governor of Virginia and revealing the contents to the patriots—became too much for his masters, and he was dismissed. However, on July 26, 1775, Congress agreed

> that a postmaster General be appointed for the United Colonies ... [and] that a line of posts be appointed ... from Falmouth in New England to Savannah in Georgia.

Franklin was given the job. The new postal system was a rival to the existing one, the British Crown Post; by Christmas of that year, the Crown Post had gone bankrupt.

Postmaster Franklin was one of the fifty-six signatories to the Declaration of Independence. In 1787, he also signed the U.S. Constitution.

The Declaration had talked of "Free and Independent states," and this model had been put into practice via the Articles of Confederation, an early constitution framed in 1781. However, this loose federation soon began to fracture. Pennsylvania and Connecticut fought a kind of guerrilla war over state boundaries for most of the 1780s. In 1786, a rebellion in Massachusetts broke out, led by a bankrupt farmer, Daniel Shays, and had to be put down by a private militia, as the 625-man U.S. Army was guarding the Canadian border. (It was close to mutiny itself, as nobody had been paid for months; Congress had no money, as it did not have the power to raise taxes.)

Elsewhere, the world proved an unfriendly place. The

Spanish banned American ships from New Orleans—in the 1780s, a part of their empire—and the same vessels found themselves attacked on the high seas by pirates.

A few new endeavors went well, however—for example, the national postal system, which flourished under the robust, imaginative leadership of its third postmaster general, Ebenezer Hazard. His example (in part at least) led many Americans, including Franklin, to the conclusion that there was only one answer to the federation's problems: stronger and better central government.

Not everyone agreed, of course. Patrick Henry thought such a change would take away the liberty for which he had been prepared to give so much. But pressure to create a federal government grew, and in 1787 a Constitutional Convention convened in the Philadelphia State House. Franklin, now aged eighty, was to be a leading participant.

The State House soon became a battleground. There were various factional struggles, but the principal one was between those who wanted to minimize the power of individual states and those who wanted to maximize it. At one point, disagreements became so violent that Franklin called for daily prayers at the start of each session. (This never happened: The Convention had no money to pay a parson.) In the end, however, enough compromises were made, and a committee was chosen to draft a constitution. Its main brief was to avoid tyranny, not just by a new George III but by any subsection of the new nation.

The resulting draft constitution was based on the separation of powers into three branches: legislative, executive, and judicial, a model practiced in pre-Imperial Rome, then rediscovered and promoted by European Enlightenment philosophers. After a preamble that noted that the Constitution was "ordained and established" by the people, a series of articles followed. Article I created the legislature, a new two-tier Congress with the two houses we know today. It gave this body the main duties of government, to frame and pass federal laws and to decide on foreign and economic policy. Article II created the executive, in theory a subsidiary function whose job was to make sure the will of Congress was effectively carried out. At its head was the president, who was also to be the ceremonial Head of State. Article III created the Supreme Court, the judiciary. A set of checks and balances cut across these three functions. The president had the power to "recommend" measures to Congress and could veto congressional legislation (which then had to return to Congress and earn a two-thirds majority, in which case the presidential veto would be overturned). He—a female president was not on the agenda in 1787—would also be commander in chief of the armed forces, as well as being in charge of government appointments (including, of course, the postmaster general, a job that soon became more about political loyalty than about Ben Franklin–style knowledge of the post and how it worked). Congress, in turn, could dismiss any president it impeached and found guilty of "Treason, Bribery, or other high Crimes and Misdemeanors." The Court could rule congressional legislation unconstitutional.

Debate resumed once the draft document was produced. On the last day of the Convention, Franklin made a speech—or at least wrote one to be delivered by a colleague, as he himself was in poor voice on that day—calling for delegates to bury their differences and accept it. He admitted to having substantial disagreements with certain aspects of the Constitution, but concluded:

> *On the whole, Sir, I cannot help expressing a Wish,*
> *that every Member of the Convention, who may still have*
> *Objections to it, would with me on this Occasion doubt a*
> *little of his own Infallibility, and to make manifest our*
> *Unanimity, put his Name to this instrument.*

Thirty-nine of the forty-two eligible signatories signed.

The Constitution still had to be agreed upon by the states, and vigorous public debate ensued. The pro-Constitution argument was put best by the *Federalist Papers* written by James Madison (a former central figure in the Constitutional Convention), Yorktown hero Alexander Hamilton, and New York lawyer John Jay. Opponents fought back, often using Roman pseudonyms—"Cato" and "Brutus" argued that the Constitution posed a danger of power being taken away from the citizen by a congressional oligarchy. The anti case was also made on the streets: There were riots in many cities, with copies of the Constitution being set alight and prominent supporters hung in effigy. Against this backdrop, the states slowly voted, some with more enthusiasm than others. By the end of June 1788, nine had signed, which was enough to make the Constitution into law. The remaining four states soon followed.

The passage of the Constitution made it necessary to elect a president. There was little doubt who would fill this role. The election, with its unwieldy electoral college system, took about a month, but on April 30, 1789, George Washington rode to Federal Hall in New York in a yellow carriage pulled by six white horses and was sworn in on the balcony, using a Masonic Bible opened randomly but appropriately to a chapter from Genesis. In his acceptance speech he declined any payment for the job—expenses only, please. Less admirably, one of his first actions was to remove Ebenezer Hazard from

the job of postmaster general and replace him with a medio-
cre politician, Samuel Osgood, who is now best known for
sacking the nation's first female postmaster, Baltimore's Mary
Katherine Goddard, on the grounds that the job involved too
much traveling for a woman. (She'd been doing it successfully
since 1775.)

The Constitution's opponents continued to argue that it
didn't do enough to protect individual liberty. Madison, in
particular, understood this concern and set about convincing
his fellow legislators to frame and pass amendments dealing
with personal freedoms. The first ten of these became the Bill
of Rights, which was passed in 1791. The First Amendment
guaranteed freedom of speech, the press, assembly, and religion. The Second asserted the right of the people to "keep
and bear Arms"—essential, given that the new nation's military strategy was based on the idea of the ever-ready local
minuteman. (A standing army was distrusted as a potential
source of unelected power.) Other amendments protected legal rights such as public trials, prohibited random seizure of
goods by government officers, and banned official use of "cruel
and unusual" punishment. The Tenth Amendment sought to
curb central power by asserting that the "powers not delegated
to the United States by the Constitution . . . are reserved to
the [individual] States . . . or the people." That "or" would
cause much debate in the future.

Ben Franklin did not live to see the Bill of Rights become
law, but he probably would have approved, being a champion of
individual liberty. One of his concerns with the Constitution
was a fear that the president would come to wield too much
power, and he preferred the executive branch be governed by a
committee. He had died peacefully in his sleep on April 17,
1790. Since then, he has appeared on more than 130 American

stamps—more than any other individual apart from Washington and Abraham Lincoln—as well as on foreign stamps, notably those of France, Britain, and (twice) the former Soviet Union. He was featured in almost every U.S. definitive series until 1954. This includes the 1938–54 "Prexies" set featuring every president from Washington to Coolidge—plus Franklin and Martha Washington. Like the 1¢ that opens this chapter, Franklin definitives are often the lowest denomination in a series—but my guess is that the self-made author of *Poor Richard's Almanac,* who later advised his colleagues to "doubt their own Infallibility," would not have minded this one bit.

FOUR

Smithsonian National Postal Museum

EMPEROR OF LIBERTY

Thomas Jefferson 5¢, 1856; Scott catalog no. 12

THOMAS JEFFERSON BECAME THE THIRD PERSON to be featured on a U.S. stamp in March 1856, with a design based on a portrait by Gilbert Stuart. By then, the postal service was booming, with three times as many letters being sent as had been in 1847. This allowed rates to drop: Americans could now send a letter weighing half an ounce up to 3,000 miles for 3¢. A Washington 3¢ was issued for this, and it became standard for the nation's first president to be on the basic national letter-rate stamp, a tradition that lasted—with a brief, irreverent interruption by a steam locomotive—for the best part of a century. The 5¢ Jefferson was for overseas mail. Of the envelopes that still exist and bear this stamp, the majority are addressed to France, a destination of which the stamp's subject would have approved.

Few would doubt Jefferson's right to this philatelic honor, as the main author of the Declaration of Independence and third president of the United States. He was, like Franklin, a man of restless intellect. But his mind was more philosophical and theoretical: His original phrasing for the first line of the Declaration had been "We hold these truths to be sacred and undeniable," which the more down-to-earth Franklin changed to "self-evident." Jefferson's vision was also geographical: The son of a mapmaker, he sent his imagination roving beyond the Appalachians to the Pacific, across great lands where Americans might one day build what he called an "Empire of Liberty," a process he surmised might take a hundred generations. Jefferson also looked East; a lover of European culture, he flourished in the role of America's ambassador in Paris between 1785 and 1789, and his great personal project, the building of his house at Monticello, was based on the work of the Italian architect Palladio. Monticello was, of course, financed by revenue earned from the work of slaves. The liberty-loving Jefferson is a complex figure.

On returning from France, Jefferson was made secretary of state in Washington's cabinet. He soon found himself embroiled in arguments with Alexander Hamilton, the cabinet's other senior figure. Their disagreements ran so deep that they led to the formation of political factions. Hamilton—and Washington, too, when a choice had to be made—wanted to increase the role of federal government. He understood, in a way that the more idealistic Jefferson didn't, that government could not work without powerful centralized institutions such as a standing army and a national bank. Behind this practical debate lay an even deeper philosophical split, about what kind of life Americans should lead. Jefferson's vision was essentially rural, expansionist, and democratic; his America was the world of the small farmer, settler, and volunteer, proud, independent-minded, but ready to do his or her duty whenever their country called. Hamilton looked to Britain's industrial revolution and wanted to emulate its urban modernity, even if that meant a more unequal, organized, city-led society. To the hero of Yorktown, the Jeffersonian idyll was too vulnerable in a world of aggressive imperialist powers.

The factions soon became political parties, Jefferson leading the Republicans (nothing to do with the modern GOP) and Hamilton the Federalists. These two groups contested the 1796 presidential election, much to the disappointment of Washington, who in a farewell address warned against factionalism and its capacity to seduce public figures away from working for the greater public good and toward the scoring of partisan points. The departing president also warned against excessive government debt and against involvement in other nations' politics, commenting:

> *The great rule of conduct for us in regard to foreign nations is in extending our commercial relations, to have with them as little political connection as possible.*

The 1796 election was won by Washington's former deputy John Adams, a Federalist. As the Federalists also controlled Congress, it might seem the party was triumphant, but they soon made themselves unpopular. Spooked by the collapse of the once-admired French Revolution into Robespierre's Terror, Congress sought to clamp down on dissent. The Sedition Act effectively gave the president the power to silence opposition newspapers. This did not go down well with liberty-loving Americans, and Jefferson coasted to victory in the 1800 election. In his inaugural address, he called for an

end to squabbling: "We are all Republicans, we are all Federalists."

But some people enjoy squabbling. Duels were not uncommon at that time: Alexander Hamilton had already fought
ten. An exchange of increasingly acrimonious letters led to his
fighting an eleventh, with Jefferson's vice president Aaron
Burr. (Technically, Burr challenged Hamilton, but only after
great provocation and a refusal to use any other means of de-
fusing the situation.) Dueling involved a complex code whereby
the person challenged, who had the right of first shot, would
"delope," or fire into the ground, after which honor was seen
to have been satisfied: The challenger had exposed himself to
the possibility of being shot, and the person challenged had
acknowledged this. However, the Burr-versus-Hamilton duel
went wrong. There is no definitive version of what happened,
but the most accepted one is that Hamilton fired into the air
rather than the ground and that Burr, hearing a bullet zing
past him, thought that Hamilton had aimed at him and
aimed back. Some people say Hamilton had been aiming to
kill. Others say that Burr, firing back, intended to miss but
was a lousy shot. What is certain is that Burr hit Hamilton in
the abdomen and that Hamilton died of his wounds the next
day: a bizarre end for one of the most able politicians never to
be president of the USA. The Federalist Party effectively died
with him, though it limped on for a number of years. What
did not die was the conflict between visions of America: one,
that of Hamilton—urban, industrial, and with a powerful,
protective nation-state; the other, that of Jefferson—rural,
democratic, and decentralized.

These visions still duel today—though traveling around
modern cities or along modern interstates, one would have to
argue that Hamilton's vision won in the long run. However,

Jefferson has been featured on nearly four times as many stamps, which perhaps shows that he scored a moral victory: Is his America what the nation would still like, in its heart, to be?

Jefferson's presidency was a strange mixture of success and failure. Before assuming office, he had been an opponent of war. After it, he fought a successful naval campaign against North African pirates and founded West Point, now the most prominent military academy in the nation. Arguably, his greatest achievement was a piece of opportunism.

In 1802, he wrote:

> *There is on the globe one single spot, the possessor of which is our natural and habitual enemy. It is New Orleans, through which the produce of three-eighths of our territory must pass.*

That possessor had been France; then after 1763 Spain; then after 1800 France again. Jefferson sent a delegation to Paris to offer to buy the city (and perhaps West Florida, too, if the right deal could be struck). The initial offer was to be $2 million, but the negotiators had permission to go up to $10 million if necessary. However, while the delegation was crossing to Europe and establishing itself in the French capital, the situation of France's new leader, Napoleon Bonaparte, was deteriorating. Slave rebels under Toussaint Louverture drove the French out of their colony of Saint-Domingue, now Haiti. A costly war with Britain was looming. Bonaparte had once had plans for a new American empire, but this had become unrealizable; what he needed instead was cash, quick. On April 11, 1803, the visitors sat down to negotiate their $2 million deal and received a different offer: all of French America for $15 million—828,000 square miles, half a billion acres, north to the Canadian border and west to the spine of the Rockies. This would effectively double the size of the United States.

Delegation leader Robert R. Livingston had no power to transact such a deal but signed it anyway, concerned that Napoleon would change his mind. It was sent back to Washington—the nation's capital since 1800—to be confirmed. Jefferson understood at once the amazing nature of this opportunity and overcame his usual scruples about whether the purchase was strictly constitutional. Others, however, objected. A motion in the House of Representatives to oppose the deal was nearly successful, ultimately being defeated by fifty-nine votes to fifty-seven. The Senate's reaction was more favorable; it ratified the deal in October, and the Louisiana Purchase entered the history books. Livingston commented, "From this day the United States take their place among the powers of the first rank." (At the time, people used the plural, "their," when talking about the United States, something that did not change until after the Civil War.)

The postal system duly grew to meet the challenge. Two years after the Purchase, you could send a letter from Washington to New Orleans along the new post road. The road was only four feet wide, but that was wide enough for a postrider. It had relay stations every 16 miles, where riders would change horses. The post would reach its destination in thirteen days. Ominously for Native Americans, it crossed Creek and Choctaw lands. Its arrival split these communities: Some thought they would prosper from the trade it would bring; others feared the cultural dissolution that would come, too.

Jefferson also sent expeditions to map out the wilder parts of the new lands and to see what lay beyond them. Thomas Freeman and Peter Custis led their 24-man team 615 miles up the Red River, from where it enters the Mississippi to what is now New Boston, Texas, before being sent back by the Spanish authorities. Captain Zebulon Pike explored the Great Plains and modern Colorado before getting lost, ending up on the Rio Grande, and also falling foul of the Spanish. His party was arrested and taken to Chihuahua—a diversion that enabled him to learn even more about the Far Southwest. However, the greatest of these ventures was that of Lewis and Clark.

Meriwether Lewis had been the president's personal secretary. Jefferson admired his learning and tact and thought he was the ideal man to lead a great expedition to the Northwest. Lewis chose his friend Lieutenant William Clark to be his second-in-command. Lewis was given free run of the library in Monticello—probably the best on the continent at that time—to find out all he could about the journey ahead. But the president's books could only teach him so much. The expedition would be a risky venture into unknown, dangerous territory.

The members of Lewis's newly-established Corps of Discovery formally set off from Camp Dubois, near St. Louis, Missouri, on May 14, 1804. By November they had followed the Missouri River to the middle of what is now North Dakota, where they stopped to build a stockade, Fort Mandan, out of cottonwood trees and to spend the winter there, enduring temperatures of −45 degrees. They were joined at the fort by trapper Toussaint Charbonneau and his Shoshone wife, Sacagawea, who subsequently gave birth to a son; legend has it that Lewis assisted with the birth. In the summer of 1805, the expedition mapped the headwaters of the Missouri and researched the local flora and fauna, the latter including a 600-pound grizzly bear with which Lewis came face-to-face.

What they did not find was an easy "north-west passage" to the eastern coast—but they decided to cross the Rockies anyway, despite the fact that it was already August. Crossing the first great spine of mountains, which we now know to be the Continental Divide, they found more mountains ahead of them. Their late start would have cost them their lives but for help from local tribes—the Shoshone (luckily a band they encountered turned out to be led by Sacagawea's brother) and the Nez Perce. Instead of starving, the explorers were fed, taught how to build canoes, and taken to the Clearwater River, down which they started on October 7, reaching the Snake River on October 10 and the Columbia River six days later. On November 7, Clark made his famous journal entry, "Ocian in view! O! The joy!" In fact, what he saw was the Columbia estuary. It took them eleven days to reach the actual "ocian." After building another winter quarters, Fort Clatsop, the expedition headed for home in March 1806, reappearing in St. Louis six months later.

Lewis and Clark became national heroes. There are conflicting stories about what happened to Sacagawea; some say she died young, others that she lived until 1884. She was also immortalized on stamps, appearing with other expedition members on a panoramic Lewis and Clark 150th in 1954 and getting her own 29¢ commemorative in 1994. Her little boy, Jean-Baptiste, grew up to lead an adventurous life, living on the frontier like his father and prospecting for gold.

Having triumphed in his first term by looking west, Jefferson found his second term overshadowed by events to the east, thanks to blockades and counterblockades by Britain and France, now at war again, each trying to sabotage the other's sea trade and ending up doing most harm to that of America, which still lacked the naval strength to fight back against these two superpowers. Like Washington before him, Jefferson was happy not to run for a third term of office. His secretary of state, James Madison, already famed for his work on the Constitution, the *Federalist Papers,* and the Bill of Rights—and with a vivacious, intelligent, attractive wife, Dolley, who became one of the great first ladies—was the obvious man to replace him and won a sweeping victory in the 1808 election.

Jefferson retired to Monticello, where he spent time improving the estate and working on a new project, the University of Virginia, which he saw finally open in 1825. His gentleman-scholar lifestyle meant he got ever deeper into debt. He had to sell his library to Congress and even considered the idea of a public lottery to help him pay off his debts. Unlike Hamilton, with whom he had fought so many political duels, Jefferson did not enjoy holding a grudge: In old age he corresponded with his adversary in the elections of 1796 and 1800, John Adams, and they became friends. By a strange twist of fate, both men died on the same day in 1826. By an even stranger twist, the date was the Fourth of July.

FIVE

Smithsonian National Postal Museum

BORN FOR A STORM

Andrew Jackson "Black Jack" 2¢, 1863; Scott catalog no. 73

ANDREW JACKSON, SEVENTH PRESIDENT, became the fourth person to be featured on a U.S. stamp in 1863—during the Civil War. The stamp soon became known as the "Black Jack." (The Confederates also issued a Jackson 2¢, the "Red Jack." Both sides were eager to co-opt this formidable character.) The image on the Black Jack, based on a portrait of Jackson by self-taught miniaturist John Wood Dodge, makes him look rather melancholy and, with his Franklin-like high forehead, cerebral. This does not reflect the seventh president's character, which was charismatic, energetic, practical, martial, and combative. He once said, "I was born for a storm; calm does not suit me." The portrait does, perhaps, reflect his constitution: He suffered from chronic intestinal problems, a condition some experts put down to the amount of lead in his body, which had accumulated during many military battles and duels.

Unlike the elite Virginian presidents before him, Andrew Jackson came from humble origins. He was genuinely born in a log cabin, in the rural Waxhaws district of the Carolinas. His Ulster-born father was killed in a logging accident shortly before his birth. As a boy, he fought in the War of Independence and was briefly a British captive, during which time he was ordered to clean an officer's boots and was struck with a sword when he refused. As a young man, he studied law, then went into politics, before returning to the military, where he came to national prominence in America's Second War of Independence.

This name given this war doesn't quite do justice to the complex motivations for it. It was certainly fought to reassert independence from the old colonial master, who was still stationing troops in the remote American North and stopping American ships on the high seas to press any former Britons into the Royal Navy. But it was also an attempt to grab land: Canada from the British and western territory from the Indians. It was also nearly a disaster.

A group in Congress that became known as the "war hawks" thought they could secure a quick win in Canada while Britain was preoccupied with fighting Napoleon. But the Canadians, many of whom were former crown loyalists who had fled north after 1781, fought back. Worse, Napoleon was defeated, and Britain turned its full energy to the conflict. In a humiliating episode, the city of Washington was captured by the newly arrived professional, battle-hardened Redcoats. The Senate, the House of Representatives, and the White House were burned. The famous Gilbert Stuart portrait of the first president, now on the dollar bill and often used on stamps, had to be rescued from the last of these by Dolley Madison. However, Britain had no real desire to rule the United States again, and talks soon began, essentially about securing the border with Canada.

While the talks went on, fighting continued. American pride, badly damaged by the burning of the capital, began to recover. A successful defense of Baltimore inspired Francis Scott Key to write "The Star-Spangled Banner." Pride was restored in full by Jackson's destruction of British forces at the Battle of New Orleans in 1815. This battle was actually fought *after* a peace treaty had been signed, but due to the time it took news to cross the Atlantic, neither side was aware of this fact. Jackson would have been bitterly disappointed had he been told to cease hostilities, as he had a hatred of Britain that dated back to the boot-cleaning incident. In New Orleans he was able to express this to the full, improvising an army—he even co-opted local pirates—and trouncing a numerically superior but ineptly commanded force.

Thanks to his military exploits Jackson became known as "Old Hickory." It's a fitting name. Hickory is native to America, not a foreign import, and Jackson represented a new kind of politics that was uniquely American. Hickory is tough, too. The wood has a unique combination of strength and rigidity—other woods may be stronger but at least partially get their strength from being able to bend under pressure; hickory doesn't bend.

As a result of New Orleans, the nation entered the postwar period in a mood of optimism: The decade that followed is referred to as the "Era of Good Feelings." There was little party factionalism, with the Republicans in charge and the Federalists now a distant memory. With the country's boundaries secure, the U.S. economy began to grow, especially in New England, where textile mills led the way. Other industries—sawmills, breweries, ironworks, brickworks, tanneries, clothiers—followed. The postal system grew with it. The era produced another great postmaster general, the colorfully named Return Jonathan Meigs Jr. (His father's name allegedly came from an incident in his grandfather's life, when he went to pay court to a young lady, who sent him away, then changed her mind and called out "Return, Jonathan.") Meigs insisted the post was there to serve the growing nation, not just to turn a profit, and he energetically expanded the system. By 1823, there were nearly 85,000 miles of post road. Post was also using the new steamships pioneered by Robert Fulton. (By 1820 there were sixty steamers plying their trade between Louisville, Kentucky, and New Orleans.) It used the Erie Canal, a 363-mile triumph of civil engineering that linked the Atlantic and the Great Lakes. (The canal, opened in 1825, slashed the cost of carrying foodstuffs to the East and manufactured goods to the West.) It would soon start using the new railroads: On September 15, 1831, the *John Bull* locomotive, newly imported from Britain, got up steam for the first time in its new home.

These were largely northern developments; the South remained dominated by vast, hierarchical cotton or tobacco plantations, with an aristocratic landowner at the top and slaves at the bottom. Animosity began to build between states where slavery was accepted (and lay at the heart of the economy) and those where slavery was illegal. The Missouri Compromise of 1820, which had balanced the number of slave and nonslave states in the Union, papered over this ever-expanding crack. In the Compromise debate one Georgia representative had shouted at his opponents, "You have kindled a fire which all the waters of the ocean cannot put out, which seas of blood only can extinguish."

So it wasn't good feelings all around. The presidential election of 1824 got rid of any remaining such emotions altogether. Four candidates, all Republicans, ran for president. Jackson was one; the others were established political figures from the East, including John Quincy Adams, the son of the second president. Jackson won 41 percent of the votes cast and Adams 30 percent, but the easterners used the electoral college system to gang up on Jackson and give Adams the job. Jackson was furious and spent the next four years criticizing the president at every possible opportunity, even Adams's best moves, such as purchasing Florida and settling a large part of the boundary with Canada.

In 1828, Jackson stood against Adams again. His supporters now called themselves Democrats, and the name stuck. The gloves really came off in this election—and it was Adams's theoretically more dignified establishment supporters who fought the dirtiest, making slurs against Jackson's wife, Rachel, who was a divorcée and who, due to a misunderstanding, had remarried before the divorce was finalized. She died shortly after the campaign, many said as a result of the calumny she had had to endure.

Jackson won easily, and with him began a radically new political era. The change started on Inauguration Day, when the celebration at the White House was gatecrashed by thousands of previously apolitical rural supporters. (Turnout at the 1828 election had been double that of 1824.) Muddy boots charged up and down the elegant corridors once graced by Dolley Madison; glassware and furniture were smashed; fights broke out. Calls to evacuate the building had no effect, and the only way to get people out proved to be the provision of free alcohol on the lawn. It was like a debutante dance at the Waldorf Astoria being overrun by bikers.

Old Hickory fled the chaos—as a military man, he took no pleasure in such disorder. But he continued to fight for the ordinary people against any group he felt threatened their freedoms, be they imperialist Brits, East Coast big shots, or congressmen representing narrow local interests. He built up the role of the president, arguing that his was the only official role that every voter got to choose. He often used his veto over Congress, something his predecessors had been unwilling to do. He sacked swathes of government officers—including Meigs's successor, John McLean—regarding them as complacent supporters of the old hierarchy. He replaced them with his own men (Jackson's postmaster general, the politician William T. Barry, proved incapable of running a large organization), commenting as he did so, "To the victor, the spoils." Jackson was a passionate supporter of the Union, seeing state influence not as democratic Jeffersonian regionalism but as an attempt by local elites to usurp power that rightfully belonged to the people. An attempt in 1832 by South Carolina to nullify a federal tariff was met by the threat of full-scale invasion of the state. At the same time, he fought a long-running battle with the first U.S. central bank, founded by Alexander Hamilton, which he saw not as a unifying force but as a tool of a small, moneyed elite. He withdrew federal funds from it and placed them with state institutions, which became known as his "Pet Banks." When the central bank's charter came up for renewal, he vetoed it. Jacksonian populism— blunt, irascible, patriotic, meritocratic, and fiercely protective of both equality and liberty—has been at the heart of American life ever since.

Jackson's protection of equality and liberty did not extend to Native Americans. The founding fathers' policy had been to encourage them to assimilate, slowly picking up American ways. But not all of them wanted to do this. Some, such as the Creek and the Shawnee, even took the British side in the 1812 war, which earned them Jackson's hatred. All Indians found their territories being increasingly infiltrated by settlers—then gold was found on Cherokee territory in 1829. A legal battle ensued, which Jackson cut through with his usual forcefulness. The Indian Removal Act meant that the five main tribes in the South would be given new lands in what is now Oklahoma and were effectively ordered to move there. Jackson's act was hotly debated in Congress, where one of its main opponents was David Crockett from Tennessee. (In Illinois, a novice politician named Abraham Lincoln also spoke against it.) But the act was passed, and during the 1830s, various Indian communities were herded into camps and then made to walk hundreds of miles to their new homes. Many died, of hunger, of exhaustion, from harassment by settlers, and, one suspects, of simple heartbreak. The route west became known as the "Trail of Tears." It was not the last indignity to be laid upon America's first inhabitants.

By modern standards, the era's intellectuals made little protest at this. They were more interested in their inner lives than in outer political events, inspired by the philosophy of transcendentalism, best summed up by Ralph Waldo Emerson in an 1836 essay called "Nature," in which he told readers: "Build your own world . . . Conform your life to the pure idea in your mind." Emerson's most famous disciple was Henry David Thoreau. Thoreau's *Walden; or, Life in the Woods* describes two years spent living away from human society—Thoreau prided himself on his ability to "do easily without the post office"—in an attempt to distill what he called the "essential facts of life." Walden was the name of the lake by which he lived in a simple hut, earning a living by doing odd jobs and cultivating crops to eat or sell, reading voraciously and walking in the woods daily. The "essential facts" that Thoreau distilled were the importance of the inner life, the irrelevance of wealth, and the uniqueness of the individual: *Walden* contains the immortal line "If a man does not keep pace with his companions, perhaps it is because he hears a different drummer." Thoreau later developed a political philosophy to match, encouraging peaceful individualism and insisting on civil disobedience if the individual considers the state to be wrong.

Thoreau can be seen as part of an intellectual movement that was sweeping across Europe at the time, but he added a uniquely American touch. European intellectuals tended to have private means or wealthy patrons; Thoreau was self-sufficient and proud of the fact. Though he and Andrew Jackson were in many ways polar opposites, Jackson a public man of action, Thoreau a private thinker, both men shared an unflinching belief in individual self-improvement. Jackson was born in a log cabin; Thoreau found his adult self in one. Both felt the cabin conveyed dignity and a kind of manliness that no amount of East Coast or European sophistication could match. Both have also been rather inadequately represented on stamps. The Black Jack doesn't do justice to Jackson's true nature. Thoreau appeared on a 5¢ stamp in 1967, a year when his ideas were being revisited by the hippies, but the image, with its oddly placed left eye, is bizarrely unflattering.

Old Hickory did not stand for reelection in 1836, but the new Democratic Party continued in office thanks to his former vice president, Martin van Buren, known as "the Little

Magician" for his political skills. (One can't imagine George Washington or Thomas Jefferson sporting folksy nicknames like this.) Van Buren's presidency was overshadowed by his feisty predecessor's. Jackson's Pet Banks had not made good use of the funds he had deposited with them and had backed massive land speculation; a few months after the new president took office, America's biggest financial crash thus far, the Panic of 1837, took place. The Little Magician used up most of his magical powers trying to clear up the mess. Jackson continued to exercise influence in his new Democratic Party up to his death in 1845. His funeral was interrupted by his pet parrot, Poll, which let loose a selection of swear words learned from its master and had to be removed from the church.

Starting with the stamp at the beginning of this chapter, Andrew Jackson has featured on twenty-nine issues—most recently in 1994—making him the fifth-most-represented individual on U.S. postage. Now he is best known for his appearance on the $20 bill—a role that is currently controversial. Liberals object to his part in driving Native Americans off their lands, and conservatives to his battle with the national bank and distrust of paper money generally. If Old Hickory's ghost is watching, it will no doubt be fully enjoying the controversy.

SIX

Smithsonian National Postal Museum

MANIFEST DESTINY

James K. Polk 32¢, 1995;
Scott catalog no. 2587

ALL THE STAMPS in this book are in historical order—except for this one. The reason is that President James Knox Polk never had his own stamp issue until 1995. He did appear in the 1938 Prexies and 1986 AMERIPEX issues, both of which featured every president, however obscure or inept; apart from that, he went uncelebrated until the 200th anniversary of his birth provided the opportunity for a single stamp to appear. He deserves better than this.

Polk was given the nickname "Young Hickory," because he was an admirer and protégé of Jackson. He shared Jackson's background—up to a point, anyway. He was also born on a Carolina farm to Scots-Irish parents, though the Polks were much more prosperous than the Jacksons. Like Jackson, he had a strong will. However, in many other ways, the two men were very different. Polk was what modern management theo-rists call a "Level Five Leader," a quiet, unassuming person unswervingly dedicated to the success of the organization that he or she serves. Such people are often mistaken for weaklings or dullards—until they are faced with some kind of confron-tation, when they turn out to be shrewd and iron-willed. Polk might not have had the deep moral and political imagination of the leaders and thinkers we have seen on U.S. stamps so far, but he was, in his own way, a great president: hard-working (he would start at 6:00 A.M. every day), possessed of both an overarching vision and the ability to attend to detail—and, above all, successful in the ambitious goals he set himself.

Polk was inaugurated in 1845. In the same year, the Young America group was formed, a collection of bright young men with fresh ideas about the nation's future. They rejected the split between Jeffersonian and Hamiltonian thinking, bor-rowing from the former a passion for westward expansion and from the latter a belief in commerce, industry, and tech-nology. They were also convinced democrats. In the twenty-first century we are used to one adult, one vote, but in 1845 this idea, even in its watered-down form of one adult white male, one vote, was still radical, when compared to the aristo-cratic systems that prevailed in Europe and its empires. Young America—and Young Hickory—felt the need to disseminate these values in a world they still perceived as backward and hostile. This feeling was summed up by journalist John L. O'Sullivan, who wrote in the July–August 1845 edition of the *Democratic Review* about America's

manifest destiny to overspread the continent allotted by Providence for the free development of our yearly multiply-ing millions.

The millions certainly were multiplying. The nation's population in 1815 had been around 8 million. By 1845 it was more than 20 million. The economy had recovered from the 1837 panic and was entering what historian Walt Rostow called the period of "sustained takeoff," with its virtuous circle of industrialization, profitability, and reinvestment. The volume of post reflected this, with 38 million letters sent in 1845, as opposed to 5 million in 1814.

Not everyone wanted to work in the new factories, however. The mid-1840s also saw more and more American families selling off their existing homes, buying and provisioning wagons, and heading for the Far West, motivated not by articles in the *Democratic Review* but by a sense of adventure and the conviction that a better life awaited at the end of the trail. Many of them made for Oregon Territory, a vast area that included all of modern Oregon, Idaho, and Washington State and parts of Wyoming, Montana, and Canada. Oregon Territory was in theory under British control but was in practice wild, open, free country. The adventurers took a route—the Oregon Trail—pioneered by the fur trappers who had lived rough in the Rockies since before the days of Lewis and Clark. Others took the original California Trail, which followed the Oregon route about two-thirds of its way, then split off south to Sacramento. Farther south, the Santa Fe Trail led from Independence, Missouri, into what is now New Mexico. After 1846, the Mormon Trail took members of the persecuted sect to Utah.

A family wanting to follow one of these would need to spend about $1,000—around $25,000 in modern money—on a wooden covered wagon, two (ideally four) oxen to pull it, supplies for a journey that would take six months, and basic tools for setting up a home on virgin land: an ax, saws, a plane, hammers and nails, spades, hoes, ropes, cooking utensils, cloth, leather, seeds, knives, guns, and ammunition. The best depiction of a settler wagon on a stamp is probably on the Swedish Pioneer Centennial 5¢ of 1948. (The Conestoga wagon, feted in a later series in 1987–88, was actually too heavy a vehicle for pioneer use.) Once the wagon was loaded, there was little space for items of sentimental value—or passengers: Able-bodied men and women walked or rode alongside. Pioneers set off in trains, usually of around thirty vehicles. It is estimated that 10 percent never reached their destination. The main killer was disease, especially cholera, but also typhoid, influenza, and food poisoning. Fording rivers was particularly dangerous, and accidents involving firearms were common. Childbirth was, of course, hazardous. What hardly ever happened was attacks by Native Americans, especially of the kind once beloved by Hollywood with warriors riding around and around circled wagons making whooping noises and presenting easy targets. The Indians were usually more interested in trading with the settlers, swapping food or handmade clothes for knives and other manufactures.

President James K. Polk wanted to ensure that the destinations sought by the pioneers were also part of the United States. In his one term of office he was responsible for bringing three huge chunks of land under U.S. control—over a million square miles, an expansion even greater than Jefferson's 1803 Louisiana Purchase.

First, Texas. Texas was originally Tejas, part of the Spanish Empire. This ancient empire was crumbling. In 1821, Mexico became independent; in 1836, Texas in turn declared independence from Mexico, which immediately launched an army 3,000 strong to reclaim it. The new state was not ready for war, but a group of 189 independence fighters, both Anglo (including David Crockett, now fed up with politics) and Tejano, decided to take a stand in the Alamo, an old mission not designed for defensive purposes. After a thirteen-day siege, this improvised fort fell. Little quarter was given—a show of ruthlessness by the Mexican commander, General Antonio López de Santa Anna, which spectacularly backfired. "Remember the Alamo!" instantly became a war cry for young men from all over America, who came to rally 'round the Lone Star flag.

The thirteen days proved enough for an impromptu Texan army to be raised and for Sam Houston—a colorful character who had been governor of Tennessee, then married into the Cherokee Nation before migrating to Texas—to be put in charge of it. Outnumbered and outgunned, Houston fought a slow defensive campaign, trying to weary the enemy while gathering his own strength. Finally, he trapped Santa Anna in a river bend at San Jacinto and launched a surprise attack. Legend has it that Santa Anna was "entertaining" the Yellow Rose of Texas, Emily West (a freed slave captured by the advancing Mexican army), when the battle started. He was certainly unprepared, and the fighting ended in eighteen minutes. Santa Anna fled but was captured the next day. He was treated with greater mercy than he had shown others; once he had agreed to Texan independence, he and his troops were allowed to return to Mexico. (The Rose, who had been among a group of indentured servants captured by the Mexican forces, was given her freedom and moved to New York—where she disappears from history into the anonymity of the fast-growing city.)

Texas then applied to join the Union—after which, nothing happened, due to fear in Washington of reigniting war with Mexico. In 1844, James K. Polk made Texan admission part of his election campaign. When he won the election, the outgoing president, John Tyler, changed his policy—but it was Polk who had been the driving force, and fittingly Polk who signed the documents admitting the state, on December 29, 1845.

Polk was also determined to sort out the far western boundary with Canada and bring Oregon into the United States. Extremists in his party wanted him to claim the entire territory, which extended right up to an old border along the latitude of 54°40' with Russian Alaska—"Fifty-four forty or fight!" they cried. Polk realized that a fight with Britain, now the dominant world power and the United States' biggest trading partner, would be crazy. Instead, he instructed his secretary of state, James Buchanan, to negotiate a settlement. The Oregon Treaty, finalizing the U.S.-Canadian border, was signed on June 15, 1846.

Polk's third territorial ambition was to secure the land west of Texas, including California. Once again, he found himself outflanked by party extremists; here the call was for "All of Mexico!" Polk knew what he wanted—in essence, the current boundary with America's southern neighbor—and set out to achieve it. Money was offered, which Mexico rejected. So Polk went to war.

Henry David Thoreau protested the war by refusing to pay his taxes and was put in prison for a day. (An aunt then bailed him out.) Abraham Lincoln spoke out against it. A young officer named Ulysses S. Grant obeyed orders and fought in the conflict but considered it "one of the most unjust ever." The issues were complex, however. The contested lands were sparsely populated, and what inhabitants there were felt little loyalty to Mexico, which they considered a distant power, autocratic but ineffective. Invading American forces were largely welcomed north of the Rio Grande. In addition, other, bigger imperialists were sniffing around the area: The British hadn't given up all hope of grabbing land in California, and in the 1860s Mexico itself was invaded and briefly controlled by the French. And had this war not been fought, what would have happened? Informal skirmishes between settlers and Mexicans would have broken out throughout the disputed territory; these would have been bloody and would probably have escalated into a formal war anyway. Polk's detractors call him a warmonger; his supporters say that he did everyone a favor by creating firm, clear, lasting boundaries between the booming United States and its proud but overextended southern neighbor.

The war was fought on several fronts. California soon fell, and an informal treaty—between combatants rather than nations—was signed by American and local Californio forces. Farther South, attacks were launched across the Rio Grande in several places, most notably by General Zachary Taylor, who captured Monterrey and defeated Santa Anna, despite being outnumbered nearly two to one, at the Battle of Buena Vista. Another general, Winfield Scott, landed a force at Vera Cruz and fought his way up to Mexico City, which fell in August 1847. A formal, international agreement, the Treaty of Guadalupe Hidalgo, was finally signed on February 2, 1848, whereby Polk ignored the increasingly loud cry to grab all of the conquered country, took the lands that he had originally wanted, and paid Mexico for them. Mexicans in the taken lands were promised full rights of U.S. citizenship. Sadly, this was not put into practice, and many of these new Americans found themselves dispossessed and disenfranchised. I do not believe that Polk wanted or intended them to be treated this way; others disagree.

As well as greatly increasing the size of the nation, the Polk presidency also saw radical reform of the U.S. postal system. This was growing ever faster as the nation became larger, more populous, and more prosperous, but its essential nature hadn't changed since 1711. Recipients paid for postage; it was expensive (in 1834, when picking up his mail, a farmer paid his local postmaster for thirty-two letters with a "good milch cow"), and the pricing structure was complex. In 1840, Britain, which had had a similar system, revolutionized its post. Reformer Rowland Hill introduced a low, national, prepaid rate and—happily for generations of philatelists—stamps: the famous Penny Black and Twopenny Blue. A number of American entrepreneurs picked up on Hill's idea: Privately run "penny post" systems began operating in several major cities, the best known being Alexander Grieg's City Despatch Post in New York, which issued its own 3¢ stamp in February 1842, bearing a picture of Washington—the first American, though not official or national, stamp.

As was becoming standard, President Polk brought with him his own postmaster general, in this case Cave Johnson, an admirer of Hill. Congress—still the ultimate lawmaker, despite Andrew Jackson's boosting of the executive's powers—was less impressed by the British example, which meant that reform of the system would be slow. However, 1845 saw the introduction of cheaper, simpler postal rates. Prepayment began creeping in, though payment on receipt remained the norm. Robert H. Morris, postmaster in New York, began issuing his own adhesive stamps (also featuring the image of Washington). Other major-city offices started using these, and a number of outlying offices issued their own designs.

"Postmasters' provisionals" from Alexandria, Annapolis, Baltimore, Boscawen, Brattleboro, Lockport, Millbury, New Haven, New York, Portsmouth, Providence, and St. Louis are now valuable collectors' items. Examples of Alexandria and Millbury provisionals both sold for $550,000 in 2012.

The cause of a nationwide system based on prepaid adhesive stamps was taken up by Massachusetts senator Daniel Webster. Webster is best known as an aristocratic opponent of Jackson and as a master of oratory; his 1830 "Second Reply to Hayne," a defense of the Union against a rising mood of state secessionism, is regarded as one of the finest speeches ever given on Capitol Hill. But he is also a key figure in postal history. His campaigning led to the Post Office Act of March 1847, which authorized Cave Johnson to prepare stamps for nationwide use. A contract was quickly awarded to the printers of the New York provisionals, Rawdon, Wright, Hatch, & Edson, to produce America's first official stamps, the 10¢ Washington we saw in chapter 2 and a 5¢ Franklin. These went on sale on July 1, 1847, from one post office in New York. There are no known first day cover envelopes (ones bearing the date stamp of the first day of issue), and precious few envelopes dating from any day in July: For a long time, the earliest date known was July 10, and then in 1990 an envelope dated July 2 was found; it sold for $100,000. The new system soon began to take off. By the time James K. Polk left office, the number of letters sent per annum had risen to 81 million. America was becoming a nation of correspondents.

The last major event in the Polk presidency took place in Northern California. On January 24, 1848, a week before the Treaty of Guadalupe Hidalgo was signed, a settler named James W. Marshall was building a sawmill on the American River. He noticed a glint in the channel beneath the mill, pulled out a lump of metal, and took it to his business partner, John Sutter. The two men agreed: It was gold. Sutter wanted to keep quiet about it, but the message began to leak out. In March, the editor of San Francisco's local paper marched through the streets of that still-small town—it had about 1,000 inhabitants—holding out a sample of the metal and proclaiming, "Gold from the American River!" By August the news was in the East Coast press, and in December President Polk confirmed the find to Congress. The stage was set for the "forty-niners," who would change the American West forever.

Polk had promised to serve only one term, as part of a deal with rivals in his party. He stuck to that promise—as he did to all his others. The 1848 election was dominated by successful generals from the recent war. One of them, Zachary Taylor, nearly did not compete, as he neglected to pick up the letter informing him that he had been selected as his party's candidate. Taylor overcame this uncertain start to be elected the nation's twelfth president, but he died after just over a year in office. The cause of his death is uncertain but was probably cholera, a hazard of life in Washington, D.C., at that time. This allowed an unremarkable deputy, Millard Fillmore, to accede to the office. Fillmore is probably best known to modern readers for giving his name to a funky district in San Francisco; a venue there, also called the Fillmore, became world-famous for psychedelic rock gigs in the mid- to late 1960s. James K. Polk retired to Tennessee but, like many others who retire from a life of hardworking service, did not live long, becoming another cholera victim in June 1849. He had been an ardent teetotaler, refusing to serve wine at White House gatherings; on hearing the news of his death, the hard-drinking Sam Houston commented that this showed the dangers of relying on water as a beverage.

The man belatedly celebrated on this chapter's stamp was one of the creators of the modern United States—he gave it its modern shape (excluding Alaska and Hawaii) and the basis of its modern postal system—but the country he left was not united. The North was growing ever more entrepreneurial and industrial, its burgeoning cities pulsing faster and faster to the rhythms of mills and railroads. The South, by contrast, plodded on, its sounds the mournful chant of slaves and the crack of the overseer's whip. Polk's massive westward expansion highlighted this divide, opening a fierce debate on whether the new American lands should be worked by slaves or by free men. This debate was to grow ever more bitter.

SEVEN

Smithsonian National Postal Museum

THE REBEL YELL

Confederate 5¢, Jefferson Davis, 1862 (London Printing); Scott catalog no. CS7

ON FEBRUARY 18, 1861, the man featured on this stamp stood on the steps of the statehouse in Montgomery, Alabama, and took the oath of office as president of the Confederate States of America. Less than two months later he was at war with his own former countrymen. The war was to be one of horrific brutality, with a death toll fifteen times greater than that of all America's previous conflicts, including the War of Independence, added together.

Jefferson Davis was born not in the Deep South but in Kentucky, only moving to Louisiana at age sixteen. Like many other American leaders of the time, he shifted between the military, agriculture, and politics: Initially a soldier, he retired to run a plantation after the death of his first wife, Sarah—an event that turned him into a recluse, until politics lured him back to public life. He subsequently resigned public office to fight in the Mexican War, acquitting himself bravely at Buena Vista (where he was shot in the heel), then returned to politics as a senator for Mississippi, serving for a few years as secretary of war under the nation's undistinguished fourteenth president, Franklin Pierce. Such a career might point to a forceful, driven individual, but Davis appears to have been someone who rose up the ladder by being talented enough and by being in the right place at the right time. He was certainly no firebrand secessionist: He described the day Mississippi left the Union as the saddest of his life, and rather than leap on the bandwagon of the newly forming southern nation, he simply placed himself at the disposal of the governor of the state to do "what Mississippi requires of me." Davis hoped this meant a return to a military role but accepted the CSA presidency as a second best. It's easy to see him as a melancholy but sympathetic outsider, plagued by illness (he suffered from an eye disease and bouts of malaria), never quite over the loss of his wife, and thrust into a job that was ultimately impossible. But one must also remember he was an eager advocate of slavery.

By 1860, there were nearly 4 million slaves in America—13 percent of the entire nation and 33 percent of the population of the South. About three-quarters of these worked in the fields, long hours spent both in fierce heat and perpetual fear: Any attempts at escape, insubordination, or even just resting were punished with savage beatings. Behind this physical cruelty was psychological bullying: Slaves were forever being humiliated to remind them of their inferior status and to create a mind-set of what one slave code (state laws) called "unconditional submission." Young men who showed any sign of

rebelliousness would be sent to "slave breakers" who specialized in physical and psychological abuse. Female slaves were
often raped. Slave families could be split up at the whim of
their owners; brothers, husbands, wives or sisters could be—
and often were—taken in chains to a market at a moment's
notice, sold, and never seen, or heard from, again. Those supposed enemies of freedom, the British, had outlawed the
practice in 1807, yet here it was, half a century later, flourish-
ing in the land created on the self-evident truths that all men
had inalienable rights to life, liberty, and the pursuit of happiness.

There had long been protests, but the campaign to abolish
slavery really only took off as a passionate, grassroots political
movement in the 1830s. William Lloyd Garrison founded
the *Liberator* newspaper in 1831 and cofounded the American Anti-Slavery Society in 1832. Books also promoted the
cause: Frederick Douglass, an escaped slave and friend of
Garrison, wrote a bestselling autobiography, and 1852 saw
the appearance of Harriet Beecher Stowe's *Uncle Tom's Cabin*,
which sold 300,000 copies in its first year and became the
bestselling novel of the entire nineteenth century. (Only the
Bible outsold it.) Abolitionism became a crusade, with meetings, anthems (often new words set to well-known, stirring
tunes such as the "Marseillaise"), leafleting campaigns, and
boycotts of slave-produced goods. The movement organized
an "underground railroad" to help escaped slaves find freedom in Canada. (A shabby attempt to placate the South in
1850 had made it a legal obligation for "free" northerners to
return fugitive slaves.) Many of the leading abolitionists were
women, who had previously played little role in public life
and who went on to campaign for women's rights.

In 1854, two great chunks of Jefferson's Louisiana Purchase were organized into territories, Kansas and Nebraska, and these were given the chance to vote to be slave or free. Nebraska—then a huge area stretching up to the Canadian border—would have nothing of slavery. Kansas became a battleground. The violence began with the elections: Armed "border ruffians" from slave-owning Missouri infiltrated the territory and rigged voting so effectively that the proslavery candidate won. Militant abolitionist John Brown and his sons responded by entering a proslavery settlement and butchering five men. Slavers then fought a pitched battle with Brown and his followers at Osawatomie, where more than twenty people died, including one of Brown's sons. And so on: "Bleeding Kansas" descended into tit-for-tat guerrilla violence, which didn't really let up until 1865. Brown fled the territory but reappeared in Harpers Ferry, Virginia, where he and a group of followers stormed the newly expanded national armory, hoping to both incite and arm a slave rebellion. They got virtually no support from the slaves and were surrounded by the local militia, ending up barricading themselves in a small engine house with nine hostages. Next day this was stormed by U.S. Marines led by a dashing colonel named Robert E. Lee. Brown was tried and hung for treason—against the State of Virginia, not the USA—watched by a crowd of spectators that included an actor, John Wilkes Booth, who took the day off from playing a bit part in a Richmond theater to watch. Bizarrely, the fanatically pro-South Booth admired Brown for his implacable commitment to violence. By and large, however, southerners regarded Brown as a terrorist getting his due. To many northerners, including Henry David Thoreau, Brown became a martyr. The latter reaction increased southern paranoia: What other violence would the Yankees support?

While these events were going on, new political groupings were emerging. The old Whig Party that had opposed
Jackson and James K. Polk had become dated and elitist;
more popular movements were forming. The Free Soil Party
and the Know-Nothing Party soon disappeared into history,
but a third new organization, the Republicans, caught the
wave of northern opinion and is still with us today: the modern GOP. One reason for the new party's success was its
nominee for the 1860 presidential election. Abraham Lincoln
has appeared on almost as many stamps as Washington; he
deserves a chapter to himself, so that is what he will get. Suffice it to say here that he won the election, and on hearing of
his success the southern states prepared to secede.

On December 20, South Carolina led the way. If America's outgoing president, James Buchanan, had been as forceful
with this secession as Andrew Jackson had been back in 1832
when the same state had tried to nullify a federal tariff, maybe
none of what follows would have happened. But he wasn't,
and probably the gulf between North and South was now
so wide that such an action would have made no difference
anyway. We will never know . . . Instead Mississippi, Florida, and Alabama followed in early January 1861. A peace
conference in Washington failed. Even as it was going on,
representatives of the breakaway states were meeting in Montgomery, Alabama. Among the decisions they made was one to
elect a president for the Confederacy.

Jefferson Davis was inaugurated two weeks before Lincoln. In his speech, he drew parallels between 1861 and 1776
and stressed his belief in the constitutional nature of the new
government. He held out an olive branch to the North, arguing that, as their economies were so different, there was no
need for rivalry between the two American governments.

However, he went on to say, "If we may not hope to avoid war, we may at least expect that posterity will acquit us of having needlessly engaged in it," and announced the setting up of a standing army. No mention was made in his speech of slavery.

One of the first things Davis did as president was to institute a Confederate Post Office. Texan congressman John H. Reagan was put in charge and proved an able administrator. At first, old U.S. stamps were used, but supplies began to run out. Initially, southern postmasters improvised, either just hand-stamping mail or producing their own locally printed provisional stamps, of which the best known are from New Orleans. Confederate provisionals are collectors' items, but many fakes were produced around the turn of the last century, so they have to be bought with great care. The first official Confederate stamp, a green 5¢ for letters traveling less than 500 miles, appeared on October 16, 1861. It was printed by a small firm in Richmond, Virginia. The stamp is of variable quality, depending on the "stone" from which it was printed; while some are sharp, on others, a ghostly figure of Davis looks out from a swirling mass, as if he had drowned in a pool of duckweed. With its appearance, Davis became the first living person to be featured on an American stamp— and since then, nobody has officially joined him. (The rule that no individual should feature on a U.S. stamp in his or her lifetime was formally made in 1886 and remains theoretically in force, though it has effectively been breached by a 2013 series showing actors from the Harry Potter movies.) A Thomas Jefferson 10¢ followed the 1861 Davis 5¢ three weeks later. The man who wrote that "all men are created equal" might seem an odd choice for a Confederate stamp, but Jefferson had been a keen supporter both of the agrarian way of life and of states' rights. The "Red Jack" appeared in 1863; Andrew Jackson might have been a fierce opponent of secession, but he was a southerner and had owned slaves. George Washington completed the quartet of men featured on CSA stamps shortly afterward. (A 1¢ featuring Jackson's second vice president, Carolinian John C. Calhoun, was prepared but never issued.)

The stamp that inspired this chapter, a new design featuring a mellower Davis, was issued on April 16, 1862. The designer was a Frenchman, Jean Ferdinand Joubert de la Ferté, and a number of the stamps, including the example shown, were printed in London; Europe still did brisk trade with the Confederate states. Later stamps of Davis—10¢; inflation soon began eating away at the Confederate economy—were to show him in classical profile, the man seeming to disappear and a figurehead replacing him. (With a large beard in these later stamps, the southern president appears to be turning into his northern nemesis.)

In March 1861, Davis's initial war strategy was to go for a quick win. Virginia needed to be persuaded to take his side, after which Washington could be attacked. Many southerners thought the northern Yankees were soft and would quickly sue for peace. The Civil War began with General P. G. T. Beauregard's attack on Fort Sumter, near Charleston, at 4:30 A.M. on April 12. The fort could not stand long bombardment with modern artillery and surrendered after a day and a half. Virginia, seemingly impressed by Davis's aggressiveness, joined the Confederacy. The Confederates were now within striking distance of Washington, and the two armies, both hastily assembled, marched toward each other and met at a small tributary of the Potomac, Bull Run Creek.

Southerners weren't alone in underrating their opposition.

Washingtonians came out to watch the armies meet—they even brought picnics and parasols—and to see Johnny Reb get his comeuppance. Instead they heard the infamous "rebel yell" of charging Confederate troops. No recordings exist of this yell, but it seems to have started low and moved up, in three steps, to an elongated, high-pitched screech, described by one combatant as "penetrating, rasping, shrieking, [and] blood-curdling." It shattered the morale of the Union troops, who were routed. At this point, the southerners could have given pursuit and history would have been different. However, the Confederates had suffered losses, too, and were insufficiently organized to follow up their success. The northern army—and the picnickers—made it back to a well-defended Washington.

The year 1862 began with an attempt by the North to capture the southern capital of Richmond, Virginia. It failed, due to the excessive caution of Union general George B. McClellan, whose perpetual unwillingness to commit to battle earned him the nickname of "the Virginia Creeper." However, on the other side of the Appalachians, things began to go less well for the South. Northern general Ulysses S. Grant advanced down the Mississippi, intending to split the Confederacy in half. In early April, he was surprised by Confederate forces at Shiloh, a small village whose name, taken from a local church, means "Place of Peace." Here, the armies slugged it out for two days, before the Union eventually won.

The slaughter at Shiloh was shocking: Each side lost about 1,700 men, with another 8,000 wounded. Many of these wounds were terrible. This was due to changes in weaponry since Polk's Mexican War. Rifles had replaced traditional muskets and were accurate over 500 yards rather than the previous hundred or so. (William Prescott, an American commander in the War of Independence, had ordered his troops not to fire until they saw the whites of the British eyes.) They fired the new Minié ball, which was not only heavier than the old musket ammunition but, made of soft lead, came apart on impact. Entry wounds might be small, but exit ones were massive. People struck by this projectile suffered shattered limbs rather than just flesh wounds. Yet tactics had not kept up with this change. Charging the enemy was still thought to be the way to win battles. Despite the noble efforts of volunteer nurses like Clara Barton, who went on to become first president of the American Red Cross, there was limited support for the wounded, as in previous wars more wounds had been superficial. On hearing the casualty figures from Shiloh, Jefferson Davis must surely have wondered what he had started at Fort Sumter.

Immediately, however, Davis understood that the losses meant that he needed a larger army—and he had fewer eligible males than the North from which to recruit it. He proposed conscription of all men between eighteen and thirty-five. Existing soldiers were to have their terms of service automatically lengthened by two years. This measure was hugely unpopular and also inconsistent with the southern cause, which was supposed to be all about freedom, especially states' freedom to defy central government: This was a Yankee-style central government order. The governor of Georgia, Joseph Brown, fumed that it was unconstitutional but was unable to prevent its application.

This was not Davis's only battle with state governors. The only living president to be portrayed on a stamp turned out to be aloof, inflexible, and prone to meddle and micromanage in some areas (usually military) and ignore others (usually civil). Davis's defenders point to the huge strain he was under. They also point out that he may have argued with his state governors but was good at choosing and motivating generals. On June 1, 1862, he made a particularly inspired appointment, that of Robert E. Lee as commander of the Army of Northern Virginia. He and Lee devised a new invasion of the North, hoping again for quick wins that would give them back the initiative after Grant's successes in the West. In August, the armies met at Bull Run Creek again, with a similar result: a Southern victory. This time, however, Lee followed the win by marching on, not directly to Washington but northwest, attempting to surround the capital. He met with regrouped Union forces near the town of Sharpsburg, Virginia.

Historians argue about which battle had most effect in the Civil War. Gettysburg is a favorite, but it can be strongly argued that the most significant was fought here, on the banks of a small river called Antietam Creek. To understand why, we need to leave the world of Jefferson Davis and look more closely at that of his opponent.

EIGHT

Smithsonian National Postal Museum

FOREVER FREE

Abraham Lincoln 15¢, 1866;
Scott catalog no. 77

THIS DARK STAMP TELLS a tragic story. From it stares the face of a great man gunned down at his moment of triumph—and, worse still for the nation, at a moment when his skills were desperately needed to heal the wounds of war.

Like Andrew Jackson, Abraham Lincoln was born in a log cabin. His father was an archetypal settler, moving in search of better land four times in Lincoln's life. Thomas Lincoln put little stock in education, but his son—despite only enjoying a year of formal schooling—was an avid reader and left home at twenty-one, the age at which frontier tradition allowed a son to cease working for his parents. A local merchant employed him, first as a boat pilot, then as a clerk in his store. Later Lincoln bought his own shop in New Salem, Illinois, but it did not prosper. (When it went bankrupt, he insisted on paying all the debts; most people in such situations headed out of town at great speed.) He volunteered for military service in a brief Indian war; he never saw action but was elected captain of his company by its members. As a result of this new status, he managed to secure the job of postmaster of New Salem. This made him an important figure in the community, but the position was not full-time. He had to supplement his income with casual work of various kinds. This included surveying, rail-splitting (preparing logs to make fences), and delivering letters. Delivery was not part of a postmaster's standard duties, but many rural ones performed it at that time, as they could charge for this service. Lincoln became known for carrying the letters in his hat. He also became interested in politics, and in 1832 he stood for election to the state legislature. He polled eighth out of thirteen candidates.

This hardly looks like a man destined to become the nation's sixteenth president. Nevertheless, in 1860 he became the Republican candidate for president. Since his first election battle he had become a successful lawyer while climbing up the ladder of local politics. For most of that time, however, he was little known outside Illinois; he only came to national attention in 1858 via his debates with proslavery Democrat Stephen A. Douglas, when both men were standing for the Senate. These were amazing public shows, which demonstrate the country's passion for politics in post-Jacksonian America. Special trains were laid on to take people to the seven events where the two men dueled with words. Other spectators traveled for days from outlying farms. They then stood and listened, in their thousands, in rain, hot sun, or wind. The format for each debate was the same: First one man would speak for an hour, then his rival for an hour and a half, then the first man for half an hour. Douglas, the better-known politician, was to have the first slot at four of the events, Lincoln at three. The debates were not about the evils of slavery (though that was a subtext) but about the desirability of its spread. Lincoln was keen not to be seen as an "extreme" abolitionist; his expressed policy was that slavery should be contained in the southern states. Douglas wanted states, especially those in the fast-expanding West, to be free to choose. The debates were also about that perennial topic, state versus federal rights. Though Lincoln became a stronger candidate as they went on, Douglas ended up the winner in the Senate election. But Lincoln's reputation was made, and in 1860 he was elected president (in a turnout of over 82 percent). His votes came almost all from the North: He won 2 out of the 996 counties in the South.

The southern decision to secede after his victory was in many ways surprising. Lincoln's platform had been one of moderation. He was by nature a conciliator and had made his name as a lawyer by finding solutions to problems rather than relentlessly pursuing and breaking opponents. He often went out of his way to see the southern view, once commenting that both sides should "be at the table." However, on his election the southern media decided he was the next John Brown. "This is a declaration of war!" thundered the *Richmond Enquirer.* Lincoln appeared to believe this was merely talk. The South, he was sure, would see sense. Then South Carolina seceded, and less than four months later, the guns opened fire on Fort Sumter.

By mid-1862, the North was in trouble. Lincoln's generals, apart from Grant, seemed inferior to those of the South. Europe, running short of cotton and eager that supplies return to their prewar level, was beginning to assert diplomatic pressure for the two sides to come to a negotiated settlement, which would be a humiliation for the Union. Popular opinion in the North, horrified by the casualty rates, was starting to divide. Lincoln had to do something to regain the initiative. In July 1862, he wrote the first draft of a new proclamation:

That on the first day of January, in the year of our Lord one thousand eight hundred and sixty-three, all persons held as slaves within any State or designated part of a State, the people whereof shall then be in rebellion against the United States, shall be then, thenceforward, and forever free.

It was a masterstroke: The war would no longer be against secession but against slavery itself. However, Lincoln still needed an appropriate moment to announce it. After Lee's triumph at the Second Battle of Bull Run, the proclamation would seem desperate and last-ditch. What the president wanted was a victory that he could follow up with his Emancipation Proclamation: a double punch, right to the guts of his opponent. But that opponent was on his soil, marching up into Maryland . . .

Hence the importance of Antietam. The battle is, of course, significant in its own right. It produced the greatest loss of American life in a single day in U.S. military history, more than Pearl Harbor or D-day, with 6,500 men killed outright and more fatally wounded. One cornfield was so full of dead that observers claimed they could walk across it without touching the ground. The result of this slaughter was a marginal victory for the Union: Lee had to retreat, but McClellan's forces were unable—or unwilling—to follow. But it was victory enough. Five days later, Lincoln issued the Proclamation. At once, Britain and France lost interest in brokering peace; they did not want to side with the slave owners against the liberators. It was the beginning of the end for the rebels.

However, the war still had to be won. Lee marched North yet again in 1863. He was initially successful, as in the previous year, but came up against Union resistance at Gettysburg. The battle was spread over three days: The armies essentially blundered into each other, and it took time to establish fighting positions. By day three the Union forces were entrenched on Cemetery Ridge, and the Confederates launched their famous attack, Pickett's Charge. More than 12,000 men advanced across half a mile of flat, open territory, in the face of sustained fire. It was breathtakingly brave, but the rifle and the Minié ball now meant that such tactics were doomed to end in annihilation. At the same time, Ulysses S. Grant was successfully concluding his siege of the Mississippi fortress of Vicksburg on behalf of the Union. Militarily, the tide had turned.

Four months after Gettysburg, a cemetery was dedicated on the land where the battle had taken place. A well-known orator, Edward Everett, was invited to give the speech and the president to "add a few appropriate remarks" after it. Everett spoke for two hours and eight minutes, at one point confusing the Union general Meade with Lee. Lincoln then got up and said 272 words. His speech was so short that there are no photographs of him speaking—by the time the cameramen had got their equipment ready, the president had sat down again. But those 272 words are arguably the most famous speech in American history. Lincoln spoke of the creation of a new Union, not from scratch, but continuing the work of nation-building (the word "nation" is used five times in the address) begun by "our fathers" who, back in 1776, "brought forth, on this continent, a new nation, conceived in Liberty and dedicated to the proposition that all men are created equal." This work was "unfinished": The war was being fought to bring about a new birth of freedom.

If Lincoln was economical with his words, others let theirs flow in a new way—via the post. The Civil War was the first conflict in the age of mass correspondence that developed after the 1847 postal reforms. Letters to and from combatants still bring it alive to modern readers. Most heartbreaking are those sequences that end suddenly or on deathbeds. G. H. Stephens, sickening of typhoid fever in 1864, wrote to his wife feeling "that this will be the last words, that you will have from me," and enjoining his children to love their mother and look after each other. He died two days later. Private Newton R. Scott, of the 36th Iowa Infantry, was more fortunate, writing on August 19, 1865, that his commander had orders to muster out the regiment and that he would "probably leave for home in ten days." One of Scott's other missives, from 1864, describes the execution of a Confederate spy, David O. Dodd—from whom we also have a letter written to his mother after his capture and sentence, which concludes:

I Know it will Be Hard for you to give up your only Son But you must Remember that it is Gods will.

Many Civil War last letters share both this family focus and this fatalism. Few show much enthusiasm for the cause—on either side—for which the writers were about to lose their lives.

The postal system was, of course, the way in which most families were informed of military deaths. The sight of someone bursting into tears at the post office, having just collected such a letter, became distressingly common, and Lincoln's dynamic postmaster general, Montgomery Blair, organized a free home delivery service in urban centers so people could open mail in private. On the same day that battle was first joined at Gettysburg, 449 letter carriers began their first rounds in the forty-nine largest cities in the Union. Blair also instituted money orders that enabled troops to send and receive money by post without the risk of anyone actually putting cash in envelopes. He introduced the railway mail service, where post was sorted in special cars while in transit along the Union's rail network, and was an early advocate of the Universal Postal Union, which standardized the world's postal system, enabling international mail to travel freely without attracting surcharges in recipient countries. Blair was also a close adviser to the president on military and political issues, which made him many enemies. In the run-up to the 1864 election, these enemies ganged up on him and forced a reluctant Lincoln to remove him from office.

If that year saw Lincoln lose his postmaster, he did—at last—find generals to match the South's Lee and Jackson. Ulysses Grant was made head of all Union forces, while William Tecumseh Sherman was given command of the army in the West. Sherman's capture of Atlanta came just in time to ensure Lincoln's victory in the 1864 election. Following that, he ravaged the South in his March to the Sea, destroying military and civilian infrastructure as he cut a swathe 50 miles wide all the way from Atlanta to Savannah. The song "Marching Through Georgia" was written in honor of this campaign; Sherman loathed it for its glorification of actions he felt to have been vicious but necessary. His own view was much darker: "War is hell."

In spring 1865, Sherman headed north into the Carolinas, moving with his usual speed and destructiveness. By contrast, Grant, farther north, found himself in a war of attrition with Lee at Petersburg—the beginnings of trench warfare, the logical consequence of the new technology that had made the

Civil War so deadly. In the end, Petersburg fell, then the Confederate capital of Richmond, Virginia. On April 4, Lincoln went to the Confederates' version of the White House on East Clay Street and sat at the desk once occupied by Jefferson Davis, who had fled south two days before. Lee tried to break out west toward the railhead at Lynchburg but was surrounded at Appomattox. He had no option but to surrender. Grant and Lee met in the front parlor of the house of Wilmer McLean, a grocer who had moved to Appomattox to escape the war. Lee wore full dress uniform; Grant, workclothes and muddy boots. They shook hands. then began reminiscing. Grant wrote, "Our conversation grew so pleasant that I almost forgot the object of our meeting." Generous terms were agreed, Grant's view being that the defeated men were now U.S. citizens again.

Lincoln's reaction to victory—for this was victory, though fighting in other theaters of war continued for several months—was downbeat, partially due to exhaustion but largely from an innate dislike of triumphalism. Even before the conflict ended, he had made his postwar ambitions known in his Second Inaugural Address:

> *With malice toward none, with charity for all ... let us strive on to finish the work we are in, to bind up the nation's wounds ... to do all which may achieve and cherish a just and lasting peace among ourselves and with all nations.*

A few nights after Appomattox, Lincoln had had a dream of seeing a corpse and being told it was the president's. He was not a man to let such things affect his actions, though he admitted to being "strangely annoyed by it" afterward. On

Good Friday, April 14, he and his wife, Mary, went to Ford's Theatre to see the comedy *Our English Cousin*. On arrival in his box—late—he was given a standing ovation by the crowd. Around 10:25, John Wilkes Booth approached the presidential box; well respected as an actor, he was not stopped. Booth knew the play and waited until its most popular line, when people would be laughing loudest, before bursting into the box and shooting the president in the head at point-blank range with a .44 derringer pistol. He then leaped down onto the stage, shouted *"Sic semper tyrannis"* ("That is what always happens to tyrants"), and made his escape backstage. Lincoln was taken to a boardinghouse across the road—his condition made it impossible to transport him any farther—and died at 7:30 the next morning.

This stamp, created by the National Bank Note Company from photographs by C. S. German and Mathew Brady, was issued exactly a year after Lincoln's death, a year being the standard period of mourning at the time. It is halfway between a commemorative and a definitive: Issued with a specific purpose (to commemorate the president), it became part of the standard set of stamps one would buy at a post office year in and year out (the definitives); its main use was to send letters overseas. On it, the great man seems gaunt and worn down by the responsibilities of war.

Lincoln was a visionary; he understood his country's need to reengage with its past, not in a narrow way but in a way that constantly refreshes and reinvigorates. He understood America's massive potential for power but also a deeper truth, that without moral force behind it, such power is meaningless. When people are asked to nominate the greatest president, the man on this 15¢ stamp is still the most common choice.

NINE

Smithsonian National Postal Museum

IRON HORSE, WILD WEST

Locomotive 3¢, 1869;
Scott catalog no. 114

THE LAST CONFEDERATE GENERAL to surrender was Stand Watie, a Cherokee, on June 23, 1865. Less than a month later, the first rails were spiked (attached to the ground with iron pegs) on the westward arm of the Transcontinental Railroad.

The stamp above was not issued to celebrate this project, though it came out in 1869, the year of the railroad's completion. It was just an ordinary definitive—or perhaps I should say an extraordinary definitive, as it was part of a groundbreaking series. Up until this point, every American stamp had borne the likeness of a national figure. The 1869 issue was different. The men destined to be the "big three" of U.S. stamps—Franklin, Washington, and Lincoln—featured, but so did a whole new set of subjects selected to instill pride in the newly reunited nation. These included a Pony Express rider at full gallop on the 2¢, the American shield and eagle on a 10¢, a steamship on the 12¢, the landing of Columbus on the 15¢, the signing of the Declaration of Independence on the 24¢, and the shield, eagle, and flags on the 30¢. The "flagship" standard letter rate 3¢ featured this mighty machine, a 24-tonner from the Baldwin works in Pennsylvania, then the biggest locomotive manufacturer in the USA.

In 1860, a railroad map of America was a strange lopsided thing, with the East, especially the Northeast, crisscrossed with lines but almost nothing west of the Mississippi. However, a transcontinental rail link had long been imagined. The Young America group had campaigned for it. Land was bought from Mexico in 1854—the Gadsden Purchase—to accommodate a southern railroad, but as North-South tension rose, the project became politically impossible. A suggested northern route essentially followed that of Lewis and Clark but was considered too vulnerable to winter. A central route became the winner by default—but nobody was sure how it would cross the Sierra Nevada, the massive wall of granite that hems in California.

A trail had already been blazed by the rider on the 2¢ stamp. The Pony Express is a key part of both postal and frontier history. During its eighteen months of operation—the legend has lasted much longer than the actual service, which never became profitable—brave young men carried over 30,000 items of mail from St. Joseph, Missouri, to Sacramento, California. They did so in all weather conditions, proving that the great barrier could be crossed. However, their route had taken them high into the mountains, up and down steep slopes. No railroad could imitate them. Was there an alternative?

In July 1860, Theodore Judah, an ambitious engineer,

climbed the Donner Pass in the high Sierra. Fourteen years earlier a wagon train had been trapped here by snow and the travelers had ended up resorting to cannibalism to survive, but Judah realized that, with bold civil engineering, this was a route that a railroad could use. He then found backers for the project and took the idea to Washington, where Lincoln, eager to link free California to the North, signed the Pacific Railroad Act on July 1, 1862. Judah later fell out with the money men and ironically died of fever contracted on a journey east from San Francisco by what was at the time still the most practical passenger route—via Panama.

The railroad would be built by two private companies, the Central Pacific working eastward from Sacramento and the Union Pacific working westward from Council Bluffs, a planned railroad terminus just across the Missouri River from Omaha. But this vast private undertaking would benefit from huge federal support. The government granted bonds to the companies at a fixed rate: $16,000 per mile across flat lands, $32,000 per mile in foothills, and $48,000 per mile in mountains. (A professor of geology was persuaded to declare the gently sloping Sacramento Valley "mountainous.") In addition, wildly generous land grants were made to the companies, 10 miles on either side of the track.

The Central Pacific began work on January 8, 1863. Progress was slow until Chinese immigrant miners were recruited. These men were soon blasting and hacking their way up into the Sierra. They had to build thirteen tunnels through the granite, a feat that had never been accomplished before. (The longest, under the crest of the mountains, was 553 yards long.) They had to carve routes out from the sheer sides of gorges, in one case with a drop of 2,000 feet below: Workers would be lowered down the cliff face in handwoven baskets, drill holes and fill them with powder, light the fuse, then yell to be pulled up. Fatalities were not uncommon; it is estimated that over 1,200 Chinese died building the railroad.

Meanwhile the Union Pacific had started west from Council Bluffs. Initially, they had an easier time of it, following the old Oregon Trail up the valley of Nebraska's Platte River. But they ran into trouble with Indians, who understood the destruction the railroad would bring to their way of life. Sioux or Cheyenne raiders would attack mail trains and surveying parties, and the line was often sabotaged. But this was not enough to stop progress: The Union Pacific's largely Irish workforce proved as dogged as the Central Pacific's Chinese. At what is now Cheyenne, Wyoming, the railroad began to climb into the Rockies; by April 1868, it had reached Sherman Summit, 8,242 feet above sea level, the highest point on the line—and at the time, the highest railroad track in the world. The two companies then found themselves in a race across the rough land between the two great ranges. A newspaper described the process of speed-laying track:

> A light car, drawn by a single horse, gallops up to the front with its load of rails. Two men seize the end of a rail and start forward, the rest of the gang taking hold by twos, until it is clear of the car. They come forward at a run. At the word of command the rail is dropped in its place . . . Less than thirty seconds to a rail for each gang, and so four rails go down to the minute . . . Close behind the gang come the gaugers, spikers, and bolters, and a lively time they make of it.

The lines grew ever closer, and in April 1869 the government forced the companies to agree on a meeting place,

Promontory Point in Utah. A month later, in a grand ceremony, the governor of California (and president of the Central Pacific), Leland Stanford, raised a mallet to drive home a golden spike, the last of over 7 million on the line. He brought the mallet down with a fulsome swing—and missed. Nevertheless, the word "done" was telegraphed both east and west, and the 1,776-mile (what other length could such an American icon be?) Transcontinental Railroad was declared open. The nation, North and South, united to celebrate with cannons, parades—Chicago's was 7 miles long—fireworks, church services, and the ringing of the Liberty Bell.

Locomotives like the one on this stamp began making their journeys across the West. They were built for transcontinental endurance, not speed. There was no need for aerodynamic streamlining, so features on the outside of the boiler could mushroom: the huge smokestack; the wide-windowed cab; the clanging bell; the cowcatcher at the front to push aside impediments on the line, from rocks to wandering buffalo. The only small things were the wheels at the front, which, articulated to negotiate winding tracks across difficult terrain, made the engine hard to derail.

The railroad brought settlers, building materials, manufactured goods—and, of course, the post: public and private communication via newspapers and letters. The railroad changed geography; it created new stories and archetypes, including that of the cowboy. These men herded cattle a thousand miles across the open plains from the ranchlands of Texas to the railroad, to be put on wagons and shipped east, notably to Philip Danforth Armour's vast meatpacking factory in Chicago, which had opened in 1867. While cowboys are often depicted as "rugged individualists," herding was in fact a team business. A dozen or so men would be responsible for moving several thousand animals, working around the clock, herding by day and keeping guard at night. The journey took about two months across sparsely populated land.

When they reached the railheads, the boys wanted to enjoy themselves. The first of the West's "cow towns" was Abilene, Kansas. By 1870, it had a population of fewer than 1,000—and seventeen saloons and twelve dance halls. Abilene's first marshal, Thomas J. Smith, was shot when trying to serve a summons for murder to two local farmers, one of whom then hacked his head off with an ax; he was replaced by "Wild Bill" Hickok, famous for his run-ins with Phil Coe and John Wesley Hardin (to whose name Bob Dylan added a *g* a century later). Hardin shot a man in a hotel for snoring too loudly and was run out of town by Hickok. Coe, who owned one of the seventeen saloons, had a sign outside his bar that showed a bull with a huge penis. Local residents objected, and Hickok sent men in to repaint the sign. The affair ended in a gunfight, in which Hickok killed not only Coe but his own deputy, whom he mistook for an outlaw.

If the Baldwin 24-tonner helped make the cowboy, it destroyed the Indian. (Not that cowboys and Indians were real enemies; some cowboys were Indian, and Indians let the herds cross their land, charging a small fee for permission.)

One way it did this was by hastening the extermination of the buffalo. The Great Plains once swarmed with these creatures, as many as 50 million according to some estimates. The Plains' original inhabitants relied on them for survival (for meat, obviously, but no part was wasted; even the brains were used to soften the hide for clothing) but also saw buffalo as sacred; Native American culture had a profound sense of unity with the land and its creatures. However, the great beast was no match for the modern bullet. The buffalo also had an odd habit: Once one was killed, its fellows clustered around it, making them ridiculously easy prey. The new railroad began to take eastern city-dwellers to live the raw, pulsating adventure of the Wild West by sitting at a train window shooting large, stationary animals at close range. Then commerce of a different kind moved in. Just like the Indians, the developing industrial system found a use for every part of the creature— the meat for food, the hides for leather, the bones for fertilizer, the horns for buttons, the hooves for glue—all on a massive scale, and all hauled east on the railroad. Numbers began to plummet.

The other way the railroad destroyed Indian life was through settlement. The Black Hills of Dakota were sacred ground for the Lakota people, a tribe of the Sioux, and had been promised to them in the Treaty of Fort Laramie in 1868. But there had also long been rumors of gold in the hills, and in 1874 a U.S. Army lieutenant colonel named George Armstrong Custer led an expedition to investigate. (As was customary, he was frequently addressed as "General," the brevet rank he held during the Civil War.) They only found small quantities, but enough to attract prospectors, who found much more. Word got out, and trainloads of gold-seekers poured into the sacred lands; by fall of that year, 15,000 were there. The army tried to evacuate them while protecting them from the angry Lakota but did not have enough soldiers for this complex task—a legacy of the founding fathers' dislike of large standing armies: There were no eager irregulars waiting to join the troops at a minute's notice in the middle of South Dakota. The government then offered to buy the Black Hills but was turned down by the Lakota chief, Sitting Bull. By December 1875, the government had decided it would no longer try to stop the settler invasion and ordered the Lakota onto a reservation by the end of January. Given the wintry conditions, this was an impossible task for the Indians to comply with—even if they wanted to, which Sitting Bull did not. War became inevitable.

In the spring of 1876, three army columns marched into the Black Hills. One was the 7th Cavalry, led by Custer. Custer was a brave fighter but took his aggression too far. Finding the Lakota encamped on the Little Bighorn River, he attacked with men still tired after a long march. The Lakota were ready and fought back; the general and his troop of 270 men were forced to retreat to a ridge and to make their famous Last Stand. No exact details of the fighting are known, as neither Custer nor any of his soldiers survived.

Little Bighorn was a defeat for the U.S. Army, but a battle lost in a war that would ultimately be won by sheer numbers and by technology. In the same month as Custer's death, June 1876, the Transcontinental Express made its first unbroken journey from the Atlantic to the Pacific. (Between 1869 and 1876, passengers had had to change trains to make the trip; up until 1873 this had included taking a ferry across the Missouri.) Lewis and Clark had spent a year getting from Camp Dubois to the West Coast. Similar journeys had taken the pioneers of the 1840s three to six months. The Pony Express had needed ten days to get mail across the western half of the country. The new railroad service, pulled by the subject of the stamp that opens this chapter, went from Grand Central Station to San Francisco in 83 hours and 39 minutes.

TEN

Smithsonian National Postal Museum

RECONSTRUCTION

Edwin M. Stanton 7¢, 1871;
Scott catalog no. 138

SURPRISINGLY, THE 1869 PICTORIAL definitive issue described in the last chapter was not a success, though the stamps are nowadays much loved by collectors. People at the time thought that pictures of engines, steamships, and Pony Express riders lacked gravitas. Maybe displacing George Washington from the standard 3¢ letter rate had not been such a great idea . . . After thirteen months of criticism, the Post Office was so stung that it went back to portraits of dead, eminent men. It did so in a particularly formal way, too: The luminaries were all shown in stiff, sculptural profiles like marble busts in a museum. It wasn't till 1875 that former president Zachary Taylor was allowed to turn and face the stamp user. By the 1890 issue, half the subjects had been unfrozen; things softened further in 1902 when Martha Washington was allowed to join this exclusive all-male club. Only in 1922 did pictorial definitives reappear on the U.S. Mail.

The stamp above comes from the high point of this marble bust period: 1873. It features Edwin M. Stanton, Lincoln's secretary of war and the man who, at the president's bedside when he died, made the famous comment "Now he belongs to the ages." (He may have said "angels"—but the generally accepted quote is much more resonant.) Stanton is a key figure in the story of the impeachment of Andrew Johnson, which is in turn a key event in the postbellum history of the South. To understand these stories—and this stamp—we have to go back to that tragic morning of Easter Saturday, 1865.

In the preceding weeks, Lincoln had made plans for peacemaking. The Thirteenth Amendment was already making its way through Congress, outlawing slavery and effectively making the Emancipation Proclamation law. A Freedmen's Bureau had been set up, to help former slaves in various ways such as by enforcing proper employment contracts, reuniting split families, and, most importantly, setting up free schools. He also had a plan under way to get the southern states quickly back into the fold: Once 10 percent of a state's population swore an oath of allegiance, that state could be readmitted to the Union.

Looking back, these plans were overly idealistic. The nation was still reeling from the war and deeply polarized. Had he lived, one feels, Lincoln would have become aware of this and, in his usual way, changed policies to suit the emerging needs of the time. However, the vice president who replaced him, Andrew Johnson, lacked Lincoln's capacity for self-criticism and change. Johnson simply followed the existing plans. He also copied Lincoln's approach to Congress, which had been dictatorial—necessary, perhaps, in time of war, but not what was required in peace. Again, one feels Lincoln would have adapted his leadership style to the new realities. Johnson didn't.

The southern states soon made it clear that they had no intention of playing the role of humble losers grateful for Lincoln's and Johnson's magnaminity. Instead, they began passing laws, on a state-by-state basis, that ostensibly dealt with vagrancy but actually sought to re-create the conditions of slavery as closely as possible without actually violating the Thirteenth Amendment. African Americans were not allowed to carry weapons, testify in court against whites, or serve on juries. If unemployed, they could be prosecuted and set to work on a plantation for a tiny wage.

Johnson's reaction to this was to do nothing. Congress passed a civil rights act making all U.S. citizens equal before the law; Johnson vetoed it. (Congress then overturned the veto.) A bill to extend the Freedmen's Bureau—it had originally only been planned to last a year—went through the same process. Meanwhile Johnson pressed ahead with Lincoln's plans to readmit former Confederate states into the machinery of government with few conditions. Soon many in Johnson's Republican Party had had enough. Thaddeus Stevens and Charles Sumner, passionate abolitionists who were horrified that the slaughter of the Civil War seemed to be fast turning into an irrelevance, founded a splinter group, the Radical Republicans, and their candidates scored huge gains in the 1866 congressional elections. On January 3, 1867, Congress introduced the Military Reconstruction Act, dividing the old Confederacy into five districts and appointing commanders for each, who were to oversee the registration of voters, black and white, and who could impose martial law if this process were resisted. Johnson responded by trying to fire these commanders and their boss, the man on this stamp, Secretary of

War Stanton. Congress, in turn, impeached Johnson for "high crimes and misdemeanors." In a dramatic impeachment vote, seven Republicans broke party ranks and voted not guilty; Johnson was cleared by a majority of one. However, the presidency lost the power it had gained under Jackson, Polk, and Lincoln; For the rest of the century, Congress would be the more powerful arm of government.

Not surprisingly, Johnson did not stand for reelection in 1868. The Republican candidate was General Grant, victor of Vicksburg and Fredericksburg, who won, though by a smaller proportion of the popular vote than expected. The work of reconstruction accelerated. In 1870, the Fifteenth Amendment declared that "the right of citizens of the United States to vote shall not be denied or abridged by the United States or by any State on account of race, color, or previous condition of servitude." (Gender remained a different matter.) In the same year, Hiram Rhodes Revels became the first African American to sit in the Senate, representing Mississippi. During Grant's eight-year presidency the Freedmen's Bureau set up more than 4,000 schools, which were attended by 250,000 children. Two thousand black men achieved public office. By 1873, South Carolina's House of Representatives had 123 members, 100 of them of African descent.

Despite these strides, life for most black southerners remained harsh. The system of slavery was largely replaced by sharecropping: Freedmen were lent land, basic accommodation, seed, tools, and (if they were lucky) a mule, in return for which they had to yield a proportion—often half—of the crop to the lender at harvest time. The cropper had to borrow money to survive during the year. Although the Ku Klux Klan was outlawed in 1871, white supremacist groups continued to flourish, driving black farmers off land, intimidating black (or any

Republican) voters, and trying to close schools and churches by whatever means they could, including murder and arson.

Southern whites suffered, too. More than a quarter of a million young southern men had died in the war, and many others had been horribly wounded. The land had been devastated; the economy had collapsed; old values had collapsed as well, and with them a whole way of life—one doesn't have to be an apologist for slavery to feel sorry for Ashley and Melanie Wilkes. Southerners saw an influx of northern "carpetbaggers," named after a popular kind of luggage made from old carpet, which the new arrivals intended to fill with money as soon as possible, buying southern assets at fire-sale prices or grabbing political office in the name of Reconstruction. (Hiram Rhodes Revels wrote a furious letter to Grant complaining about this.) They saw southern "scalawags" (a term originally used for farm animals) co-operating with these people and making fortunes. Meanwhile the price of cotton on world markets kept falling, which did nobody in the South any good, black or white.

In 1873, the momentum of Reconstruction began to falter. The nation suffered a financial crash, after which the North's priorities became more about reconstructing its own economy. In the 1874 congressional elections the South voted Democrat, appearing to endorse an anti-Reconstruction ticket. Northerners, seeing this but not realizing that the results were skewed by rampant voter intimidation from white supremacists, thought that the apparently enfranchised black voters didn't want Radical Republican rule any longer. On top of this, the party of Reconstruction began to lose moral authority through a series of financial scandals, including one involving Postmaster General John Creswell and a mail contractor, George Chorpenning, where $267,000 of public money mysteriously disappeared.

The 1876 presidential election appeared to be won by Democrat Samuel J. Tilden, but there were problems with a number of the results—especially in Florida—and in the end, Tilden offered a deal to the Republican candidate, Rutherford B. Hayes: Take your troops out of the South and you can have the presidency. The deal was done. Reconstruction was over.

As the century continued, southern states began passing "Jim Crow" laws—the name of the first popular blackface minstrel character, created by Dan Rice around 1830—segregating schools and other public places, and reintroducing antebellum bans on mixed marriages. Barriers to black voting were erected: poll taxes and literacy tests, the latter complete with "grandfather clauses" that allowed illiterate white voters to avoid them as long as they could prove they were descended from someone who could have voted in 1867. A nadir of race relations was reached in 1895 with the *Plessy v. Ferguson* judgment, in which the arrest of a mixed-race man for traveling in a whites-only railroad carriage was upheld by the U.S. Supreme Court. The State of Louisiana, the Court argued, had a perfect right to maintain such "separate but equal" facilities. The lynchings of African Americans who dared stand up to the old order—for example, men seen walking out with white women—continued.

However, new ways and new ideals began slowly to sprout from the old cotton fields. On July 4, 1881, a school for black teachers was opened by two men, one a former slave and the other a former slave owner, in Tuskegee, Alabama. The premises were a shack with a leaky roof, but the principal (who gave his first lessons under an umbrella) was the twenty-five-year old Booker T. Washington. Washington was ambitious for the school. The next year, he organized a loan to purchase an abandoned plantation nearby—a symbolic act, though the pragmatic Washington was much more interested in what he could do with the land than in any gesture. He set students to work turning this into a campus: Washington was a passionate believer in the elevating power of skilled manual labor and in self-sufficiency, both for the individual and the institution. He was also a shrewd fund-raiser. By 1888, the school—which would eventually become Tuskegee University—had 400 students, and by 1906 more than 1,500. If President Rutherford B. Hayes couldn't reconstruct the South, Booker T. Washington was going to do it, craftsman by craftsman.

Washington's approach was to call for African Americans to ignore politics and get on with making their way in the world. Others argued for a different route: Historian and sociologist W. E. B. du Bois believed in a political struggle led by an elite, the "talented tenth." Still others found support in communities via their churches, which also doubled as schools and colleges.

During this period, the South made some economic progress, too. In the 1880s, the region doubled its railroad mileage. The city of Birmingham, Alabama, boomed because of its new steel industry. Old industries, like tobacco, were modernized by men like James B. Duke, who built the American Tobacco Company, amassing a huge fortune he later bequeathed in order to found Duke University. Textile mills moved south, in search of cheaper labor and to be nearer the cotton.

Overall, however, the story of the South, from 1865 into the new century and beyond remained a troubled one. Though Edwin M. Stanton himself cannot be accused of so doing, having died in 1869, his cold, official stamp can be seen as a kind of turning away from the unhappiness, as if it is all too much to bear.

ELEVEN

Smithsonian National Postal Museum

NUMBER ONE

Columbus 400th Anniversary $5, 1893; Scott catalog no. 245

FOR NEARLY HALF A CENTURY, the U.S. Post Office did not issue commemorative stamps. The 1866 15¢ Lincoln was a commemoration of the slain president but took its place among the nation's definitive stamp series. The same happened when, in 1881, President James A. Garfield was assassinated, this time by a disappointed job-seeker—the curse of Andrew Jackson's politicization of the government appointments system. But as the nineteenth century drew to a close, other countries began issuing illustrated stamps for special occasions. Peru was the first, celebrating the twentieth anniversary of its first railroad. The British colony of New South Wales followed, commemorating its centenary. A big anniversary for America was coming up in 1892, the 400th of Columbus's arrival.

Having been slow off the mark in the global commemorative stamps stakes, the Post Office produced the finest set of special stamps the world had yet seen. Sixteen magnificent specimens, with values from 1¢ to $5, tell the story of Columbus's voyages (in rather bizarre order: the series begins with the 1¢ showing him sighting land, and the 2¢ has him landing, but the 5¢ shows him soliciting funds to start his expedition). The $4 features Columbus and Queen Isabella, making her the first woman to appear on a U.S. stamp. The $5 at the head of this chapter, the most prized of the set for modern collectors, features allegories of Liberty and America flanking a portrait of the explorer by Charles E. Barber, chief engraver of the U.S. Mint. This portrait was also used on the expo ticket (see below) and on a special commemorative half-dollar. The "Columbian issue" was not cheap—the stamps have a face value of $16.34, around $500 in modern money. A $5 stamp had little postal use, and the Society for the Suppression of Speculative Stamps was founded soon after, to lobby against future high-value issues.

The stamps did not actually appear on the market until January 1893. Formally, they were issued to celebrate the opening of a vast commemorative event, the World's Columbian Exposition in Chicago—and the expo opened a year late: Its planners had gotten carried away, and it took much longer to set up than had been initially envisioned. However, both the stamps and the exposition proved worth the wait. The latter covered 640 acres of central Chicago, now Jackson Park (named in honor of the man on the Black Jack). During its opening period of summer/early autumn of 1893, it attracted 27 million visitors, over 700,000 coming on October 9, "Chicago Day," which celebrated the rebuilding of the city after the disastrous fire of 1871. There were pavilions from nineteen other nations. (Norway's featured a Viking boat that had been rowed across the Atlantic for the expo, and which later served as a model for an odd 1925 stamp, where a Viking longboat, circa A.D. 1000, is seen flying the Stars and Stripes.) All the U.S. states exhibited. Idaho's giant log cabin was probably the most popular, though California's statue of a conquistador made out of prunes also attracted attention. Pennsylvania produced the Liberty Bell and John Quincy Adams's baby clothes. The centerpiece of the expo was the White City, an area of wide boulevards and neoclassical Beaux Arts architecture, which paved the way for future urban (and philatelic) design. This was surrounded by vast pavilions. Some of these impressed with their sheer size: The Manufactures and Liberal Arts Building covered eleven acres. Others whisked you into the future, such as Louis Sullivan's modernist Transportation Building, or the Electricity Building with two strange machines that showed you "moving pictures" and a life-size house full of new gadgets: electric fans, stoves, irons, sewing machines and elevators. The Post Office, as a department of the executive, exhibited in the U.S. Government Building. The Palace of Fine Arts featured classical art and is the only pavilion from the expo still standing—it is now Chicago's Museum of Science and Industry. When visitors had grown tired of these, they could go to the Midway Plaisance, a boulevard of entertainments which included "hoochee coochee" dancing by "Little Egypt," the chance to ride a camel, and, most popular of all, George Washington Gale Ferris's great steam-driven wheel that took you 264 feet above the ground, from which point you could enjoy the panorama of the biggest show the world had ever seen.

The world's biggest commemorative stamp issue, the world's biggest expo, the world's biggest wheel—big, big, big . . . This was America in 1893. It wasn't just braggadocio: By that time, the United States, which 112 years earlier had been made up of a few colonies clinging to the Eastern Seaboard of a vast unexplored continent, was now the most prosperous nation on earth. It could be said that the previous holder of that title, Britain, had willfully surrendered the baton of global economic leadership in the 1880s by choosing to invest in spreading old technologies around the world (especially within its own empire) rather than to develop new ones at home. But it took a dynamic nation like America to seize that baton and forge what most historians regard as a second industrial revolution, built on two of the technologies on display at the expo celebrated on this stamp: steel and electricity.

The most prominent American steelmaker was Andrew Carnegie. Carnegie was the son of Scottish immigrants. After starting work at $1.20 a week in a cotton mill at the age of twelve, he became a messenger boy at the local telegraph office, then worked for the Pennsylvania Railroad, where he rose fast to become a divisional superintendent. He invested his savings in a diverse series of successful ventures, including an oil well, but his great interest was in metal. In 1872, he traveled to England to see the new furnace developed by Henry Bessemer that turned iron into steel. This "converter" enabled alloys to be made both with unmatched precision and in unprecedented amounts. He brought the technology back to the USA and invested massively in it, despite the financial panic of 1873. In 1875, he opened the J. Edgar Thomson Steelworks, named after his boss at the railroad—a thank-you for mentoring him. By 1880, the plant was producing

100,000 tons of steel a year. Carnegie continued to expand the business both vertically, by buying up suppliers of coke and iron ore, and horizontally, by buying other mills. In 1901, he would sell it for half a billion dollars.

Carnegie steel was used to make the rails for the railroad system that was now crisscrossing America. It was used to build more powerful locomotives to haul ever more people, goods, and mail along these lines. It was used to build new steel ships that carried ever more people, goods, and (especially after the 1874 founding of the Universal Postal Union advocated by Montgomery Blair) mail across the oceans. It was used to build bridges, cranes, factories, warehouses, and, perhaps most dramatic of all, into the skeletons of ever taller buildings. In 1885, the Home Insurance Building, a brief walk from the Columbian Exposition site, had amazed everyone with its ten stories. The expo's organizational HQ was in another steel-framed Chicago tower, the Rand McNally Building. By 1893, such edifices were now rising to more than 300 feet and had earned themselves the name "skyscrapers."

Carnegie was not an inventor but an entrepreneur, a man who saw a brilliant technical idea created by someone else and turned it into a money-making machine. The titan of the electrical revolution, Thomas Alva Edison, was both. Like Carnegie, he worked as a young man in the telegraph industry. He experimented with the technology both in his spare time and at work: He was fired from his first job for causing an explosion. At age twenty-one, he became a full-time inventor. One of his earliest creations was a "ticker," a machine for telegraphing the movement of stock prices, which brought him to the attention of Franklin L. Pope, who worked for an information service on Wall Street. Pope hired Edison; a few days later Pope's system crashed and nobody could work out how to fix it. Edison repaired it in a couple of hours.

In the spring of 1876—a few months before George A. Custer made his Last Stand at Little Bighorn—Edison bought land in Menlo Park, New Jersey, and set up his "Invention Factory." He began working on voice technology, improving the new "telephone" of Alexander Graham Bell. In November 1877, he was able to record the nursery rhyme "Mary had a little lamb" on a "phonograph," the first-ever recording of sound. Another subject that fascinated him was electric light. The principle of the lightbulb was understood, but nobody could get a filament to last more than a few minutes. Edison tried thousands of materials—or rather Edison and his team did. He was a great motivator of bright young men and formed a kind of tribe at Menlo Park, where he and his "muckers" worked long hours, in love with the adventure of it all. On October 21, 1879, a filament made of bamboo glowed for thirteen and a half hours. Christmas 1879 in the Edison home was illuminated by these bulbs; by summer 1880, he was mass-producing them; by 1882, he was ready to light an entire street. This had required the development of a bigger generator and a better electrical transmission system. At 3:00 on September 4, 1882, the lights of Pearl Street, New York City, went on, and Edison became world-famous. A bizarre "war of currents" followed with his rival George Westinghouse, in which Edison electrocuted animals to show the dangers of Westinghouse's alternating current—a demonstration that led to the development of the electric chair by two of Edison's workers.

After the death of his first wife in 1884, Edison moved from Menlo Park and set up a new lab in West Orange, New Jersey, about 40 miles away. He continued to grow his lighting and electricity generation and distribution businesses. In 1892, these were merged, together with those of a competitor, Charles Coffin, to form the General Electric Company, now the global giant GE.

As well as invention and mass production, the growing wealth of America was built on advances in retail and marketing. The master of these arts was John Wanamaker. Wanamaker set up his first store, in Philadelphia, in 1861, with the slogan "One price and goods returnable." (At most other shops at this time, customers were expected to haggle with counter clerks.) He opened a second store in 1869 and the Grand Depot, one of the first department stores outside New York, in 1875. In 1879, he was the first retailer to take out a full-page advertisement in a newspaper, and in 1880, he broke another mold by hiring a full-time ad copywriter, John E. Powers, who did away with the hype of earlier advertising and concentrated on clear, factual statements of customer benefit. Later, Wanamaker installed in the Grand Court atrium of his store a huge pipe organ and a giant statue of an eagle, which became a favored meeting point for Philadelphians. "Meet you at the eagle," they would say—and having met, would wander through Wanamaker's store and spend, spend, spend.

In 1889, Wanamaker was appointed postmaster general by the twenty-third president, Benjamin Harrison. He did not get the job because of his passion for the postal service but because he had been a leading fund-raiser in Harrison's successful 1888 campaign. Andrew Jackson's spoils system was by now under attack—the Pendleton Civil Service Reform Act of 1883 had insisted that certain ranks in the government service must be appointed on merit—but this did not extend to postmasters, or their boss.

Wanamaker proved an energetic postmaster general. Probably his most lasting achievement sits at the head of this chapter: He was responsible for the Columbus commemoratives. Wanamaker also tried to set up a special delivery service for parcels and a bank for small savers run from post offices similar to the one set up in Britain back in 1861 by Rowland Hill, but he found his efforts blocked by railroad and banking lobby groups. A third reform, Rural Free Delivery, met with more success. Since 1863, ever more mailmen had been delivering in ever more cities and towns. In 1893, the year this stamp came out, country folk still had to collect their mail and newspapers from the local post office, just as they had done in the days of Ben Franklin and Abraham Lincoln. A rural delivery system was tested in West Virginia, and it worked; the system was rolled out across many parts of the nation, and by 1903, a third of Americans were receiving mail delivery direct to their homes. The light blue, horse-drawn cart would take all day to clop around a regular route of about 25 miles, with about a hundred mailboxes to drop letters and newspapers into. The carts stopped longer where items such as registered post or money orders had to be delivered in person—or where someone on the route wanted to talk. For the inhabitants of isolated farmsteads, the postman or postwoman became an invaluable link with the rest of the nation.

Less successfully, Wanamaker dismissed many competent postal officials and replaced them with political appointees. He then became involved in a controversy involving a uniform he commissioned for letter carriers, to be made by a company with which he had financial links.

Carnegie, Edison, Wanamaker: great men, great deeds. But the true spirit of the World's Columbian Exposition was democratic. This was a show for anybody and everybody, and America's public responded, attending in droves. Imagine an ordinary American family paying the admission price of 50¢ each—maybe they paid with the special half-dollars that bore the same image as this stamp—to walk down the great neoclassical boulevard, around the massive pavilions and along the Midway Plaisance, amazed and proud at their nation's stunning technological and economic achievements in the thirty-eight years since Appomattox. They had every right to feel that way.

TWELVE

Smithsonian National Postal Museum

DANCE OF THE GHOSTS

Trans-Mississippi Exposition commemorative $1, "Western Cattle in Storm," 1898; Scott catalog no. 292

AMERICA'S SECOND SET OF COMMEMORATIVE stamps celebrated another exposition, the Trans-Mississippi of 1898. The event was no match for the great expo of 1893; it covered about a quarter of the land and attracted a tenth the number of visitors. It was held in Omaha—cynics said it was just a piece of boosterism for Nebraska rather than a celebration of America and its place in the world. However, the 1898 expo spurred the Post Office to produce nine stamps, including the one above, which is regularly voted by philatelists as America's most beautiful ever. The issue was created by Raymond Ostrander Smith, chief designer of the government Bureau of Engraving and Printing, which had taken over stamp design and production in 1894, and featured images of the West: cattle, explorers, prospectors, pioneers, a Sioux hunting a buffalo, the Eads Bridge across the Mississippi (built by one of Andrew Carnegie's companies). The issue is a treasure, artistically and, now, commercially—a mint set is worth around $5,000. However, it has been accused of showing a mythological West rather than the real one.

There was certainly plenty of mythologizing going on by 1898.

Two stamps in the series—the 8¢, showing troops guarding a train, and the 50¢, showing a gold prospector—were based on paintings by Frederic Remington. Remington was an easterner who had gone to try his hand at ranching, failed, and returned to the East with an unquenchable passion for the West and a determination to paint it. He was not the first artist to do this—painters such as Albert Bierstadt already had reputations for vast, glowing, romantic western panoramas—but Remington preferred to show individual dramas: tough, dignified males battling, alone or in small groups, against the odds. The West as it was, or the West that the East wanted to see? He toured the region regularly in search of subject matter but did most of his work in his Gothic Revival mansion in Westchester County, New York. One of his most famous pictures was a self-portrait: It shows a lanky *hombre* in a cowboy hat and batwing chaps, rifle at the ready, astride an even lankier horse. The real Frederic Remington was rather more portly; the unfortunate horse might well have ended up on its knees.

Another source of the mythical West was the "dime novel," in which heroes like Edward Lytton Wheeler's Deadwood Dick fought for justice, or at least fairness, against corrupt, manipulative bad guys. Deadwood Dick is technically an outlaw, but a man of principle: The law doesn't work; it's up to men like him to see that right prevails. If this involves holding up a stagecoach and relieving its effete, double-dealing East Coast passengers of their ill-gotten cash, well, so be it. (One Wheeler villain is even worse than an easterner—the Hon. Cecil Grosvenor from England.) Humbly born, convinced of his own rightness, prepared to use violence when necessary, hating big East Coast money: Deadwood Dick is Andrew Jackson in a Stetson. Wheeler's other creations included Sierra Sam, Denver Doll, Captain Crack-Shot, Nobby Nick, and Wild Edna the Girl Bandit. Like many other popular authors, he was very prolific. Unlike many popular authors, little is known about his life, other than that he died around 1886, but Deadwood Dick fought on for many years, courtesy of ghostwriters. (Fans claim the later books lack the fizz of Wheeler's originals.)

King of the mythological West, however, was "Buffalo Bill" Cody, who played a starring role at the Trans-Mississippi Exposition. Cody had really lived the frontier life. His father had been an anti-slavery crusader in the days of Bleeding Kansas and died as a result of stab wounds sustained in an attack by a border ruffian. Cody left home at eleven and became a "boy extra," a kind of messenger on a wagon train. At fifteen he became a Pony Express rider, then earned a living as a buffalo hunter, stagecoach driver, and army scout before getting a role in one of the first Wild West shows in 1872. In 1883, he formed his own touring show—its first performance was in Omaha, home of the exposition. By 1898, it was the market leader. A typical Cody extravaganza at that time would begin with a parade of riders: cowboys, scouts, *vaqueros*, Indians, and representatives of other cultures centred around the horse, such as Georgians and Mongolians. At the head, of course, rode Buffalo Bill himself, six feet tall in an era when most men were five foot six, sporting his trademark mustache, goatee, and flowing hair. There would then be displays of equestrian derring-do. Sharpshooters like Annie Oakley showed off their skills. (A rather less sharp Cody shooter at the 1898 expo managed to put a bullet through an electric cable and put out the show's lighting for the evening.) There would be races and reenactments of supposedly typical western scenarios such as a raid on a wagon train, a stagecoach robbery, and the Pony Express ensuring the mail went through. In a dramatic climax, viewers saw an Indian attack on a settler's cabin and a rescue by a posse of cowboys. No prizes for guessing who was the leader of the rescuers.

If this was myth, what was really going on?

We left the West in 1876; let's pick up the story there. Custer's Last Stand was effectively Sitting Bull's last stand, too. In 1877, the army went after him and he had to escape to what he called the "Land of the Great-Grandmother": Queen Victoria and her Dominion in Canada, where there was still territory free. The once-sacred Black Hills filled with mining towns like the real Deadwood and with people like the real Deadwood Dick, Nat Love, a black cowboy famed for his shooting skills. There were few free-roaming buffalo in Canada, and in 1881 hunger forced Sitting Bull to return to the United States and surrender, the great chief's son handing his Winchester carbine and revolver over to Major David H. Brotherton, commander of Fort Buford. After two years as a prisoner of war, Sitting Bull was allowed to live on a reservation 150 miles south of his former home. He even took part in Buffalo Bill's show for four months in 1885, during which time he met President Grover Cleveland and shook his hand. Some say that he muttered curses in Lakota at the audiences during the shows; he certainly made a lot of money signing programs, then gave most of it away to poor people, of any ethnicity, that he met.

At the same time as Thomas A. Edison was installing electric street lighting in New York, lawmen like Wyatt Earp, Bat Masterson, and Pat Garrett were keeping the streets of Dodge City or Tombstone, Arizona, free of outlaws. The myth machine has worked its magic on these real-life characters, too, turning ordinary, fallible human beings into superheroes. Earp had run a brothel; Masterson earned a living by gambling when he couldn't get law work; Garrett shot Billy the Kid in 1881 when the latter was unarmed, in the middle of the night. The Kid, too, has been mythologized, into a romantic rebel in the Deadwood Dick vein, while in reality he was guilty of several murders—estimates of how many vary from four (including two law enforcement officers) to twenty-one, one for every year of his age.

In fact, the Old West was beginning to disappear. Ranching was starting to degrade the environment, with too many cattle and not enough grass. The plains were becoming crisscrossed with wire, making droving ever harder. Various patents for barbed wire were issued in the 1870s, but the man who sold it to the West was John Warne Gates, who created a monopoly. (He then became known for his gambling away of the proceeds, earning the nickname "Bet-a-Million.") The railroad moved ever deeper into Texas, making long droves unnecessary. In 1881, the Southern Pacific became the second transcontinental route.

The year 1883 saw the arrival in North Dakota of Theodore Roosevelt, a young eastern politician with a growing reputation. His move was, like the young Jefferson Davis's retreat to his plantation, driven by early personal tragedy, the death of his young wife in childbirth. Roosevelt made the

West his own. He shot bears, chased and arrested thieves who stole a boat from his ranch, got in a fight in a Montana saloon (and won). At the same time, he did something that Deadwood Dick probably never got around to: reading Leo Tolstoy's *Anna Karenina* in French. He headed back east in late 1886, where he wasn't above a little self-mythologizing. But he had found real treasure out West: energy, optimism, and a spirit of sturdy, physical fair-mindedness. He would later bring these traits to the highest office in the land.

While the Old West may seem to be a male world, this is another part of the myth. If the wild world of ranching and cow towns was largely male, farming and settling in the Midwest and Northwest were family affairs. Women played an enormous role in making the homesteads work, often combining traditional domestic roles with outdoor toil as tough as that of their menfolk. The novelist Laura Ingalls Wilder had a huge success with her *Little House* series in the 1930s, based on her real-life experiences in Nebraska and Dakota as a child and young woman sixty years earlier. If this series romanticizes things somewhat—though not as much as the 1970s TV series did—an autobiographical account of the first four years of her marriage, found in her daughter's papers and published in 1971, pulls no punches. Her husband suffered an attack of diphtheria and had to walk with a stick; various crops were destroyed by weather; a son was born but died shortly afterward—yet her tone remains optimistic: Keep at it and things will work out. Things did work out for the Wilders, too, though for many other settlers the setbacks proved too much. Her deep fortitude is hugely impressive, and another essential part of the western spirit.

Things did not work out so well for the Native Americans. Idealistic but uninformed "Friends of the Indians" came up with ideas for giving them individual plots of land and turning them into farmers—ideas that became reality after the passing of the Dawes Act in 1887. Life on the reservation may have been stultifying, but at least the first Americans had been able to keep their traditional, communal social structure there. Isolated farms did not suit them at all. Not all Indian lands stayed in Indian hands, either. In 1889, large swathes of former territory in Oklahoma—to which the current inhabitants' forebears had been forcibly moved by Andrew Jackson—were handed over to settlers. In what must have been one of the most bizarre sights of U.S. history, an estimated 50,000 settlers lined up to begin a race for land, to start at noon on April 22, 1889. On a signal from a cavalry bugle, the race began—though many participants reached remote locations to find people already encamped there: "sooners," who had ignored the rules and who had no intention of getting off the land they now claimed.

Too disparately settled and demoralized to fight back physically, the Native Americans found a kind of inner resistance through the Ghost Dance movement. In 1889, Wovoka, a Paiute shaman, had a vision. It was an essentially peaceful one: The tribes should cooperate with each other and the white man. A ritual was to be followed, which would bring back dead Indians and make the white man head back east of his own accord. The buffalo would return to the plains. Wovoka taught the ritual, a five-day dance, to members of various tribes (including a representative of the Mormons), who interpreted it in light of their own culture and experience. The warlike Lakota added the idea of the Ghost Shirt, a ceremonial garment that made the wearer immune to bullets. Lakota began to perform the dance. The authorities took this as a sign that they were planning an uprising; in 1890, the army was dispatched to arrest tribal leaders, including Sitting Bull. The great chief had had a vision, too—that he would be killed by one of his own people. In a bungled attempt to arrest him, he was shot by a Lakota policeman.

At least Sitting Bull was spared the pain of hearing about Wounded Knee. Two weeks after his death, a group of Lakota tried to leave the reservation and were pursued by Custer's old unit, the 7th Cavalry. The cavalry caught up with them at Wounded Knee Creek and demanded they surrender their weapons. This they did, but a scuffle broke out between a Native American and a cavalryman. A shot was fired, and the soldiers turned their weapons—which included cannon and Hotchkiss machine guns—on the unarmed Lakota. It is estimated that up to 300 died; 146 ended up in one mass grave.

The year 1890 also saw the U.S. Census Bureau officially declare that the frontier—a line beyond which the population density was less than two persons per square mile—no longer existed. America was now populated with U.S. citizens coast to coast. Thomas Jefferson had predicted this would take a hundred generations; it had taken just over a hundred years.

If the era of the frontier was history nearly a decade before the Trans-Mississippi stamps came out, its legacy lived on. In 1893, a young historian named Frederick Jackson Turner published his now-famous thesis that the frontier had created the American character. He argued that it was not the struggle for independence, nor the Civil War and the eradication of slavery, but the adventure of the West that had given Americans

> *that practical, inventive turn of mind, quick to find*
> *expedients; that masterful grasp of material things . . . that*
> *restless, nervous energy, that dominant individualism . . .*
> *that buoyancy and exuberance which comes with freedom.*

This message beams loud and clear from the 1898 Trans-Mississippi stamps. Yes, they are steeped in myth. Men outnumber women, who appear on only one of the nine stamps, the 10¢, which shows "hardships of emigration." The Native American shown on the 4¢ is hunting a buffalo, which by 1898 was virtually extinct. (The image comes from a painting from 1854.) The $1 stamp at the head of this chapter isn't exactly authentic, either: It is based on a picture by a Scottish artist; the cattle we see braving the storm actually lived in Callander, 40 miles from Glasgow. But at its heart, the issue embodies noble and very American truths, which F. J. Turner pinpointed with great clarity. These stamps—and the myths of the Old West which they mirror—may be a dance of ghosts, but those ghosts were once real people, and subsequent generations of Americans have lived their lives in their bright, clear light.

THIRTEEN

Smithsonian National Postal Museum

PAINTED LILIES

Pan-American Exposition 10¢, 1901; Scott catalog no. 299

AMERICA'S THIRD SET of commemorative stamps, also designed by Raymond O. Smith, dovetailed with an exposition as well, this time the Pan-American Expo in Buffalo, which ran from May to November 1901. Appropriately for a new century, these stamps looked not to the past but to the present and the future. They featured technological achievements: steamships, the Empire State Express (Grand Central to Buffalo in seven hours, including a section where the train went more than 100 mph), bridges, canals, and an electric automobile. The stamps were technological achievements in themselves. The higher values in the 1869 series had been bicolored, but their design had been messy (except, perhaps, for a 90¢ Lincoln) and their production error-prone; for the rest of the century, stamps remained monochrome. The 1901 series returned to the two-color idea, and did so triumphantly. The example above, the 10¢, shows the SS *St. Paul*, a 550-foot-long ocean liner that could carry 1,400 people across the Atlantic. The journey took six days, though steamship companies were fighting to decrease that time: In 1907, the British liner *Mauritania* would make the crossing in four and a half days. The companies also competed in the luxury they could offer their richest passengers. Liners began to resemble floating hotels, with paneled staterooms, sumptuous meals, a ballroom, a gymnasium . . .

The vessels of this era offered such facilities because a small number of people were growing rich in a way that no one, apart from royalty, had ever done in the history of the world. Back in 1776, Adam Smith had described the emerging industrial/market system as a kind of wealth-creating machine—but he also saw it as a force that would challenge extreme private wealth, then in the exclusive hands of landed aristocrats, and distribute it more widely. As the nineteenth century headed toward its end, this machine seemed to be getting out of control, creating a tiny plutocracy. This trend had been noted back in 1873, by Mark Twain, the sharpest observer of American life of his generation, when he coauthored a book called *The Gilded Age: A Tale of Today*. The title refers to lines from Shakespeare's *King John:*

To gild refined gold, to paint the lily . . .
Is wasteful and ridiculous excess.

Twain's book deals with land speculation, whereas the real megabucks of this era were made through industry and finance.

We have already seen Andrew Carnegie amass a huge fortune. Carnegie, however, was a man of principle and believed that the accumulation of vast private wealth was wrong. He thought that the job of the successful businessman was to provide the best possible goods at the cheapest realistic prices, thereby benefiting society as a whole, then to donate the money earned to worthwhile causes. In his "Gospel of Wealth," he wrote:

> *I propose to take an income no greater than $50,000 per annum. Beyond this I . . . [shall] spend the surplus each year for benevolent purposes.*

That $50,000 then was around $750,000 now, so Carnegie wasn't exactly slumming it, but given the vastness of his fortune, it is a remarkable gesture. He set up libraries, a university—now Carnegie Mellon—and institutes dedicated to furthering world peace. (The Carnegie Foundation owns the Peace Palace in The Hague, now home of the International Court of Justice.) He also paid for the building or reconstruction of 7,000 church organs in the USA, Canada, and Britain.

The cause of plutocracy was monopoly, the control of a market by one participant. In 1776, Adam Smith had warned against the dangers of this, but his words now went unheeded. A new idea was fashionable instead: Monopoly was a good thing; it minimized "inefficient" competition and kept markets orderly. In practice, it did nothing of the sort. Railroad companies were particular abusers of their monopolies, overcharging users—including the Post Office Department—and setting up corrupt corporate structures that siphoned profits away from ordinary investors and into the pockets of the company directors. Monopoly was also seen as somehow natural, based on the new philosophy of Social Darwinism, which viewed human society as a struggle for survival; the weak would go to the wall, but the fittest and most excellent would survive, and would get ever fitter and more excellent as the process continued. In fact, monopoly was a lot less natural than its advocates thought. It took the power of big finance to fully stifle competition. Bankers such as John Pierpont Morgan earned vast fees for organizing and backing the mergers that created this supposedly beneficial system.

At the other end of the social scale, workers' pay remained low. Postal clerks, for example, earned $700 a year and had to work 365 days in that year, with an average workday of fourteen hours. Mail carriers did better, earning an annual $1,000 and in theory working an eight-hour day—but this rule was stretched: Eight hours meant eight hours delivering and took no account of time spent between deliveries. Sorters on the mobile railroad cars earned $1,000, too, but the wagons were not kept in good repair and were often damaged in accidents. If you started work in this job in 1889, there was a chance of one in twenty that after four years you would have suffered death or serious injury.

Still, it was better than the poverty suffered by many in other parts of the world. Just as the frontier was officially coming to an end, waves of people were arriving in America, no longer from the places of "old" white immigration (Britain, Holland, Germany, Sweden, and, later, Ireland) but from Southern and Eastern Europe. They came no longer in search of farmland but of industrial work. After 1892, most entered the United States via the new federal immigration station on Ellis Island. (Previous arrivals had been the concern of New York State.) Beneath the also-new Statue of Liberty—since featured on thirty-seven different stamp issues—they would be asked a simple set of forty questions, some about themselves (including the somewhat naive "Are you an anarchist?"), others about America ("What is the Constitution?" "Which president freed the slaves?"). For a few, Ellis became Heartbreak Island as they were not allowed in, usually for health reasons, but most passed through within a few hours of landing, then went their myriad ways to participate in the booming economy—and to join the fecund U.S. population (in 1892, it was around 65 million) in keeping wage rates down.

Workers began to protest their low pay by setting up unions. Early attempts at this, such as the Knights of Labor, had strange trajectories, slowly attracting recruits at first, mushrooming, then collapsing as the leadership proved unable to deal with the difficulties of running a mass institution. By the height of the Gilded Age, however, labor was beginning to organize more effectively. The National Association of Letter Carriers was founded in 1889, with Civil War veteran William H. Wood as its first president; in 1893, it successfully sued the Post Office Department for back payments of overtime.

Other struggles were much bitterer. In 1894, employees of the Pullman Company went on strike to protest a pay cut. They persuaded the new American Railway Union to stop running trains with Pullman cars on them. The national rail network began to descend into chaos. A peaceful protest rally in Chicago turned into a riot: One of the buildings from the 1893 expo was burned down, and a locomotive derailed. President Grover Cleveland sent in the army to get the railroads moving again, citing as his reason his constitutional duty to ensure the delivery of the U.S. mail. The trains ran again, and the union was broken—but thirty people died in violent incidents connected to the strike. Such were industrial relations in the Gilded Age.

The Gilded Age also saw America at war again. A century earlier, George Washington had warned the nation to have "as little political connection as possible" with foreign affairs. But late nineteenth-century America felt ready to take to the international stage. The 1880s had seen a bizarre "scramble for Africa" by European powers, with men in pith helmets drawing lines on maps and declaring themselves rulers of squared-off chunks of land. America had watched with Washingtonian disinterest, but when the Europeans started doing the same to China, a country the United States considered within its sphere of influence, this was too much. The impending final collapse of the old Spanish Empire provided the opportunity to join in the global land grab.

Newspapers, especially the "yellow" populist press of magnates William Randolph Hearst and Joseph Pulitzer, began running stories of Spanish atrocities in Cuba. On January 25, 1898, the USS *Maine* sailed into Havana Harbor to offer protection to American citizens on the island, which was degenerating into anarchy as the Cubans sought to expel the Spanish. Three weeks later, the *Maine* exploded, killing 266 men. The explosion was probably an accident, but Hearst and Pulitzer went into patriotic overdrive: The Spanish were to blame and must pay. President William McKinley, a veteran of Antietam who had no illusions about the nature of war, did not want to fight, but Congress did, and Congress had more power than the president at that time. Hostilities with Spain formally began on April 25, 1898.

The vessel on the 10¢ stamp, the *St. Paul*, played a proud role in the fighting: It was commandeered and turned into a "swift auxiliary cruiser" under the command of Charles D.

Sigsbee, former captain of the *Maine*. It took part in blockades of Cuba and San Juan. On the first of these it captured a British steamer trying to sneak in a cargo of coal; on the second it won a battle with an enemy destroyer, the *Terror*. Meanwhile in the Philippines, another disputed colony, the U.S. Navy crippled seven Spanish vessels for the reported loss of one sailor, who suffered a heart attack.

On land, the fighting was less uneven. At San Juan Hill, near Santiago de Cuba, victory cost 2,000 U.S. lives. Thanks to another Remington picture, the battle has become best known for the brave charge by a volunteer regiment, the Rough Riders, led by Colonel Theodore Roosevelt. In fact, more casualties were sustained by black professional "Buffalo Soldiers" than by the dashing volunteers, but such is the power of myth-making.

The Spanish capitulated after ten weeks. It was time to fulfill the promise of the war and give independence to the formerly oppressed colonies. However, Congress suddenly decided that these nations weren't ready for self-government. This came as a particular shock in the Philippines, where guerrillas had been fighting the Spanish for many years and felt they had earned the right to rule themselves. After a brief peace, they continued the struggle, now against America. This new war was of the kind McKinley had feared, bloody and long-lasting. Filipino guerrillas, defending their homeland against invaders from the other side of a vast ocean, proved a much tougher enemy than Old Spain. The cruelty soon ratcheted up. U.S. general Elwell S. Otis, another Civil War veteran, became notorious for his ruthlessness—toward enemy fighters and "suspect" civilians. The conflict set a bad precedent for many future engagements: lack of what we would now call a clear "exit strategy"; war fever rampant in the media; an early win based on obvious technological superiority; a subsequent failure to engage the "hearts and minds" of most locals, degenerating into a guerrilla war with all the paranoia and viciousness such struggles inevitably involve.

America's Pacific expansion also brought it into conflict with two other newly ambitious nations, Japan and Germany. Germany and the United States both tried to intervene in a civil war in Samoa; only after a typhoon wrecked most of their ships did they decide to split the islands between them. For years the Germans secretly plotted revenge. Papers discovered in the imperial archive a few years ago show that Kaiser Wilhelm II discussed plans to invade America: Troops would land at Cape Cod and Sandy Hook, then advance on Boston and New York. The aim was not to conquer the USA but to scare the government into ceding American Samoa and a naval base on Cuba to Germany. The idea was shelved in 1906 but remains a reminder of the dangerous game that global geopolitics became around the turn of the last century.

Domestically, however, things seemed to be returning to business as usual. In late 1900, two geologists, Pattillo Higgins and Antun Lucic, began drilling for oil on Spindletop Hill in the far east of Texas. Progress was slow, due to layers of sand beneath the rock: Any hole drilled would collapse once these layers were reached. The problem was solved by pumping mud down the hole; drilling continued, but no oil was found. By Christmas 1900, they had reached 880 feet and were beginning to question the project. But in the new year they resumed in a more cheerful spirit. On January 10, mud began bubbling back out of the hole; a driller reported a "singing sound," then "a noise like a cannon shot," and 600 feet of pipe flew into the air—amazingly, nobody was injured—followed by a gusher 150 feet high. Levees were dug to contain the oil, which was spurting out of the ground at a rate of 100,000 barrels a day. (Lucic had, apparently, hoped for 5 barrels a day.) The product was analyzed and found to be of excellent quality for both uses of the product, lubrication and the distillation of the lamp fuel kerosene. (A by-product of this distillation, petroleum, was often thrown away, as there was no commercial use for it yet.) The Texas oil boom had begun.

So it's not surprising that the exposition celebrated on this stamp opened on May 1, 1901, in a spirit of optimism. In theory, the event had a Pan-American theme: Its emblem was two women whose flowing dresses take the shape of North and South America and whose hands meet over the far south of Mexico. In practice, more U.S. states exhibited than Southern or Central American nations. Above all, the expo was a celebration of electricity. (Ironically, the stamp series featured a use of this new power source that was soon to become outmoded: an electric car. At that time, there were sixty-two of these vehicles acting as taxis in New York City.) The expo's skyline was dominated by the 391-foot Electric Tower, which was lit by 44,000 incandescent bulbs and had a searchlight on the top that could be seen from Canada. Power, for this and the 200,000 other bulbs that lit the venue, came partially from nearby generators but partially via cable, carried 25 miles from Niagara Falls using Nikola Tesla's recently discovered system of "three-phase" transmission.

The event's highlight was to be a two-day visit from President McKinley. On September 5 he arrived in grand style, riding in a carriage while bands played a range of tunes. (The latest marches of John Philip Sousa were particularly popular.) He gave a speech, praising scientific progress and its uses for peace: Easier communication between nations should mean fewer misunderstandings and thus fewer wars. The crowd cheered approval of these sentiments. On the sixth, he returned more informally, in the afternoon attending a reception in the Temple of Music where members of the public could shake his hand. Security arrangements were loose; a rule that people had to approach the president with their hands clearly empty was relaxed due to the hot weather and the number of individuals wiping their brows with handkerchiefs. One such apparent brow-wiper was Leon Czolgosz, a loner and anarchist, who had concealed a pistol beneath his handkerchief and shot McKinley twice at point-blank range. Rushed to a local hospital, the president appeared to be recovering. Thomas Edison sent the prototype X-ray machine that was on display at the expo to the hospital, but it was not deemed necessary to use it. On September 14, McKinley took a turn for the worse and died whispering the words of the hymn "Nearer, my God, to Thee." He was the third American leader in thirty-six years to die at the hands of an assassin.

So the elegant, forward-looking, technophilic 1901 expo stamp series turns out to tell a complex story. America entered the new century with steamships, railroads, bridges, canals, and electric automobiles—not to mention oil, electric light, a booming population, and a small empire—but with nagging questions. The plutocrats of the Gilded Age preached Social Darwinism. But did this philosophy not just mean "might is right"? And if that is the case, what can be mightier than a gun, even if wielded by a lone, half-crazy individual?

FOURTEEN

Smithsonian National Postal Museum

BULLY FOR TR!

Panama-Pacific Exposition commemorative 2¢, 1913; Scott catalog no. 398

THE UNFORTUNATE MCKINLEY'S VICE PRESIDENT was Theodore Roosevelt, whom we have already seen ranching out west and leading the Rough Riders up the hill at San Juan. Now he was president, at forty-two the youngest man ever to hold that title. He brought with him a new philosophy. TR, as he liked to be called, believed that a simplistic individualism was no longer a good enough answer to the problems of the emerging industrial world with its vast monopolies and masses of factory workers, a world that had the capacity to create amazing new things but also to destroy cultures and natural habitats. He argued that the history of liberty had once been the history of the limitation of tyrannical governmental power, but no longer—in a democracy, the power of the state belonged to the people:

> *It is theirs to use and to exercise, if they choose to use and to exercise it. It offers the only adequate instrument with which they can work for the betterment, for the uplifting of the masses.*

Good-bye Gilded Age, and welcome to the Progressive Era. It's hard to find a stamp of the time that sums up these years. One with Roosevelt on it would be perfect, but the rule preventing the depiction of living people—even presidents—makes this impossible. So what are the alternatives? In 1902, the Bureau of Engraving and Printing issued its second set of definitive stamps (but the first truly to be the Bureau's: An earlier 1894 set had been someone else's designs). These were particularly handsome—the redoubtable Raymond Ostrander Smith was the overall designer—especially the frames around the portraits, which were done in the Beaux Arts style used by the designers of the 1893 expo. The most interesting of these is the 8¢, which featured Martha Washington, the first recognizable American woman to appear on a stamp. A sign of progress, surely? However, women were not to get the vote for nearly two more decades. The era wasn't *that* progressive, so the stamp doesn't really suit. In 1913, John Wanamaker's idea for Parcel Post finally became a reality, and a set of stamps for this showcased technological achievements of the period. But, successful as it was, Parcel Post was hardly the most ambitious aspect of the Progressive Era. The stamp for this chapter is a 2¢ commemorative, issued in 1913, celebrating the extraordinary achievement that was the Panama Canal.

(It had a secondary function, to promote an upcoming expo in San Francisco in 1915; hence that date appears on it.)

TR started reforming things the moment he assumed office. After four decades of portly, bearded, frock-coated, politically weak presidents, he wanted power to rest with the executive, as it had in the days of Jackson, Polk, and Lincoln. He invited Booker T. Washington to visit him in the White House, which the Tuskegee educator duly did, on October 16, 1901, to cries of horror from the southern press. He took on the plutocrats, beginning his battle with the Northern Securities Company, a conglomerate controlled by J. P. Morgan and John D. Rockefeller that was trying to monopolize the railroad routes west out of Chicago. He resolved a potentially disastrous dispute in the coal industry, not by sending in the army but by making both sides come to the White House and negotiate. After winning the 1904 election in his own right, he spearheaded a series of acts that sought to remedy a range of social ills. The Hepburn Act addressed the railroads, removing their ability to charge whatever they wanted. The Meat Inspection Act regulated the slaughtering and meatpacking industry, and the Pure Food and Drug Act did the same to the huge business of quack medical remedies. The Antiquities Act gave the president new powers to control the use of federal land: During his time in office he created five national parks, fifty-one bird reservations, and 150 national forests. Roosevelt was not the first president to act to protect the environment—Jackson, Lincoln, and Grant had made early moves in this area, too—but he gave the issue more importance than any other White House occupant had so far.

To drive these reforms through, often against considerable resistance, Roosevelt used the media, which he manipulated with consummate skill. He turned the White House into a kind of national brand, calling it his "bully pulpit." (In the early 1900s, "bully" was a positive word, meaning lively, energetic and bull-like, as in the phrase "Bully for you!") He was assisted in his efforts by a new breed of journalist known as "muckrakers": Jacob Riis, Ida Tarbell, and Lincoln Steffens shared Roosevelt's anger at both the conditions of poorer Americans and corruption in high places, and they weren't afraid to write about these things. Upton Sinclair's 1906 novel *The Jungle* helped TR take on the food barons; Sinclair's descriptions of how rotten meat, stale water, and dead rats found their way into sausages still make horrifying reading—as do his descriptions of the psychological effects of working on the barons' soulless slaughtering lines.

Roosevelt's foreign policy seems less "progressive" to twenty-first-century readers. He was not as aggressive as Congress had been in the 1890s but still sent his fleet around the Pacific to show everyone how powerful the United States had become. In his 1904 State of the Union message he added a corollary to the Monroe Doctrine: Not only did Europe have no right to intervene in the Americas, but the United States did have such a right. Arguably this was well intentioned, with the aim to spread democracy and freedom, but as he should have seen in the Philippines, big-power intervention rarely has that effect.

The Panama Canal was TR's one international intervention that did bring unambiguous benefit to America and to the world. The idea of building a waterway across the Panamanian isthmus had been mooted by King Charles I of Spain in 1529. In the 1880s work had begun, led by the engineer Ferdinand de Lesseps, the man who had built the world's other great geopolitical canal: the Suez Canal in Egypt. But the task had proven too much—workers died in the thousands from mosquito-borne diseases—and had been abandoned. Some initial work on reviving the Panama project had been done by President McKinley, but TR didn't just "do initial work"; he completed things.

On January 22, 1903, a treaty was signed with representatives of the Colombian government. (Panama was at the time a province of that country.) However, the Colombian Senate refused to ratify it. At this point, TR suddenly felt a deep moral compulsion to support a rebellion by Panamanian nationalists. The uprising succeeded quickly: On November 3, the new nation of Panama declared independence, and three days later, it granted America the right to build the canal.

Work began in May 1904, with presidential instructions to "make dirt fly." First, however, the mosquitoes that had wreaked such havoc in the 1880s had to be stopped. An enormous campaign of eradication was launched. Pools of standing water, where the creature's larvae hatch, were either drained or covered with a film of oil. House-to-house searches were made for larvae. Victims of malaria or yellow fever were quarantined in portable "fever cages," cubicles with a wooden frame infilled with insect-proof mesh, to prevent any surviving mosquitoes from biting them, then passing the disease on. The results of this campaign were stunning. Yellow fever was virtually eradicated from the area by 1906, and outbreaks of malaria greatly lessened. A hundred years later, the Canal Zone remains largely free of these terrible diseases.

TR made a visit to the canal works in 1906, making him the first serving U.S. president to leave the nation's borders. There is a famous picture of him posing on a huge steam shovel in an immaculate white suit; TR knew how to grab a photo opportunity. Later on, medals were given to any worker who spent more than two years on the project. On one side was a picture of the canal's Culebra Cut (the point at which it crosses the Continental Divide) and the individual's years of service; on the other was a picture of TR.

If the Panama Canal was an amazing public achievement, progress was being made by the era's private inventors and entrepreneurs, too. Perhaps the greatest technological triumph of the Progressive Era was that of Orville and Wilbur Wright. Neither brother's life had a particularly auspicious start: Wilbur suffered from what appears to have been depression after the death of his mother, turning down a place at Yale; Orville dropped out of high school. Instead of pursuing education, they ran a local newspaper, then a printing press, then a repair shop for the fashionable new means of transport, the bicycle. However, their greatest passion was flight. In 1900, the brothers spent October in Kitty Hawk, North Carolina, a seaside town with regular but gentle winds, where they flew gliders. Back home in Dayton, Ohio, they tested further designs and materials in a home-built wind tunnel or rode around the town on a specially designed bicycle to find out what kind of wing would create the most lift. After initial attempts to use propellers like those used in ships, they went back to the wind tunnel to design an optimal propeller for flight. They built their own lightweight engine, in collaboration with their mechanic, Charlie Taylor. In late 1903, the rather unimaginatively named *Flyer I* was ready to take to the air at Kitty Hawk. On December 17, Orville flew the plane for 852 feet. Watched by five other people, it is regarded as the first proper manned, powered flight. In September 1904, *Flyer II* covered 4,000 feet—in a circle. In 1905, *Flyer III* crashed—Orville was lucky to escape injury—but by the end of the year their flights were miles long rather than feet. While the Wrights were developing their project, the U.S.

government was investing in a rival project, the Langley Aerodrome, a machine launched by catapult. After two test flights ended up nosediving into the Potomac River, the government lost interest in air power. Like many other brilliant people, the Wrights had to go to another country to find success. It was their 1908 demonstrations in France that convinced the world of their achievement.

The year 1908 also saw another stunning technical breakthrough. On October 1, the first Model T Ford chugged out of its factory on Piquette Avenue in Detroit. Like the Wright Flyer, the Model T was the result of years of thought, trial, and costly error. Henry Ford had worked for Edison in the 1890s, and in his spare time (encouraged by his boss) he conducted experiments with the new gasoline-driven engines. In 1899, he had become a full-time entrepreneur. Although his first two companies failed, he kept going. In 1903, he set a record of over 90 mph in one of his vehicles—probably as hair-raising a ride as a trip in the early Flyer. At the same time, Ford's factory, in a converted wagon works, began making the Model A. This retailed for $750 and proved a success, selling 1,750 units in its first year. A more upmarket Model B followed, but Ford's dream was to "build a car for the great multitude." This turned out to be the Model T. (Not every letter came to market.) In 1909, 12,000 were sold; by 1912, this figure had risen to 78,000. When production finally stopped in 1927, more than 15 million had been sold. In 1968, a year, ironically, when the great car economy was beginning to implode, Ford and his groundbreaking vehicle made it into the Prominent Americans series of definitive stamps, at 12¢ squeezed in between Andrew Jackson (10¢) and John F. Kennedy (13¢).

While Model Ts were beginning to swarm up and down

the streets of America's cities, the buildings on those streets grew taller and taller. If the work on the stamp that opens this chapter is one symbol of Progressive Era optimism, another is the skyscraper. We have seen these in 1890s Chicago. They soon sprouted in other U.S. cities: Milwaukee, Philadelphia and, most notably, New York City. Here, 1908 saw the opening of the Singer Building, whose Italianate tower reached more than 600 feet into the air—beating the city's previous record holder by more than a third. It didn't hold the record for long: The next year the Metropolitan Life building broke through the 700-foot barrier. By contrast, the tallest office building outside the United States at that time was 141 feet tall.

In 1909, TR left office. He had earlier made a promise to emulate Washington and not serve a third term. (The two-term limit did not become law until 1951.) As the end of his presidency grew nearer, Roosevelt came to regret that promise. But the decision had been made. His successor was William H. Taft, now best known as the fattest president in history, who said his ambition was to achieve as much as Roosevelt, "but without any noise." As the new president squeezed himself into the old bully pulpit, TR and his family set off on a hunting expedition in Africa. J. P. Morgan wryly commented that "America expects that every lion will do its duty."

Taft soon found that presidents need to make noise. Though he continued to prosecute monopolies, the breadth and energy of the Progressive movement began to dissipate. The fire at the Triangle Shirtwaist Factory in 1911, where 150 immigrant female workers found themselves locked into a blazing sweatshop, showed how much more needed to be done. TR became ever more restless and decided to run for president again. To do so, he set up his own party. The Progressive Party—or Bull Moose Party, named after a TR comment that he was as fit as one of these creatures—had a strong modernizing agenda, which included women's suffrage, social insurance, and the popular election of senators. However, it soon fell to squabbling, and ended up simply splitting the Republican vote. The 1912 election was won by Democrat Woodrow Wilson.

America's economy continued to boom. As of 1913, Parcel Post played its part, enabling both samples and purchased goods to be sent through the mail to people's homes. Rural America, in particular, benefited from this—as did the parents of five-year-old Charlotte May Pierstorff; unable to afford the train fare for their child to visit her grandparents in Lewiston, Idaho, they stuck the requisite amount of stamps (53¢) on her coat and "posted" her. (She traveled in the mail compartment of the train.) It is not known what stamps Charlotte wore for her journey.

The year 1913 also saw the Panama Canal become a transcontinental waterway. On October 10, President Wilson dynamited the dyke between the Chagres River and the cut at Gamboa by remote control from his desk in Washington. Water flooded into the cut, and the Atlantic and Pacific oceans were joined, though work still had to be done on many aspects of the canal before it was navigable by ships of any great size. Despite Wilson's having performed this official function, nobody was in any doubt who the father of the Panama Canal was. These words are still on a plaque in the rotunda at the Canal Administration Building in Balboa Heights, Panama:

> *It is not the critic who counts, not the man who points out how the strong man stumbled, or where the doer of deeds could have done them better. The credit belongs to the man who is actually in the arena; whose face is marred by*

dust and sweat and blood; who strives valiantly, who errs and comes short again and again; who knows the great enthusiasms, the great devotions, and spends himself in a worthy cause; who, at the best, knows in the end the triumph of high achievement; and who, at the worst, if he fails, at least fails while daring greatly, so that his place shall never be with those cold and timid souls who know neither victory nor defeat.

It's bombastic; by modern standards it's macho; but it will undoubtedly keep on inspiring people long after more nuanced and politically correct material has disappeared into the garbage pail of history. The author, of course, is TR.

The canal was fully ready in the summer of 1914, and a big opening ceremony was planned for mid-August. In anticipation of this, one of the ships that had helped build it, the SS *Cristobal*, traveled from one end to the other to ensure there would be no hitches and became the first vessel to make the ocean-to-ocean journey without stopping. This was a truly momentous occasion—but nobody was paying attention. The *Cristobal* completed its journey on August 3, 1914. The next morning, Imperial German troops marched into Belgium, and the Great European War began.

FIFTEEN

Smithsonian National Postal Museum

MAKING THE WORLD
SAFE FOR DEMOCRACY

3¢ Victory stamp, 1919;
Scott catalog no. 537

VICTORY? IN WHAT? The day of the German invasion of Belgium, President Wilson issued a statement of neutrality—the first of ten issued in the next two years. The U.S. Navy was told to prevent American ships delivering munitions to either side. In his December 1914 State of the Union message, Wilson told Congress: "We are at peace with all the world."

Who wanted to go to war, anyway? On the same day that Wilson addressed Congress, one could have attended the opening of a new revue on Broadway. *Watch Your Step* featured music and lyrics by the latest songwriting sensation, Irving Berlin. Berlin's parents had been among those arrivals on Ellis Island, in 1893, and the young lad had grown up in poverty but surrounded by New York's wealth and opportunity. At age eight, he was selling newspapers on the streets and found that if he sang snatches of popular songs, he'd sell more. He graduated to being a singing waiter in Chinatown's Pelham Café, serving drinks and making up rude parodies of current hits. After hours, he'd write melodies on the restaurant's piano, using only the black keys. In 1911, he had his breakthrough with "Alexander's Ragtime Band." Technically the song is not ragtime, the syncopated piano music raised to beautiful sophistication back in the late 1890s by Scott Joplin. (Unlike Berlin, Scott Joplin was always pushing the boundaries of his art, often beyond commercial success. In 1915, when crowds were flocking to *Watch Your Step,* Joplin's ragtime opera *Treemonisha* had its one performance, a readthrough at Harlem's Lincoln Theater.) From then on, Berlin produced a succession of classic popular hits—though an attempted follow-up to his breakthrough, called "Alexander's Bag-pipe Band," was not one of them.

Besides, if Americans wanted a war, there was one—in Mexico. A civil conflict had been raging there since 1911. Wilson resolved to sort this out, intervened, switched sides, switched sides again, and found himself embroiled in a guerrilla struggle with the charismatic Pancho Villa, who even invaded New Mexico at one point.

But worse violence was exercising its sinister magnetism across the Atlantic. America kept trading with combatant nations, especially with its old commercial partners Britain and France. Passengers continued to cross the ocean. But on February 4, 1915, the German navy declared the waters around Great Britain and Ireland a war zone. On May 7, the American Cunard liner *Lusitania* was sunk by a German U-boat off the Old Head of Kinsale in southern Ireland. The

Lusitania was not carrying explosives or shells, though there was small-arms ammunition among the cargo (material not covered by the U.S. Navy embargo). The liner was armed, but only with two rather insubstantial guns. And it was sunk without warning, in contravention of the Hague conventions on maritime warfare. More than 1,000 people died, 128 of them American citizens.

Wilson still did not want to fight—and neither did the majority of Americans, for whom life went on untroubled by wars and sinkings. (Many people were more concerned about the enforced introduction of the new tunnel-shaped mailboxes. After July 1916, this was the only design you could have installed, a rule that did not please some freedom-loving postal recipients.) In the November 1916 election, Wilson's slogan was "He kept us out of war." He won, becoming the first Democrat to secure a second term since Jackson. He kept trying to mediate between London and Berlin, but history was not on his side.

On January 22, 1917, Wilson gave a speech about achieving "peace without victory." But on February 1, Germany announced that any vessels were fair game for its U-boats. The American merchant ship *Housatonic* was sunk on February 3. Three weeks later, Wilson was handed a copy of a telegram that had been sent by German foreign minister Arthur Zimmermann to Germany's ambassador in Mexico City. In it, the ambassador was instructed to approach the Mexican government and suggest that in the event of America joining the war, Mexico should ally itself with Germany; Germany in turn would help Mexico recover those lands lost back in 1848. The sinking of ships continued: the *Algonquin*, the *City of Memphis*, the *Vigilancia*, the *Illinois*, the *Healdton*... It was too much. On April 2, the president asked Congress to declare war on Germany—not for "conquest" or "dominion" but because "the world must be made safe for democracy." Congress did as asked.

America was not prepared for war on the scale being waged in Europe. Its standing army was small, given its size and economic power—just as the founding fathers had wanted. So while the first soldiers of the American Expeditionary Force (AEF) landed in France on June 27, 1917, they did not launch straight into battle. Most of that year was spent building up support and supply lines. Where U.S. forces did see action, it was as reserve units, helping out struggling, exhausted allies at particularly weak points in their lines.

Meanwhile, the president continued to develop his position on the war. On January 8, 1918, he announced his Fourteen Points, a bold attempt at creating what would later be called a New World Order. According to this manifesto, the postwar world would be ruled by "open covenants of peace," not secret treaties by Great Powers. There would be "freedom of navigation upon the seas," not the rule of British battleships or U-boats. Nations would disarm "to the lowest point consistent with domestic safety." Empires would be broken up, with "the populations concerned" having an equal say with their colonial masters as to how. There would be a "general association of nations," where differences could be settled. There was no talk of punishing Germany; instead, Wilson concluded:

> *We have no jealousy of German greatness, and there is nothing in this programme that impairs it . . . We do not wish to fight her either with arms or with hostile arrangements of trade if she is willing to associate herself with us and the other peace-loving nations of the world in covenants of justice and law and fair dealing. We wish her only*

to accept a place of equality among the peoples of the world—the new world in which we now live—instead of a place of mastery.

U.S. commander John J. Pershing wanted his men to fight as a unified army. Its allies were less keen, but events forced their hand. Germany, aware that as ever more American troops and equipment arrived across the Atlantic, time was running out, launched a massive surprise offensive in northern France. It surmised that if its armies could capture Paris, the Allies would be forced to negotiate. The initial success of this attack led the British general Douglas Haig to issue his famous order that "every position must be held to the last man." May 28 saw the first full American action, the Battle of Cantigny: At 6:45 A.M., men of the 28th Infantry regiment stormed a hilltop village; they took it in forty-five minutes, then held off fierce counterattacks for the rest of the day. One hundred ninety-nine U.S. soldiers were killed, including Matthew B. Juan, the first Native American to die in the combat. Most of June saw U.S. Marines fighting the bitter battle of Belleau Wood, suffering losses of nearly 2,000 men but finally securing victory. On July 18, U.S. and French troops counterattacked the Germans across a 25-mile front. This operation, known as the Battle of Chateau-Thierry, was a turning point in the war. The German advance turned into a retreat, and on August 8, the Allies began their victorious "Hundred Days Offensive."

Through all this, the AEF was well supported by its postal service, which at the height of the conflict employed 1,600 people. Parcels from home containing luxuries were great morale boosters; letters back were subject to censorship and tended to play up the optimism of the fighters. Sergeant Norman S. Thomas, for example, wrote of seeing ambulance carts full of men with

> *wounded arms legs and heads bandaged up, but each one with a smile on his face and a cheery word, tickled to death to be able to do their bit in knocking H*** out of the hun.*

On October 4, the German chancellor, Prince Max of Baden, telegraphed President Wilson requesting an armistice. Wilson said he would only deal with a democratic government. The Germans produced a new constitution; Wilson insisted the kaiser abdicate. On November 10, the armistice was signed, in a railway carriage north of Paris. Hostilities would cease at 11:00 A.M. the next day. Less war-weary than his allies, Pershing insisted on fighting to the very end—attacks were launched on November 11 itself. Private Henry Gunther was killed charging a machine-gun post at 10:59. It was reported that "almost as he fell, the gunfire died away and an appalling silence prevailed." Gunther joined 53,401 other U.S. combat deaths in the conflict: more than double the amount of men killed in all America's previous external wars and the War of Independence combined—though still only one-fifth of the combat death toll of the Civil War.

This costly victory was celebrated with the single stamp that opens this chapter in March 1919. A grand celebratory issue had been suggested, but the Bureau of Engraving and Printing was still busy producing Liberty Bonds, which had been the main vehicle for financing the war. The stamp, which shows "Liberty Victorious" holding a sword and the scales of justice, against the background of Old Glory and the flags of Britain, Belgium, Italy, and France, was not a great success with the public. They didn't like the color (the ink fades in light), the fussiness of the design, or the fuzziness of its execution. The fact that it represented the new 3¢ basic letter rate, which had been introduced in 1917 to aid the war effort, wasn't popular, either. (In July 1919, the rate went back down to 2¢, where it had been since 1883.) Maybe, also, people were tired of war and didn't want a great celebration every time they mailed a letter.

Or maybe it was the influenza.

On March 11, 1918, a cook at Fort Riley, Kansas, a staging post for new recruits on their way to France, went down with what was quickly diagnosed as influenza—too late for forty-six other recruits, who also soon died of it. A similar illness was then reported in other camps, on troopships, in France . . . The disease soon spread throughout Europe. It was most virulent in Spain (or appeared to be; the rest of Europe had censored presses at that time, from which news of the flu was kept out) and became known as "the Spanish Lady." It spread to the rest of the world, then appeared to die down. But in late August 1918, a mutation appeared in three port cities at once: Brest in France, Freetown in Sierra Leone, and Boston. The strain quickly proved to be of a totally new intensity, as contagious as the earlier flu and twenty-five times more lethal. The effects were horrifying. Victims' lungs would fill incredibly rapidly with a mixture of blood and pus; death, a release from spasms of coughing and what survivor Katherine Anne Porter described as a "terrible compelling pain," was by asphyxia; doctors compared it to the effects of the worst poison gas used in the war. (Conspiracy theorists blamed the outbreak on German agents using gas.) It struck with terrifying speed: Tales began to circulate of people setting off for work in good health and never returning home, or of a bridge party of four ladies meeting one evening—next morning three were dead. Most diseases target the very young and the very old, but the Spanish Lady claimed half her victims from those between twenty and forty ("thus imitating the war itself," as one commentator observed). In one month, October 1918, the flu killed 200,000 Americans—almost four times the number of AEF combat fatalities in the entire war. Through it all, the post kept on being delivered, and with it educational material on how best to avoid infection. The value of such material, however, was limited. Nobody really knew what to do. Victor Vaughan, surgeon general of the U.S. Army, commented that doctors "knew no more about the flu than 14th century Florentines had known about the Black Death."

Then the pestilence disappeared, as quickly as it had arrived. Nobody knows why. The virus probably mutated into something less deadly. (A third wave, a few months later, was much less virulent.) The total death toll in the United States was 675,000. Yet it is little written about—for example, compared to the huge amount of material about the Great War. Maybe that is because its story involves little human agency. We can all learn from the mistakes and achievements of Pershing, Haig, Wilson, or the kaiser, but the story of "the Spanish Lady" tells the layperson nothing beyond the scary truth that life can be fragile. Perhaps after all this, the flag-waving on 1919's 3¢ Victory stamp seemed hollow.

Victory soon became hollow politically, too. President Wilson set off for Paris to participate in the great peace conference to be held in Versailles, stopping en route in London to receive an ecstatic welcome (and to remind Britain that the old colonial master's days of empire were over). It was downhill from then on. Wilson had played hardball with the enemy but was completely outflanked by his former allies, especially the French. He wanted to put the Fourteen Principles into action; they wanted revenge. On February 14, he presented his idea for a "general association of nations," now named the League of Nations, where world leaders would meet and sort out their differences in peace. The suggestion was ignored. In the end, Wilson threatened to leave the conference if it was not accepted, and the League was reluctantly voted into being. Most of the rest of his Fourteen Points were ignored, and a suitably vengeful "treaty," ceding large tracts of Germany's most productive land to neighbors and insisting the defeated nation pay vast reparations for the war, was signed on June 28, 1919.

The next day, a young German corporal named Adolf Hitler read in the press of the humiliation that the Treaty of Versailles had heaped on his nation and swore he'd get revenge. On that same day, in Moscow, Joseph Vissarionovich Dzhugashvili was busy with his new job as commissioner of nationalities in the Bolshevik government that had seized power in 1917—though Dzhugashvili, or Stalin as he was better known, had greater ambitions.

A world safe for democracy? No wonder this stamp is so muted.

SIXTEEN

Smithsonian National Postal Museum

GOLDEN BEGINNINGS

"Fourth Bureau Issue," Golden Gate definitive 20¢, 1923; Scott catalog no. 567

IN 1908–09, THE BUREAU of Engraving and Printing replaced its Raymond Ostrander Smith Beaux Arts definitives with a rather dull series depicting Washington and Franklin. The nation was saddled with these for more than a decade, but in 1922–23, the Bureau came up with a fresh, vibrant new issue, designed by Smith's successor, Clair Aubrey Houston. This series featured a variety of portraits (including McKinley, Sioux chief Hollow Horn Bear, and TR, who had died in 1919) and, on higher values, pictorials, which made their appearance again after half a century. The stamps were issued on different days and in specific places, with official first day covers being prepared for the first time. These soon became essential collectors' items. The 20¢ was issued in San

Francisco on May 1, 1923. It features a painting of the channel between San Francisco Bay and the Pacific Ocean—the Golden Gate—by local maritime artist William A. Coulter.

California has always been a place of beginnings. The great Gold Rush of 1848–49 had turned the state from an outpost to a center of population. The Gold Rush had made a deep mark on America's mind-set—in some ways not for the best: A hardworking, patient people suddenly got the idea that one could get rich quick. But in other ways it added to America's already strong sense of optimism, of abundance, of being blessed by the land.

On June 15, 1878, Leland Stanford—the man who had (on his second attempt) hammered home the golden spike to complete the Transcontinental Railroad—summoned the press to his stud farm in Palo Alto, California, for a demonstration of a new technology designed by inventor Eadweard Muybridge. A set of cameras on split-second timers would record a galloping horse, and the photographs would then be put into a machine called a zoopraxiscope, which would produce an image of the horse in motion. At the time, nobody knew exactly how a horse galloped. The most common idea was that it stuck its front and back legs out at the same time—which is how a galloping horse had traditionally been depicted, and how it appeared on the 1869 2¢ Pony Express stamp. Governor Stanford's Sallie Gardner thundered past the cameras; the images were developed and loaded into the zoopraxiscope; the world saw a "motion picture" for the first time. Slowing the motion down revealed that the 1869 stamp had gotten it wrong. The actual gallop is much more complex.

Needless to say, Thomas Edison soon got involved in this technology. He developed a rival system, the kinetograph, which was demonstrated, in competition with the zoopraxis-cope, at the 1893 Columbian Exposition. Other inventors were on the trail, too: Take your pick from the phantoscope, the pleograph, the mutoscope, the cinematograph, the electrotachyscope, the eidoloscope . . . People flocked to see the offerings of these machines, simple clips where a movie camera was set up and recorded whatever was happening in front of it. Slowly the offerings became more complex. In 1903, audiences were thrilled by Edwin S. Porter's *The Great Train Robbery,* especially the last sequence, where the chief villain turns to the camera and fires straight at it. In 1905, the first "nickelodeon," a venue dedicated to showing moving pictures, opened in Pittsburgh: Your nickel got you the chance to sit on a hard wooden bench and watch a set of short, flickering films to live piano accompaniment. By 1908, there were 8,000 of these moving-picture houses in the USA. There was also a monopoly in the business of making the films, a trust based in New Jersey called the Motion Picture Patents Company (MPPC).

To escape this monopoly, filmmakers began heading west. California had been traumatized by the 1906 earthquake that wreaked havoc in San Francisco. (William A. Coulter, artist of the 20¢ stamp that opens this chapter, painted a dramatic picture of the subsequent fire.) But this land of beginnings was not downhearted for long, and embraced the new industry. In 1909, "Colonel" William N. Selig built his studio in Edendale, a suburb of L.A. (now Echo Park, though there is still an Edendale post office), where he made westerns featuring Tom Mix, the Buffalo Bill of the silent screen. Mack Sennett set up nearby; from 1912 the Keystone Kops could be seen charging around Edendale's streets. As the new decade advanced, more and more independents joined these pioneers. California rewarded the rebels with its sunshine: perfect for location shooting.

The monopolists didn't want actors getting ideas above their station; actors in their films were anonymous. But the public wanted names, so Hollywood (which quickly became the new epicenter of filmmaking once Edendale ran out of space) provided them. *Motion Picture Story Magazine* and *Photoplay*, the first magazines to feature film stars, appeared in 1911. Their first idol was Mary Pickford, who starred in a series of movies such as *Tess of the Storm Country* and *Rags*, in which she played feisty heroines defying ill fortune. She then formed her own production company, United Artists, with director D. W. Griffith, action hero Douglas Fairbanks (whom she later married), and Charlie Chaplin. Chaplin was the greatest star of silent comedy. His Little Tramp character made its debut in 1914, in an improvised Sennett short called *Kid Auto Races at Venice* (essentially a six-minute running gag of Charlie trying to hijack film coverage of a car race). The character came into being when Chaplin was asked to quickly put on "funny make-up." He chose a ragbag of clothes—oversized hat and shoes, tight coat, gentlemanly walking stick—and found that the outfit inspired him. His Little Tramp became a symbol for the simple, ordinary, well-meaning man trying to get by in a tough, complex, unfriendly world.

Before 1914, if there was a global culture, it had been European; exactly what flavor of "European" depended on who had invaded or colonized your country. This changed in 1914, both philosophically and practically. Philosophically, the old European dominance had, despite those invasions, been partly moral: People around the world thought that Europe was somehow "more civilized." Once the slaughter of the trenches began, thoughtful individuals like Sun Yat-sen and Mohandas K. Gandhi began to disagree. Practically, the Great War destroyed the European film industry; after 1918, the world's cinemas began to show Hollywood films, and by 1920, 80 percent of the world's movies were made in California. The era of American global "soft power" had begun. While Woodrow Wilson failed at Versailles, Mary Pickford and Charlie Chaplin were charming the world, cinema by cinema, telling it that the USA was a place where integrity and energy overcame malice and deviousness.

Mary Pickford's message that America's women were strong and free might have resounded around the world, but before 1920 she couldn't vote. In that year, however, the Nineteenth Amendment was ratified and universal suffrage finally became a reality. It had been a long time coming. The amendment had been drafted by trailblazing activists Susan B. Anthony and Elizabeth Cady Stanton back in the 1870s and put before Congress in 1878 by Senator Aaron A. Sargent of California. It then disappeared into the machinery of government, reappearing nine years later, when it was voted down by the Senate. After that, suffrage campaigners turned their attention to states; California was one of the first to change its laws. (The West generally voted for change, the South and East against.) Though votes for women had been espoused by the Progressive movement, what really changed things was the war. Women worked in factories and showed themselves just as capable as men at doing many jobs. Over 10,000 nurses, many of whom volunteered through the YMCA, supported the army in France. A similar number of women enlisted in the navy. (The army would not accept female recruits.) And wasn't the war about democracy? Protests grew in intensity, with groups of suffragette "Silent Sentinels" picketing the

White House. The Sentinels were initially fined for obstructing the traffic, but as official patience grew thin, they began to receive prison sentences. Many were sent to the Occoquan Workhouse in Virginia, where they were kept in insanitary conditions and given putrid food. On the night of November 15, 1917, thirty-three suffragette prisoners were viciously beaten up by guards. When news of this got out—the *New York Times* carried a piece on the brutality ten days later—public opinion quickly turned in favor of the protesters. In January 1918, Wilson asked Congress to pass a bill giving women the right to vote. Congress still fought the change for two years before finally conceding.

Genuine universal suffrage did not make much difference to the outcome of the 1920 election, which could have been predicted by a time-traveler from 1865, the South voting solidly Democrat and the North and West equally Republican. For the latter party, Warren G. Harding campaigned for "normalcy," and this won the hearts of voters. Once he was in power, however, "normalcy" turned out to be corruption—not on Harding's part but among the "Ohio gang," a set of cronies from his home state whom he had appointed to national office and over whom he proved incapable of exercising control.

One Harding appointment that did work out was William H. Hays as postmaster general. Hays later became known for imposing a restrictive censorship code on Hollywood, but as a postmaster he was a success. His predecessor, Albert S. Burleson, had been a bully, and many of Burleson's appointees had been the same: The postmaster of St. Louis insisted his employees salute him like a military officer and composed cheers in praise of himself that employees were expected to yell. Hays, in an introductory speech that could have come from the HR department of a twenty-first-century software company, announced his intention to "humanize" the service and to make its 300,000 employees (the Post Office Department was the nation's biggest civilian employer) "partners" in "a great human institution touching every individual in the country." Labor, he added, was not a commodity. Morale in the service soared.

America's economy had done well during the war, with its manufacturing capacity expanding. Along with the rest of the world economy, this took a tumble in 1920, but it soon recovered and began to grow at a startling new rate. The 1922–23 issue of definitive stamps is a sign of this regeneration, with its confidence and energy. Nowhere was the new boom more visible than in California. Hollywood itself was a major driver of economic growth—its famous hillside sign was erected in 1923 to market real estate—but many light industrial businesses were setting up in the Golden State, too. Its population grew by 65 percent in the 1920s. In 1923, plans were formally put in motion to build a bridge across the beautiful entrance to San Francisco Bay shown in this stamp. Many people doubted this could be done—the Gate was over a mile wide, full of swift currents and 350 feet deep at its center. But in the emerging postwar decade, and especially in California, land of new beginnings, anything and everything seemed possible.

SEVENTEEN

Smithsonian National Postal Museum

ROAR!

Lindbergh commemorative 3¢, 1927; Scott catalog no. C10

THE POST OFFICE HAD BEEN experimenting with Air Mail since 1911. The first scheduled service opened on May 15, 1918, between Washington and New York. It didn't get off to a great start: The first pilot got lost, made a forced landing, and broke a propeller; the mail was loaded onto a truck and driven back to D.C. But future flights went better, and the service was soon extended to Chicago and, in 1920, to San Francisco. Special stamps were issued for Air Mail. In keeping with the wobbly start of the service, some were printed incorrectly with the aeroplane, the barnstorming Curtis "Jenny" JN-4, upside down. One sheet of these found its way into public hands—the rest were destroyed by officials—and the "Inverted Jenny" is now one of the rarest collectors' items. Examples can fetch $1 million at auction. In 1926, further

Air Mail routes were contracted out to commercial organizations. On one of these, from St. Louis to Chicago, the chief pilot was Charles A. Lindbergh.

Lindbergh, a former army and stunt pilot, wanted to do more than just take mail across the Midwest. In 1919, hotelier Raymond Orteig had offered a prize of $25,000 to the first person to fly nonstop between New York and Paris. This was a dangerous challenge. Already, six men had died trying to meet it: four while testing specially adapted planes and two in an actual attempt (two French war heroes who had perished somewhere between Ireland and the American coast). Despite this, there was strong competition. Little known and with no financial backing apart from a loan and the enthusiastic support of a small aircraft manufacturer based in San Diego, who built the plane featured on this stamp, the *Spirit of St. Louis,* Lindbergh was an outsider. But the day-to-day challenges of carrying the post had made him a master aviator. He knew exactly what he wanted from the plane, which he codesigned. The cockpit was cramped—but he didn't want to be too comfortable, in order to keep himself awake. There was no front windshield: To make the craft better balanced, he had instruments in front of him and could only see forward by looking out of the side window (a skill he had learned flying the mail, in which the pilot often sat at the back of a fully loaded plane to keep it balanced). He was fanatical about cutting down on weight to ensure enough fuel for the journey; even his maps had the edges trimmed off.

The former Air Mail pilot took off from Roosevelt Airfield on Long Island at 7:52 A.M. on May 20, 1927. As the stamp shows, he flew up the coast of the United States and Canada. Ten hours into his flight he left land and headed out across the ocean. Here, he encountered fog, ice, and storm clouds—at one point having to fly as high as 10,000 feet to avoid the latter, at another finding himself 10 feet above the water—all the time battling fatigue. Twenty-seven hours into his flight he spotted the coast of Ireland. Two hours later he crossed the French coast at Cherbourg, and an hour and half after that he landed at Paris's Le Bourget aerodrome, having been airborne for thirty and a half hours. The exhausted Lindbergh was lifted from his plane and given a rapturous reception by the French, in one of their fanatically pro-U.S. moments.

Back home, this stamp was quickly issued in his honor. It is a rare exception to the rather unexciting stamps that characterized the mid- and late 1920s. After the promise of the 1922–23 definitives, the rest of the decade saw a few, almost all monochrome, commemoratives trickling off the Bureau of Engraving and Printing presses. (President Harding's successor, Calvin Coolidge, thought colorful special stamps were an unnecessary expense.) These stamps do not tell the story of their time well, for this was a vibrant, innovative, colorful era: the Roaring Twenties. So let's close the stamp album for a moment and just listen to the roar . . .

Perhaps the decade's loudest roar was that of the automobile. By 1923, there were 13 million on America's roads, and this figure would double by 1930. The booming auto industry boosted its suppliers, too—providers of steel, rubber, glass, leather, and gasoline. Drivers created demand for new services such as garages and motels. On a larger scale, the automobile enabled suburbs to stretch out into the countryside, with bigger homes that people could fill with more new technology: vacuum cleaners, washing machines, refrigerators, phonographs, telephones, electric irons—and the communication marvel of the age, radio.

In 1920, the first commercial station, KDKA in Pittsburgh, had begun broadcasting. By the end of 1922, there were more than five hundred stations in the United States—though listening was still rather a haphazard process, as stations often cut into each other's wavelengths, and the receivers were unreliable (many came in kit form). As sets became more user-friendly and the airwaves more regulated, life began to revolve ever more around weekly sports broadcasts and shows like *Barn Dance* (later renamed the *Grand Ole Opry* to poke fun at the show that preceded it, the immaculately highbrow *Music Appreciation Hour*) and *Amos 'n' Andy*, a comedy set in a small taxi company, originally in Chicago but moved in 1929 to Harlem.

Then there was the roar of jazz. Around the turn of the century, New Orleans had become a musical cauldron into which a delicious set of ingredients was poured: work songs, gospel, marching bands, ragtime, parlor and minstrel songs, European classical music, dances from Spain, the remembered rhythms of Africa . . . Simmer for a decade in a suitably freewheeling environment—the dance hall, the bordello—and you have an amazing new art form. An early New Orleans jazz band would feature a front line all jamming over a song's basic chord pattern; later, individual soloists moved to the fore. The first undisputed king of these was Louis Armstrong. Like Irving Berlin, Armstrong was born into poverty but within touching distance of opportunity. As a spirited lad in New Orleans he had to do menial work to support his mother and sister but could sneak off to dance halls in the evenings with his cornet. At one of these he impressed bandleader Joe "King" Oliver, who took the boy under his wing. As a young man, Armstrong honed his trade playing on Mississippi riverboats; in 1922, he followed Oliver to Chicago, from where his fame spread across the USA.

Armstrong, like other great trumpeters/cornetists of the time such as Bix Beiderbecke and James "Bubber" Miley, was a musician of stunning originality and talent, pushing the boundaries of the instrument and the genre, but doing so in a way that was pleasing and melodic. More alert members of the musical establishment began to take note; in 1924, Leopold Stokowski, conductor of the Philadelphia Orchestra, commented that jazz was "here to stay." In the same year, George Gershwin closed the gap between the two cultures with *Rhapsody in Blue.* However, jazz's true home remained the club, especially the speakeasy (so called because one was expected to mention its location in a hushed voice, so as not to be overheard by government agents), where illegal alcohol was served.

Prohibition—and attempts to get around it—was another defining characteristic of the Roaring Twenties. The first recorded example of the policy dates from the Chinese Xia Dynasty, around 2000 B.C. It didn't work then, and there is no record of it ever working since. America tried it in 1919, after many years of campaigning by largely rural temperance societies. (President Wilson tried to veto the Volestead Act that initiated Prohibition but failed.) Organized crime soon took over the alcohol trade. This created a huge boost for the gangsters—and greater danger for drinkers, who could never be quite sure what was in that bottle they had just bought. The government added to the danger by putting toxic ingredients in industrial-use alcohol to discourage abuse. The bootleggers used it anyway, and it is estimated that 10,000 people died as a result. Most of these victims were poor. The rich could buy illegally imported spirits from such upmarket sources as William McCoy, whose rum and whiskey were always "the real McCoy."

With the new music and these new venues came new dances: the Charleston, the Black Bottom, the Shimmy, and (after May 21, 1927) the Lindy Hop were frenetic, revealing, sexy, and above all great fun. Queen of the new dancing was Paris-based American Josephine Baker, but every young woman could have a go—though she might risk being called a "flapper." Many flappers, however, bore the name with pride. It meant being stylish, with that bob haircut, short skirt, and heavy makeup. It meant being independent: Flappers smoked cigarettes, drank cocktails, drove automobiles, went on "dates," and initiated relationships. At work, the bright '20s woman was competing successfully with men in the new, burgeoning service industries and corporate clerical departments. She even took to the air: The year after Lindbergh's flight, Amelia Earhart became the first woman to fly the Atlantic, as part of a crew of three, and in the same year flew solo across the USA and back. (She had to wait until 1968 to appear on a stamp.)

The year 1925 produced another new roar—of laughter, at the shambles of the Scopes Monkey Trial. In that year, Tennessee passed an act forbidding the teaching of Charles Darwin's theory of evolution—or at least the part of it that dealt with the origins of man. Progressives saw this as an attack on intellectual freedom, and a teacher, John T. Scopes, agreed to be prosecuted under the new law to draw public attention to this. A media circus of modern proportions descended on the small town of Dayton, Tennessee, to cover the trial. This included journalist H. L. Mencken, who proceeded to rip the prosecution to shreds day after day in his nationally syndicated articles. His unfortunate victim was prosecutor William Jennings Bryan, who deserved a better fate. Bryan had been a Democratic contender for president three times in the days of McKinley and TR. He was a populist, but one who supported many views that most modern readers would now admire, such as women's suffrage and opposition to the Ku Klux Klan. His dislike of evolution was partially based on a dislike of the Gilded Age doctrine of Social Darwinism. He paid a terrible price for his participation: Ridiculed in the press, he died shortly after the verdict—which went his way but was a Pyrrhic victory. The case and its coverage effectively took religion out of the political arena for decades.

If the movies didn't roar, they at least began to make a noise. As with silent films, the history of the talkies is full of false starts and sudden leaps. Eadweard Muybridge and Thomas Edison were involved, as were the French, another plethora of new words (the chronomegaphone, the kinetophone, movietone, photokinema, vitaphone, the audion), and happy lawyers. In 1923, Iowa-born inventor Lee de Forest started showing short "Phonofilms" in New York. It was, however, another four years before the first true talkie appeared: *The Jazz Singer,* where Al Jolson would deliver his prophetic line "You ain't heard nothing yet."

The 1928 presidential election was a runaway win for the new Republican candidate, Herbert Hoover. Hoover looked the perfect man for the job. He was born not quite in a log cabin but in a cottage in rural Iowa, to Quaker parents who owned a hardware store. A successful student of geology at the new university in California endowed by Leland Stanford, he made a fortune in the mining business, after which he devoted himself to public service. During the war he organized U.S. food aid to Europe, after which he oversaw the 1920s boom as secretary of commerce. Hoover genuinely believed that his party's policies had created a self-fueling system of perpetual economic growth, which would soon abolish poverty in the U.S. altogether; a Republican campaign ad trumpeted, "A chicken in every pot and a car in every backyard." Add to this Lou Hoover, a bright first lady—while her husband was prospecting in China, she learned Mandarin, and to this day she is the only president's wife to speak an Asian language—and you had a true "dream ticket" for the White House. Four more years of roaring, please.

True, some economists were beginning to worry about the high levels of credit that had been financing the boom, but the new president had no doubts. If you needed reassurance— well, look at the New York skyline. By 1929, two giants were in pursuit of the title of tallest building in the world. The Bank of Manhattan at 40 Wall Street was going to be 840 feet high. Automobile magnate Walter Chrysler announced an even mightier rival, at 925 feet, uptown at Forty-second and Lexington. So the architects of 40 Wall Street added three more stories to their plans, taking it to 927 feet. Chrysler insisted his skyscraper beat this, and a plan was hatched to hide a spire inside the middle of the building, which would suddenly be raised and take his HQ past the thousand-foot mark . . . The rivals rose at extraordinary speed, four stories a week, thanks to the tireless work of the "steel monkeys" who risked their lives to place and rivet the girders that made the steel skeletons. There were no safety harnesses in 1929; according to one worker, "You either get used to it, or you're dead." (It is, incidentally, a myth that Mohawk Indians worked on the skyscrapers because they had no fear of heights. The truth is that they needed the money and were extremely brave.)

The U.S. stock market was scaling vertiginous new heights, too. Back in August 1921, the leading market index, the Dow Jones, had stood at 63.9, a low point from which it began an unprecedented rise. Over most of the decade, that rise was solid but gentle, though it accelerated slightly as time went on. On December 19, 1927, it passed 200 for the first time. Shortly after, it dipped, but in March 1928 it began to climb at a new, faster rate. This acceleration affected most of the market, but in early 1929 investors began to pile into a narrow selection of the high-tech favorites of the day: David Sarnoff's RCA, Alfred P. Sloan's General Motors, and almost anything connected with electricity.

On September 3, 1929, Wall Street's Dow Jones Index hit a new high of 381.2. The market then traded downward, but many experts thought this was just a correction, shaking out some overzealous speculators, and boom times would soon be back. On October 23, economist Irving Fisher told a meeting of bankers that stock prices "in most instances were not inflated." No doubt his audience went home happy that evening, through streets filled with the roar of a tumultuous decade hurtling toward its close.

EIGHTEEN

Smithsonian National Postal Museum

BROTHER, CAN YOU SPARE A DIME?

Kansas overprint 8¢, 1929–30; Scott catalog no. 666

WHILE THE '20s ROARED through the streets of America's booming cities and suburbs, rural life stayed largely unchanged. In 1920, more than 40 percent of Americans still lived on farms, and for this population, income suffered a blow after the Great War and continued to deteriorate throughout the '20s. Fewer than 10 percent of farmers had electricity. There were no washing machines or radios for the majority, even if they could have afforded them, which most couldn't. Debts began to mount for many farmers across the country. Traditional industries such as mining suffered, too. Coal prices were falling, due to overproduction and to the substitution of oil and gas.

With increased poverty came increased criminality—including an ever-increasing number of raids on rural post offices in which both money and stamps were taken. During the middle part of the decade, U.S. Marines were dispatched to guard the most vulnerable offices, which cut the crime rate, but in 1927, they were called up to take part in an intervention in Nicaragua, and the crime rate rebounded. The stamp above was the result of another attempt to stop the mail robberies. The theory was that if stamps were overprinted with the name of the state where they were issued, post office raiders would not be able to sell them elsewhere. In 1929–30, definitives from 1¢ to 10¢ were overprinted and sold in Kansas and Nebraska.

The experiment was not a success: The robberies continued. The overprinting was stopped, and the stamps are now collectors' items—though they continue their association with crime. A good used example of the 8¢ Grant overprint opening this chapter is now worth around $70, but you can pick up a nice overprint-free 8¢ Grant for a dollar, so the issue has become a happy hunting ground for anyone with ill intent and a simple printing set.

The morning after Irving Fisher's reassuring meeting with the bankers, stock prices plunged 11 percent. The next day, Friday, a group of financiers pumped money into the market, which largely recovered. J. P. Morgan had done this in 1907, and the system had revived. But the following two working days saw the market in freefall again, losing 25 percent of its value over Black Monday and Black Tuesday, October 28 and 29, 1929: the famous Wall Street Crash.

The crash turned out to be only just the beginning. Initially, the market appeared to recover; by April 17, 1930, the Thursday before Easter, it had recouped about half the ground lost. Traders came back from their holidays in a cheerful mood, but the market fell that day and kept falling for the rest of the year (with the occasional uptick, a phenomenon that became known as a "dead cat bounce"). It continued on this path through the whole of 1931 and most of 1932, until the Dow Jones Index was just above 40, a level it had not seen since 1896.

The October 1929 crash set off a chain reaction. It scared people: Previously gung-ho about the future, Americans suddenly became prudent and stopped spending. But parking your money in a bank in 1930 was not a wise move. The year saw bank failures across the nation; with no spending, the businesses to which these banks had lent money started going bankrupt. Which, of course, made people even more terrified . . . Nature did its part, too. After a spring of unusually strong tornadoes, a drought descended on Middle America—especially on the usually fertile Mississippi and Ohio valleys, but also on Wyoming and Montana. Summer 1930 was scorching: In July, the temperature in Holly Springs, Missouri, reached 115 degrees. Farmers, many in excessive debt already, reeled under this new blow.

Economists still argue about exactly how much the government also made things worse—though the arguments are largely between those who say "a lot" and those who say "a hell of a lot." The Smoot-Hawley Act of June 1930 imposed record tariffs on imports; intended to boost American manufacturers, this caused a slump in global trade. At home, money was kept "tight" to keep America on the gold standard, a system that, in essence, linked the number of dollars circulating through the economy to the value of the nation's reserves in Fort Knox. Such measures are now known to have a deflationary economic effect, but this was not understood at the time.

Unemployment rocketed from 5 percent, a level that had been pretty constant since the turn of the century, passing 10 percent in 1931 and 20 percent in 1932. The figure does not include legions of small farmers, technically employed but actually just scraping a living off highly mortgaged and deteriorating land. Men started to wander the country in search of casual work. There had been hobos since the Civil War—by the end of the nineteenth century there had been hobo conventions, one of which, held in St. Louis, had even agreed on a code of ethics. ("Try to be a gentleman at all times," went part of its second article.) However, the Great Depression saw a huge rise in their numbers. In 1931, the Southern Pacific Railroad claimed to have thrown more than 630,000 illegal passengers off its trains. Breadlines became a feature of urban life; unemployed men would spend hours queuing for handouts of basic foodstuffs from charitable organizations. Shantytowns sprang up around American cities; these soon became known as Hoovervilles, a humiliation for the president, though he at least still had a roof over his head. Yip Harburg's lyrics to the 1931 hit "Brother, Can You Spare a Dime?" summed it all up: We fought the war; we built the railroads and the skyscrapers; now we're reduced to panhandling . . .

There really didn't seem to be a solution. Across the Atlantic, new social models were developing and being promoted. The Union of Soviet Socialist Republics was in its second decade. Its confident stamps trumpeted the sturdiness and commitment of its workers and their triumphs in fields such as heavy engineering. In Germany another form of socialism, National Socialism, was on the rise. These ideologies seemed deeply un-American, with their total submission of the individual to the all-powerful state. But the fear that maybe the old American way had had its day began to infect the nation. In the previous century, Karl Marx had argued that capitalism was a phase that societies went through, that the system would inevitably collapse under its own inconsistency, and that the most advanced capitalist nation would fall first. Few Americans went this far in their thinking—unlike European intellectuals, who headed in droves for the Marxist fold—but the doubt was there.

Historian James T. Adams hit back in his 1931 book *Epic of America*, in which he prasied the power of the American dream. This notion has been interpreted in a number of ways ever since. For some it is the notion that any individual, whatever his or her background, can become incredibly rich or achieve ultimate power. For others the dream is one of opportunity for a decent life for all, in which hard work will guarantee anyone a decent standard of living. Adams's preferred version was more philosophical:

> *It is not a dream of motor cars and high wages merely, but a dream of a social order in which each man and each woman shall be able to attain to the fullest stature of which they are innately capable, and be recognized by others for what they are, regardless of the fortuitous circumstances of birth or position.*

But he did not have as clear a vision of how America could return to this dream from its current nightmare.

In 1932—when the Post Office Department experienced an unprecedented loss of $152 million—a group of war veterans descended on Washington to request advance payment of entitlements. A bill to expedite this failed in the Senate, and most of the "Bonus Army" went home. Two thousand stayed, encamped along Pennsylvania Avenue, and became an increasing embarrassment to the government. On July 28, violence erupted, and troops under the command of General Douglas MacArthur entered the camp armed with bayonets and adamsite, a now-banned crowd-dispersion gas that is alleged to have killed two veterans' children. It's hardly surprising that Hoover lost the election later that year, with less than 40 percent of the vote.

Time for Franklin Delano Roosevelt and his New Deal. Exactly what that entailed and how effective it was, I shall let the next stamp relate. Suffice it to say here that whatever happened in Washington after 1932, in the world of the Kansas/Nebraska 8¢ overprint—the world of rural poverty and crime—the Great Depression lasted far into the 1930s.

As this ground on, a mythology emerged, centred around young, rootless, mobile criminals. Some people, possibly as a channel for the anger they felt at the system and how it had let them down, found these individuals romantic—though in real life the criminals murdered defenseless store owners or bank or post office clerks. Most famous among them were Bonnie and Clyde. Clyde Barrow was a product of the penal system: Incarcerated for a petty crime at the age of seventeen, he emerged from prison a heartless professional criminal. Bonnie Parker was a bright high school student who wrote stories and poetry but then dropped out of education, had a failed marriage, and did waitressing work until meeting and falling in love with Barrow. In August 1932, Barrow killed a police deputy after a drunken argument, and the couple began their violent trek across a world of dirt tracks and hideouts, crisscrossing state lines to avoid pursuit. Texas Ranger Frank Hamer formed a posse of six officers, including a top marksman, to track them down. The lawmen caught up with their prey on a lonely road through a Louisiana pine forest on May 23, 1934, and dispensed 150 rounds of rough justice.

If there is a soundtrack to the rural depression, it has to be the blues. In the Deep South, itinerant African American bluesmen would travel from town to town, playing at "juke joints" or on street corners; at the latter they would try to out-play each other, a process known as "cutting heads." Their music, for guitar and voice, was raw, soulful, and defiant, mu-sically only a step or two away from the public "field holler" chants of the plantations but now expressing private loves, de-sires, fears, and losses. Greatest of these, perhaps, was Robert Johnson, despite his legacy being just a handful of recordings.

Johnson lived a brief, restless life on the road, knocking back whiskey, charming women, and, if his own legend is to be believed, selling his soul to the devil in return for his musical talent—which was considerable: He could apparently hear a song on the radio once and play the tune and the orig-inal chords perfectly. Mysterious to the last, Johnson died aged twenty-seven, possibly poisoned by the husband of a woman with whom he had flirted. It is not even known where he is buried. Three-quarters of a century on, millionaire rock stars idolize this man who never owned much beyond a gui-tar, a suit, and a hat that he pulled down over one side of his face to hide a damaged eye.

In the middle of the decade, Kansas (Nebraska got off more lightly) found itself at the heart of a new scourge, the Dust Bowl. The drought that had hit Middle America in 1930 did not let up: A series of blazing summers followed. This was the climate returning to its natural state. The years before had been unusually wet, which (with the help of real estate promoters) had persuaded both government and settlers that the land in that part of the country could be intensively farmed forever. From the 1880s onward, ever more of the short, deep-rooted prairie grass had been plowed by settlers. The topsoil began to dry out, then to blow away. On May 9, 1934, a storm blew across the Great Plains. It lasted for two days and whipped hundreds of millions of tons of soil into the air. Photographs show tidal waves of whirling dirt thundering across the flat lands, engulfing anything and anybody in their path. These became regular events: Black Sunday, April 14, 1935, was even more destructive than the great storm of '34. People began to desert the Plains, especially the southern portion, in their hundreds of thousands (though many more stayed and stuck it out, with typical settler determination), heading west along Route 66 or Route 30. "Okies"—which became a generic name for these refugees, not just those from Oklahoma—did not get a warm welcome, as John Steinbeck so graphically recorded in his novel *The Grapes of Wrath*.

Would it ever end? It's time for our tale to head back to Washington. The Kansas/Nebraska overprint stamp experiment failed totally in its goal of stopping crime. Would other government initiatives prove any more effective in sorting out the economy? Or was the economy broken beyond repair, as many feared?

NINETEEN

Smithsonian National Postal Museum

NEW DEAL, NEW DAY

National Parks issue 10¢, Farley Series, 1935 (imperforate, ungummed); Scott catalog no. 765

FRANKLIN DELANO ROOSEVELT had been given a huge collection of stamps by his mother when he was ten years old—the thirty-second president of America was born to wealth and privilege; no log cabin for him—and he spent the rest of his life sorting it and adding to it. The collection eventually ended up containing more than a million specimens, held in 150 albums. (Sadly, it was broken up and sold on his death.) Even at the most tempestuous times in his life, he would find time to work on it, something he found uniquely effective in decreasing his stress. "I owe my life to my hobbies—especially stamp collecting," he once said.

FDR also understood the power of stamps as propaganda. As soon as he was in office, he got the Post Office producing commemorative stamps again and insisted they be clear, bright, and uncluttered and carry positive images. He designed a number of them himself, in outline at least: the Byrd Antarctic expedition of 1933, Mother's Day 1934 (based on *Whistler's Mother;* a Bureau designer added a flowerpot in the left-hand corner), and the 6¢ Air Mail of 1938. The National Parks set, first issued in 1934, is not one of Roosevelt's designs, but it highlights one of the key policies of the New Deal that he promised the voters, the creation of a Civilian Conservation Corps (CCC) to work on environmental projects. The Great Smoky Mountains Park, on the border of North Carolina and Tennessee—this stamp shows Mount LeConte, on the Tennessee side of the park—was set up in June of 1934 and its infrastructure built by the new Corps. It is now the most visited park in the country.

Stamps were only part of Roosevelt's propaganda effort. His inauguration speech on March 4, 1933, got straight to the point. Things could and would be fixed:

> *The only thing we have to fear is fear itself—nameless, unreasoning, unjustified terror, which paralyzes needed efforts to convert retreat into advance.*

His antidote to fear was action. The first Congress of the new administration lasted exactly a hundred days, from the day of his inauguration to June 16, and was a time of unprecedented decisiveness. Roosevelt was, of course, fortunate in having a majority in both houses—not every president has been so lucky—but he rode his luck superbly. The immediate problem he had to solve was the banking system, which looked to be on the point of total collapse. Congress gave Roosevelt control over the banks, which were immediately closed and only allowed to reopen once the Treasury had been through their books. To prevent panic, Roosevelt went on the radio and explained the situation to the nation—the first of his "fireside chats." (He understood the power of new technologies: He was also the first president to make extensive use of the telephone). The chats worked. Most banks reopened quickly and found their lobbies packed with customers wanting to put back money.

The next piece of the old system to go was Prohibition. The Beer and Wine Revenue Act legalized beverages with up to 3.2 percent alcohol content—and put a sales tax on them. Later in the year, the Twenty-first Amendment abolished the alcohol ban altogether. "I think this would be a good time for a beer," the president commented.

The Civilian Conservation Corps was next. A quarter of a million unemployed men were able to sign up for a six-month stint of work on environmental projects. Food and basic, military-style accommodation were provided. The men only got a small wage, most of which was sent back to their families, but they got work, camaraderie, pride—and a full stomach; 70 percent of CCC members were malnourished on arrival at camp. The CCC would last for the rest of the decade, employ 3 million young men, plant as many trees, set up 800 parks (of which Great Smoky was the biggest), improve existing parks, and provide relief after the disastrous flooding of the Ohio and Mississippi rivers in 1937.

Action was also taken to help agriculture and prevent further mortgage foreclosures. America was taken off the gold standard. The Glass-Steagall Act regulated banking: Depositor protection was introduced, and a split was made between banks' speculative activities and the day-to-day business of looking after people's money and making loans. The Public

Works Administration, set up to organize and finance big projects such as the Lincoln Tunnel and the Grand Coulee Dam, also built roads and schools. The Tennessee Valley Authority rejuvenated the vast, languishing Wilson Dam at Muscle Shoals, Alabama, improved the navigability of the Tennessee River, replanted forests in the valley, and brought electricity to thousands of isolated farms and communities.

The Post Office Department did its bit, too. James A. Farley was the new postmaster general. A politician, he had known as much about the postal system as John Wanamaker had at the time of his appointment (nothing). But Farley made a success of the job. Despite a fall in revenue, he laid off as few men as possible. He made the service profitable again. A $65 million building program, in conjunction with other New Deal bodies, led to the construction of over a thousand new or replacement post offices, the finest of all, perhaps, in Philadelphia. Murals were commissioned for offices around the country in conjunction with the newly created government Section of Fine Arts. Artists were asked to work in a realist style called "American Scene," to tell local stories where possible, and to be upbeat. Many of their works can still be seen and enjoyed— some still on postal premises, though most surviving murals have been moved to other sites or have seen the old post offices converted for other uses. In Giddings, Texas, cowboys are depicted receiving mail. A set in West Palm Beach, by artist Stevan Dohanos, tells the story of James Edward Hamilton, Florida's "barefoot" mail carrier. In the nineteenth century, there was no road from Palm Beach to Miami, so mailmen made a three-day journey on foot and by boat to get the post through; Hamilton was killed on one such expedition in 1887, local legend has it by an alligator.

Further initiatives followed, many spearheaded by Secretary of Labor Frances Perkins, the first woman to serve in a presidential cabinet. A "second New Deal" in 1935 concentrated more on welfare for pensioners and the unemployed but also carried on the program of public works, via Harry Hopkins's Works Progress Administration. Rural electrification, a success in the Tennessee Valley, was spread nationwide.

Hollywood joined in the mood-lifting. From 1933 onward it realized that it was in the business of taking people's minds off Old Man Depression, and it did so with gusto. People thronged to movie theaters for a taste of luxury and escape, to see dapper Fred Astaire sweep Ginger Rogers off her feet (often to the music of Irving Berlin), to marvel at the vast baroque dance sequences of Busby Berkeley, or to watch King Kong carry Fay Wray to the top of the Empire State Building—itself a symbol of resistance to the gloom. Finished in 1931, it was the tallest building in the world at 1,250 feet (1,454 feet if you include the spire). The era also saw the rise of the big swing band, the antithesis of the craggy lonesome bluesman. Unlike the smaller, freer jazz groups of the 1920s, big band music featured tight arrangements; the best of these retained the energy and syncopation of the earlier combos but hit listeners with a wall of sophisticated sound.

By the time campaigning for the 1936 election began, national income had doubled from its 1932 low, 6 million jobs had been created, farm incomes had risen by more than half, the stock market had risen 80 percent, and corporate America, operating at a loss in 1932, was making $6 billion in profits.

The New Deal was not without its critics, however. Recovery was patchy; as we have seen, large parts of rural America remained depressed. Some people, such as radical Wisconsin senator "Fighting Bob" La Follette, thought the New Deal measures didn't go far enough. Others regarded the New

Deal as socialistic and un-American. Looking at the 1934 3¢ NRA special issue stamp (National Recovery Administration, in case anyone is wondering what the National Rifle Association is doing on a New Deal stamp), one can detect a whiff of Sovietism. Four workers (three male, one female) stride toward a rising sun, above the slogan "In a Common Determination." But such imagery was part of the zeitgeist. Roosevelt could be high-handed, and his rhetoric could wander into capitalist-bashing, but he was not a European-style "the state knows everything" Socialist. He was an American democratic politician, cleverly forging an alliance between conflicting groups within the nation. He remolded his party into a mixture of traditionally minded Southern Democrats and a new, "progressive" constituency of organized labor, minorities, and liberal intellectuals. This combination, despite its inherent instabilities, was to last for decades.

Champion of the progressive wing was the first lady, Eleanor Roosevelt. She had been born a Roosevelt—she was TR's niece—so shared her husband's ultraprivileged upbringing. This background did not stop her from becoming a champion of the marginalized: women, African Americans, the unemployed. In this role she sometimes publicly disagreed with her husband, something unheard of before at the White House. Their relationship was complex. After an initial, youthful romance, the marriage soured and nearly ended in divorce. But political and family pressures kept them together, and when FDR contracted polio, which doctors expected to be fatal, she provided great support. (The illness left him unable to walk for the rest of his life.)

The 10¢ stamp at the head of this chapter is imperforate. It was not intended for postal use. Whenever the new commemorative stamps were produced, Postmaster General Farley kept a few imperforate, ungummed sheets of them as souvenirs, which he would then hand out to friends or political allies. (The president always got the first one.) The philatelic community protested that Farley was abusing his position: These rare sheets would be of great value. Farley replied that they were overreacting; the "excitement" over the stamp sheets was "a tempest in a teapot," he said. But in the end the publicity grew too negative and he had to give in. Large numbers of the sheets were produced in 1935 and offered for sale to an eager collecting community. These became known as "Farley's Follies," and this stamp is from one of them.

Another example of governmental hubris occurred in 1937 when, after Supreme Court rulings that challenged the constitutionality of some New Deal measures, FDR tried to pack the court with his own people. Again, protests were made, and the president had to back down.

The same year saw a brief but sharp recession, but in essence America had gotten its energy back. A magnificent symbol of this was the long-planned Golden Gate Bridge. Its central span was the longest in the world, a record it held until 1964. It was also an object of aesthetic beauty with its Art Deco design by architect Irving Morrow—and it was completed ahead of schedule and under budget. On May 27, 1937, "Pedestrian Day," 200,000 people promenaded across it. The next day Angelo Rossi, mayor of San Francisco, crossed to Marin on the old ferry, then rode back in a motorcade, formally opening the bridge.

The year 1937 also saw outstanding, contemporary design from the Post Office. The 1922–23 definitives, though attractive, now looked dated, and a competition was held to find a replacement. Eleven hundred artists entered; the field was whittled down to six designs, which were made into a special sheet and shown to the president. He chose the simplest, by 27-year-old artist and Bureau outsider Elaine Rawlinson. Gone were all those ornate frames, infills, and elaborate lettering. The series showed only a bust, the stamp's value, the name of the individual featured and his time as president, and the words "United States Postage." The colorful series, which became known as the Prexies, featured every president up to Coolidge, with each stamp's value being the place of the president in historical order (so George Washington was on the 1¢, John Adams the 2¢, Jefferson the 3¢, and so on).

The decade looked to be ending on a thoroughly upbeat note. On April 30, 1939, the 150th anniversary of George Washington's inauguration, the World's Fair opened in New York, with the slogan "Dawn of a New Day." The opening was celebrated with a handsome 3¢ stamp showing two futuristic fair buildings, the Trylon and the Perisphere. The Trylon was a spire more than 600 feet high, the Perisphere a concrete sphere 180 feet in diameter, containing a model of "Democracity, the City of the Future." Elsewhere on display were a 7-foot robot—Electro the Moto-Man walked, spoke in a synthesized voice, and smoked cigarettes—televisions, fluorescent light, factory farming, a 3-D movie of a Plymouth being assembled, futuristic locomotives, and, in the General Motors Futurama, a giant model of America in 1960, a nation, unsurprisingly, dominated by the automobile. Quietly located among the exhibits from electric typewriter company IBM was an "electronic calculator" that used punched cards to do mathematical calculations, though most visitors probably didn't think such an invention would have much effect on their lives.

Sixty other nations exhibited. The USSR pavilion, also trumpeting modernity but with hardly a consumer good in sight, was one of the most visited, out of curiosity rather than secret ideological admiration. The Jewish Palestine Pavilion showed the work of settlers in the Holy Land and made the case for establishing the state of Israel. Britain reminded visitors of its own traditions of liberty with a copy of the Magna Carta. There was also, of course, an amusement section. The Life Savers Parachute Jump took people two at a time 250 feet in the air, then let them float down on a carefully controlled parachute. The tower was moved to Coney Island after the fair and is still standing, though it stopped operating in 1964. Particularly popular with male visitors, the Bendix Lama Temple detailed the erotic temptations of a young Buddhist priest, and the Frozen Alive Girl had clearly frozen because she had unwisely gone out on a cold day wearing hardly any clothing.

The World's Fair closed for the year on October 31. (It was to run again in 1940.) But during that summer, the dawning new day had suddenly started looking much less cheerful than the high-tech consumer heaven that the fair had promised its visitors.

TWENTY

Smithsonian National Postal Museum

SULPHUR ISLAND

Iwo Jima issue 3¢, 1945; Scott catalog no. 929

IN THE EARLY 1930s, Germany had issued a few sober stamps each year. Halfway through the decade, many more issues began to appear, often featuring grandiose pseudo-classical architecture, swastikas, or the country's new chancellor, Adolf Hitler. In Russia, Stalin was cementing his position of absolute power. And to America's west, militaristic ideas were becoming ever more influential in Japan, leading the nation into a twisted new version of its ancient Bushido code. Japan's invasion of China, and in particular the capture of that struggling nation's capital, Nanjing, in 1937, showed the new Japan in action: 250,000—some estimates go as high as 350,000—civilians were murdered, many with horrific and deliberate cruelty. However, 1930s America had had its own issues to deal with. It did not wish to be a military power. It had cut back on defense spending after the First World War, and by 1939, its army was the eighteenth largest in the world, with 185,000 men. (Japan had 620,000 soldiers in China alone.) Its navy was half the size of that of its Asian rival. There was, perhaps, a fear that Japan would threaten the Philippines—a fear recognized by Holland M. Smith, an officer in the U.S. Marines who trained his then-small section of the defense forces to master the art of amphibious warfare. But Europe's tyrants seemed to pose little threat. They sounded ever more eager to attack each other; this would be Armageddon, but it would be someone else's Armageddon. The fight would not threaten American interests, and even if it did, there was nothing America could do to stop it. In the meantime, Hitler and Stalin's mutual antagonism kept Europe safe from the dominance of either of them and the Atlantic open for trade.

On August 23, 1939, the two dictators signed a nonaggression pact. Shortly afterward, German panzers swept into Poland—another reinvention of war, which suddenly became fast-moving again after eighty-four years of being about static attrition. By summer 1940 most of Europe was under Soviet, Nazi, or Fascist control. Only Britain remained unconquered, an island of freedom off a continent under totalitarian rule. On September 27, 1940, Germany signed the Tripartite Pact with Japan and Italy. The three nations promised to "establish and maintain a new order of things," by force of arms if necessary. America might have been the world's biggest economy, but it was suddenly surrounded by some very nasty—and now united—powers, like a rich kid who has wandered down an alleyway and suddenly finds himself faced by a gang of toughs.

Still—what to do next? Many people, remembering the

casualty list of the Great War, wanted to do nothing. They considered that America was unlikely to be invaded and that, even though it was still recovering from the Depression, the nation could flourish on its own, with its own internal market. Others disagreed. If Britain fell, what would become of Canada? Suddenly, America might have vast, land-hungry Fascist forces along its 4,000-mile northern border. They questioned the idea that America could suddenly do without trade. Added to this was a moral dimension: Could the uniquely prosperous descendants of Franklin, Washington, and Jefferson really stand by while the rest of the world was trampled by jackboots?

The resolve to do everything short of declaring war grew as the global situation became ever more perilous. This can be seen in the stamps of the era. The Famous Americans set, planned in 1939 and issued throughout 1940, featured, in groups of five each, authors, poets, educators, scientists, composers (no jazz), artists, and inventors; not a soldier or sailor in sight. By October 1940, we see the National Defense Series, whose 2¢ features a 90 mm antiaircraft gun. These latter stamps were designed, in outline at least, by the president.

FDR was playing a clever game. He was well aware of the threat to America's interests, way of life, and even territorial integrity, if Britain were defeated and the totalitarian states decided to divvy the world up between them. But he had to coax a skeptical American public into understanding this. Move too fast, and opinion could turn against him. Move too slowly, and Britain might fall. His first major act was to swap fifty aging navy destroyers for U.S. access to British naval bases in Newfoundland and the Caribbean. The Lend-Lease Act went through Congress (bill number HR 1776), a system whereby Britain, already bankrupted by standing up to Hitler, could borrow military equipment. "We must be the arsenal of democracy," the president told the nation. Morally, the war became more complex when Hitler turned on Stalin and the two tyrannies began fighting each other. However, the Axis powers of Germany, Japan, and Italy remained the aggressive, imperialist threat. On December 7, 1941, such subtleties became irrelevant.

Historians debate whether Pearl Harbor could have been avoided. Conspiracy theorists say that FDR goaded Japan into making the attack; the truth seems to be that he was keen to negotiate peace in the Pacific, despite Nanjing, but was outmaneuvered by hawks in his own cabinet. The conspiracy theorists also point to the poor defense of the base—which is true, but this was not because FDR was prepared to sacrifice U.S. lives to get a war started but because few senior military thought that Japan's Admiral Yamamoto could strike that far across the Pacific. The attack began at 7:48 A.M. Two waves of Japanese planes pulverized the U.S. Pacific Fleet. Of the eight battleships in port at that time, four were sunk and the other four damaged. Half the base's aircraft were destroyed, mostly on the ground, and 2,386 people were killed. (A third wave of bombers, which would have wreaked even more havoc, was canceled. Yamamoto thought enough damage had been done and did not want to risk them.) The next day, Congress voted to go to war, unanimously in the Senate and by 388 votes to 1 in the House of Representatives. The 1 was Jeannette Rankin from Montana, who had also voted against war in 1917; she was chased by an angry mob after the vote and had to hide in a telephone booth, from which she called the police to rescue her.

The same day that Congress voted to go to war, Japan invaded Luzon, the most northerly Philippine island of any size. U.S. and Philippine forces were forced to retreat to the Bataan peninsula. Rescue was impossible; the Japanese controlled the sea and air. After four months of resistance, Allied forces surrendered. The treatment they received ripped any civilized rules of war to shreds: An estimated 15,000 soldiers died on a forced march on which they received little food or water; stragglers were bayoneted or beheaded by officers practicing their swordsmanship. Survivors of this march faced three and a half years of continuing inhumanity, on hellish transport ships, in POW camps, or as slave labor. The Japanese swept south, capturing New Guinea and the Solomon Islands, as well as the oil-rich Dutch East Indies (now Indonesia). This advance threatened to cut off the route between the United States and its ally Australia but was halted by a naval action in the Coral Sea, fought over four days in May 1942. A second sea battle on June 4 took place around the tiny atoll of Midway. Four Japanese aircraft carriers were sunk—America lost one, the *Yorktown*—and Japan lost dominance of the Pacific Ocean.

The enemy still had to be dislodged from the islands they had so swiftly conquered. Quite how difficult this would be became apparent during the first land action, on Guadalcanal in the Solomon Islands, which began on August 7, 1942. The landing, for which Holland Smith's marines had been preparing for a decade, was largely unopposed—the last time U.S. troops would enjoy such fortune—but once battle was joined it became vicious and grueling. The enemy was largely unseen, dug as they were into huge bunker complexes, and had been indoctrinated to fight to the last man. The environment was almost as unforgiving: swamps, mountains, and jungles; heat and humidity; snakes, crocodiles, and—most dangerous of all—disease-bearing mosquitoes. It took until

February 1943 to conquer this relatively small piece of land (about 2,000 square miles in area). There were five more enemy-occupied islands of similar size in the Solomons alone.

The men captured at Bataan or slogging across Guadalcanal would not have appreciated the fact, but Roosevelt and Churchill had agreed that their first priority was Hitler. The German dictator had reneged on his pact with Stalin in 1941, and Russia was now on the Allied side; it was essential that the new ally be kept on board. Moscow—and America's generals—wanted an all-out attack on occupied mainland Europe in 1942. FDR was not convinced, and he turned out to be right: An exploratory raid on Dieppe in August was a disaster, with a Canadian invasion force of 5,000 men suffering 900 deaths and 1,900 taken prisoner. After Dieppe, it was decided instead to invade North Africa, with the aim of removing Nazi forces from the southern Mediterranean coast then striking up through Italy.

If Dieppe was a tragedy, Operation Torch, the North African landings, was farcical. U.S. troops found themselves fighting the French, who were supposed to have welcomed them, on an Atlantic coast with little strategic relevance. However, the campaign that followed began to create a united army out of the American and British forces.

Overall commander U.S. general Dwight D. Eisenhower established his mastery of both logistical planning and soothing spiky military egos. (His three best combat generals were the Americans George Patton and Omar Bradley and Britain's Bernard Montgomery. The first two disliked Brits—and each other—and the latter disliked Americans.) The American production machine was now in high gear, turning out planes, tanks, and trucks—not to mention rations and boots. After his eventual defeat, German general Erwin Rommel commented that the North Africa campaign had been "won by the quartermaster." The Allied advance, led by Patton, continued into Sicily, where another amphibious landing proved a much greater success—so much so that Italy surrendered before any Allied troops landed on its mainland. This surrender quickly became irrelevant, as the former Axis power was immediately occupied by the Germans. Talk had been of Europe's "soft underbelly," but when the invasion of Italy began on September 9, 1943, the underbelly turned out to be full of battle-hardened Wehrmacht units. A vicious campaign would follow.

Meanwhile in the Pacific, U.S. forces were inching forward; 1943 saw a series of operations against other islands in the Solomons. Some of these had bizarre names: Operation Blissful was launched against Choiseul Island and Operation Cherryblossom against the northernmost island, Bougainville. These names belie the horrific difficulty of the fighting, especially on the latter island. What did not happen in 1943 was an invasion of northern Europe. America and Russia wanted it, Britain did not; in the end a compromise was reached. The attack would take place in June 1944: D-day.

Looking through a stamp collection, one would hardly guess the nation was locked in war in a way it had never been before. A simple "Win the War" 3¢ was issued in 1942. The Flags series of 1943–44 commemorated countries occupied by Axis powers—including, rather oddly, Austria, despite the fact that in 1936 cheering crowds had lined the streets of Vienna to welcome its new Führer. The defense of the Bataan peninsula was honored with a stamp in 1944. But otherwise, the Post Office quietly commemorated anniversaries such as Samuel Morse's first telegraph message or the centennial of Florida's statehood.

This contrasts with the way that other parts of America's cultural industry threw themselves into the fray. *Casablanca* premiered in 1942. Now seen as the classic Hollywood wartime movie, at the time it was only a moderate box office success. Much more popular were *This Is the Army* with songs by Irving Berlin and a lead role for an actor named Ronald Reagan, the romantic *A Guy Named Joe*, and the World War I biopic *Sergeant York*. Musically, the era belongs to Glenn Miller (who, like those three big movies, was not really liked by critics). Miller, a trombonist, learned his trade arranging for other bandleaders. He formed his own outfit in 1938, where he developed his dense, reedy sound. During the buildup to D-day, this sound echoed around countless U.S. bases in Britain, as troops prepared for action.

That action began on June 6. At 6:30 A.M. 57,000 U.S. troops landed on Omaha and Utah beaches near Carentan in Normandy. They faced withering fire and unexpectedly difficult conditions, especially on Omaha, where currents dragged landing craft away from intended landing places so that tanks, which were supposed to blast their way across the flatter sections of the coastline, were unable to get onto the beach. In the end the only way forward was to scale the surrounding cliffs. By the end of the day 2,400 men were dead—but the 1st Division was a mile inland.

German strategy had been to concentrate defenses on the beaches, and once these were breached, Allied armies made speedy progress. Paris fell on August 25, and by December 16, Eisenhower had reached the Ardennes. (The day before this, Major Glenn Miller's plane had disappeared over the English Channel, never to be found.) The next day saw a vast German counterattack in the Ardennes, but this was beaten back; by February 1945, 3 million Allied soldiers were camped on the banks of the Rhine, ready for the final push toward Berlin.

Progress in the Pacific was slower. More islands had to be clawed from the Japanese grasp: Saipan in the Marianas (military planners had thought the liberation would take three days; it took three weeks), Guam, the Philippines. Attention then turned to taking Japan itself. The first piece of that nation to be attacked was Iwo Jima, an 8-square-mile lump of volcanic rock—its name means "Sulphur Island"—which in times of peace had been uninhabited. It was now a Japanese air base, standing between America's main bomber bases on the Mariana Islands and mainland Japan. The invasion began on February 19, 1945. Even by the standards of the Pacific war, the resistance was ferocious. Twenty thousand Japanese soldiers were dug into a network of tunnels and bunkers, and had been ordered to fight to the death. It took more than a month of hand-to-hand fighting, and more than 7,000 U.S. lives, to displace them.

Having done little to reflect the war up till now, the Post Office finally captured a powerful, defining image. The Iwo Jima 3¢ is based on a photograph taken early in the fighting, on February 23, showing five marines and one sailor raising the Stars and Stripes on the top of the island's peak, Mount Suribachi. The picture was taken by Joe Rosenthal, a journalist who had volunteered for the Army but been turned down because of poor eyesight. It was not posed, as some stories incorrectly have it, though it was the second flag-raising that day: The first flag had been rather small, and assault commander Lieutenant Colonel Chandler Johnson—who was killed on March 3—wanted one that "every son-of-a-bitch on this cruddy island can see." He got one that was seen all over the world. The image was featured in the Sunday papers two days later, used to advertise War Bonds and finally rushed onto this stamp.

Rosenthal's image is stirring—but behind it all, tragic. The capture of Mount Suribachi only gave the marines control of a third of Iwo Jima; the mountain is at one corner of a triangle. In the fight for the rest of the island, three of the six men featured on the stamp died. The marine ramming the pole into the ground, Corporal Harlon Block, died on March 1. Sergeant Michael Strank (half-hidden, in the middle of the group) also died on that day, probably in a friendly fire incident. The marine second from the back, Franklin R. Sousely, was shot by a sniper on March 21. The three survivors, like millions of other war veterans, suffered from lasting psychological effects. The man at the back, Private Ira H. Hayes, a Pima Indian—from the same small, usually peaceful tribe as World War I hero Matthew Juan—battled with alcohol and died in 1955. Private Rene Gagnon (largely hidden, near the front) also died of drink, though living into his fifties. Lionized for a while after the photograph—the three survivors met President Truman and various Hollywood stars—he ended up doing menial jobs, angry at the fickle nature of fame and the media. Only one of the men on this stamp, John H. Bradley (at the front of the group, with his back to the camera), survived to old age. He hardly ever talked about the war, even to his family. His son later revealed that he had been racked with survivor guilt: Later in the battle for the island, Bradley had discovered what was left of a buddy who had been tortured to death by Japanese soldiers.

The Iwo Jima stamp shows us the many-sided truth of war: its teamwork and courage, its moments of glory, but behind that, its amoral destructiveness and its long, painful after-effects—something General William Tecumseh Sherman understood so well. It does not, however, show a problem that was becoming appallingly apparent: If the Japanese resisted the attack on an empty island 600 miles from their mainland with such ferocity, how many lives was it going to take to invade the mainland and conquer it?

TWENTY-ONE

Smithsonian National Postal Museum

TOWARD DISUNITED NATIONS

UN Peace Conference commemorative 5¢, 1945; Scott catalog no. 928

THIS SIMPLE STAMP IS FULL of hidden, unintended irony. It features a quote by FDR dated April 25, 1945, by which date the president was no longer alive. It is a stamp of peace but was issued while war was still raging in Europe and the Pacific. It looks forward to an era of global harmony—an era that never materialized.

On its date of issue, April 25, representatives of forty-six nations gathered in San Francisco to discuss an international body to preserve future world peace. Every delegate was given a special commemorative album containing the stamp, courtesy of a presidential order, dated April 11. It was the last order FDR gave: He had a heart attack at 1:00 P.M. the next day and died two hours later. At noon on that same day, the new president, Harry Truman, had had a meeting with Secretary of War Henry L. Stimson. Rather than give a briefing, Stimson had handed Truman a memorandum that began:

> *Within four months we shall in all probability have completed the most terrible weapon ever known in human history, one bomb of which could destroy a whole city.*

On July 16, this probability became fact at Alamogordo, New Mexico. The shockwave from the test explosion was felt 100 miles away. Observers 10 miles away experienced heat "like an oven"; to one of them, J. Robert Oppenheimer, words from the *Bhagavad Gita* leaped to mind: "I am become Death, the Destroyer of Worlds." Truman had known nothing about the weapon when he entered the White House. Its development, code-named the Manhattan Project, had been carried out in extraordinary secrecy, despite involving more than 100,000 people. Now, the honest, plain-dealing president, who had run a small business in Missouri and served as an artillery captain in World War I before entering politics, had a power no other human being had ever had in the history of the world, to order the use of an atomic bomb.

After the hard-won success at Iwo Jima, the marines had moved on to Okinawa, another island closer to the Japanese mainland, to be pitted against 100,000 defenders ordered to fight to the death. As on Sulphur Island, they overcame the dire odds, despite enduring a death toll of 12,500. (The entire Japanese garrison died, too, as did tens of thousands of Okinawans, many ordered by the Imperial Army to commit suicide rather than surrender.) Military commanders had then begun work on a spring 1946 invasion of the Japanese mainland, in which estimates of Allied casualties ran as high as 1 million and beyond. (One Japanese estimate was of 20 million deaths in this ultimate struggle.)

Truman understood that the atom bomb could perhaps prevent this slaughter. Against this, a minority voice argued that using this weapon was an act of such immorality that no circumstances could justify it. More practically, its opponents argued that its use would trigger an arms race with Russia (Dwight Eisenhower was of this view): exactly the opposite of what the United Nations conference sought to bring about. Truman had to make the decision. No wonder he later put a sign on his desk that read THE BUCK STOPS HERE.

On the early morning of August 6, 1945, just over two months after the "Toward United Nations" stamp was issued, three B-29 bombers took off from the air base on Tinian Island. One of them was named the *Enola Gay* and carried an atom bomb. (Another was called *Necessary Evil*.) By 8:00 A.M. they reached Hiroshima. At 8:15, the weapon was dropped, descending on a parachute and detonating at 2,000 feet. The airmen saw a vast ball of flame, which expanded till it hit the ground, where it radiated out in all directions consuming the city. One of the crew commented. "My God, what have we done?" Thousands of people were vaporized instantly. Others died from falling rubble or sustained terrible burns; still others were so severely irradiated that they lingered on for a few agonizing weeks or months. The final death toll has been estimated at 135,000. A second such horror was visited on Nagasaki three days later. Shortly afterward, the Japanese emperor Hirohito overruled his military advisers, some of whom were happy for their country to be obliterated rather than capitulate, and ordered his generals to surrender.

The atomic bomb became the defining object of the next

half century. It undoubtedly saved hundreds of thousands of lives by ending the war and then became the cornerstone of America's defense strategy. However, the Manhattan Project has never been featured on stamps, nor have any of its leading lights, except for Enrico Fermi, who made major subsequent contributions to physics and later became an opponent of nuclear armaments. In 1995, a minisheet celebrating the fiftieth anniversary of the end of the war was announced. One of the ten stamps was to show a mushroom cloud and the caption "Atomic bombs hasten war's end." Protests, including one from the mayor of Nagasaki, arose immediately, and the stamp was replaced by one featuring Harry Truman accepting Japan's surrender. Stamps can say a lot, but there are some things that reduce even them to silence.

The Japanese surrender was announced at 7:00 P.M. EST on August 14, and America went wild. Central New York City filled with revelers, including the sailor and nurse featured kissing in the famous photograph by Alfred Eisenstaedt. In Washington, D.C., half a million people took to the streets. For others, of course, the celebrations were more muted. In the conflict, 405,366 U.S. fighters had died. Many more would come home changed: some for the better, eager to embrace the opportunities offered by the GI Bill that President Roosevelt had signed in 1944; others, like Corpsman John H. Bradley, haunted by memories.

America now held a position of global economic, political, and military power that no other nation had ever held. It had boomed during the war years—and not just in those sectors making military goods. Wartime spending had completed the job of the New Deal, boosting the economy and sending money flowing around it again. In mid-1945, more than half the world's manufacturing was in the USA. A third of the world's export trade came from America—just as well, as the nation owned half the world's ships. Two-thirds of the world's gold reserves were located in Fort Knox. But could the United States unite the world, as this stamp promised?

Russia did not want to be united. It began systematically silencing calls for democracy in the Eastern European countries it had occupied, using whatever means necessary: rigged elections, assassinations, arrests by secret police. Truman, an optimist about human nature, hoped to make personal progress with the Soviet leader. He made none. The Soviet dictator later confided to Nikita Khrushchev that he considered Truman "worthless."

On February 9, 1946, Stalin made a speech to the Supreme Soviet stating that Communism and capitalism could not coexist: His country must rearm for the next war, which would probably take place in the 1950s. Was this just rhetoric for home consumption? The president asked George Kennan, a senior U.S. diplomat in Moscow, to find out. Kennan's reply, in an 8,000-word telegram, was deeply pessimistic: Russia was above all scared, and would insist on a buffer of puppet regimes around it. A fortnight later, Truman proudly welcomed Winston Churchill to Fulton, Missouri, where the old warrior told an audience of students—and press—that an "Iron Curtain" had fallen across Europe. Many Americans were shocked: For the last four years they had been told that "Uncle Joe" Stalin was their ally, and some had seen him as a more progressive force than the descendants of George III. Truman commissioned another report about Russia, this time from his special adviser Clark Clifford. This came to an even more negative conclusion: The Soviet Union was "on a course of aggrandizement designed to lead to eventual world domination." Russia had its own Manhattan Project—Stalin had put his ruthless henchman Lavrenti Beria in charge of it the day after Hiroshima—and would do all it could to undermine democracies.

How should America react? After World War I, it had gone back to its Washingtonian/nineteenth-century roots, shrinking the standing army and staying out of international conflict. Now the United States felt impelled to stand up to Stalin. This was partially because it had just won a war against two of the three tyrannies that had threatened to overwhelm it in the 1930s, and partially because of its extraordinary economic supremacy. It would police the world because it could. Would *this* unite nations?

In February 1947, America had to shore up tottering regimes in Greece and Turkey, two nations right next to Churchill's Iron Curtain, which looked like they might go Communist unless the United States intervened. On March 12, Truman announced to a silent Congress, awed by the importance of the moment, that the United States would support "free peoples who are resisting attempted subjugation by armed minorities or by outside pressures." The help would be "primarily through economic and financial aid." The speech, which became known as the "Truman Doctrine," would shape U.S. policy for the next forty-five years. An enormous financial boost for Western Europe soon followed, on the advice of George C. Marshall, Eisenhower's former chief of staff. (Russia and its satellites were formally invited to participate in the program but walked out of negotiations after five days.) In four years, the Marshall Plan gave around $13 billion to fourteen European states, some of which was spent on food, the rest on capital goods to rebuild infrastructure and industry. Goods were also provided—including mules from Texas to replace ones killed in the conflict in Greece.

In February 1948, Stalin organized a coup in Czechoslovakia. In June of that year, he tried to cut off all supplies to Berlin, an island of shared power in the sea of Soviet-occupied eastern Germany; a massive airlift was organized, and in the end the Soviet dictator backed down—on Berlin at least. On August 29, 1949, the Russians successfully tested their own atomic bomb, *Pervaya molniya* (First lightning).

Europe might have split, but Truman had hoped that his doctrine would not be needed in Asia, which instead would prove a fertile area for the natural expansion of freedom. China—or a large part of it, anyway—had been freshly liberated from the horrors of Japanese rule. It was time to welcome the world's most populous nation into the club of modern democracies. But it didn't want to join. Instead, it was locked in a civil war, in which one side was Communist. America provided arms for the other side, the Nationalists—but found itself backing a loser. On October 1, 1949, Mao Tse-tung stood on the Gate of Heavenly Peace in Beijing and proclaimed the founding of the People's Republic of China: the world's largest Communist nation.

On June 25, 1950, five years and two months after the stamp that opens this chapter was issued, troops from Communist North Korea launched a surprise attack on the South. The scattered U.S. forces in the country were overrun. The lucky ones managed to retreat; the less fortunate were killed or captured. By September, more than three-quarters of South Korea was in Communist hands. Soon after, General MacArthur had his finest hour, launching a daring invasion at Inchon, 150 miles behind enemy lines. North Korea crumbled, and soon the U.S. forces, technically fighting under a

United Nations banner, were at the 38th parallel, the old border between the two Koreas. There should then have been a
pause for reflection, but MacArthur forged ahead. Pyongyang fell on October 19; by November most of the North was
in UN hands. Then China responded. Two hundred thousand troops poured across the Yalu River. The world looked
to be heading for war again, and the hopes expressed in
FDR's final stamp appeared to be empty dreams.

TWENTY-TWO

SALUTING YOUNG AMERICA

YOUTH
MONTH
SEPT. 1-30, 1948

3¢

UNITED STATES POSTAGE

3¢

Smithsonian National Postal Museum

ROCKING AND ROLLING

Saluting Young America 3¢, 1948;
Scott catalog no. 963

IF THE YEARS AFTER the Second World War saw the "united nations" dream souring to a divided and dangerous world, on America's home front this didn't appear to matter that much. If you look at the stamps of, say, 1948, there is no sense of a nation under threat. The overriding impression is that people were tired of war and eager to get back to life as normal. Aggressively normal, if the rather wooden-looking boy and girl in this stamp are anything to go by. Other special issues of '48 provide a diet of obscure centennials, moderately eminent people, and, wackiest of all, a giant chicken waddling into the sunrise in celebration of a hundred years of America's poultry industry. The stamp above, by prolific designer Victor S. McCloskey Jr., was issued for "Youth Month," a media event to combat juvenile delinquency. For its launch, youngsters from all over the United States assembled on the White House lawn; President Truman oversaw a ceremony in which three of them were given sheets of the stamps by the postmaster general, Jesse M. Donaldson. One, Peter Owens, had won a competition to be the "Typical American Boy."

But what did these "typical" youngsters want? On July 11, 1951, a disk jockey named Alan Freed began broadcasting on a Cleveland radio station, WJW. The airwaves were still largely segregated, but Freed, though white himself, played music mainly by black artists. He enthused about the material rather than simply presenting it, creating in what he called his "Moondog Kingdom" a sense of adventure and belonging for his young audience. Amusingly to modern listeners, he would also segue into raving about products he'd been paid to advertise, like Sulfur 8 hair conditioner, Erin Brew—apparently the No. 1 beer in the northern Ohio area at the time—and the Temple Baptist Church. The songs Freed played were "rhythm and blues," which used chord progressions and scales similar to the blues but were more upbeat and usually played by small groups: drums, bass, piano, sax, and, electric guitar, the last of these boosted by amplification technology. Like blues, lyrics could be sexual and suggestive (hopefully not just after an ad for the Temple Baptist Church). Freed started to organize concerts for his listeners. The Moondog Coronation Ball was held on Friday night, March 21, 1952. Too many people turned up, and when the first band began to play, fans who had been made to wait outside broke the doors down. Fights ensued; the police were called; the event became national news—and so did rock 'n' roll (a term invented by Freed), from the start associated with juvenile delinquency. Not what the instigators of the 1948 stamp had in mind for Young America.

By 1954, Freed had been lured to New York. The music had moved on, too, becoming lighter due to the influence of country: That year also saw the release of "Rock Around the Clock." The song was a moderate success, but a year later it was used in a film called *Blackboard Jungle*—about juvenile delinquency—and became a global hit. However, the singer, Bill Haley, wasn't exactly teenage heart-throb material: He was nearly thirty and getting a little tubby. The music needed a star.

Elvis Presley was born on January 8, 1935, in a two-room shack in Tupelo, Mississippi, from which his parents were later evicted for nonpayment of rent. When he was thirteen, the family relocated to Nashville, Tennessee; at age eighteen, he cut a demo disk at Sun Records, which brought him to the attention of Sun's boss, Sam Phillips, a man perpetually on the lookout for talent (particularly "a white man with the Negro sound"). Phillips organized a session on July 5, 1954, with Presley and two backing musicians, which was unremarkable until Presley launched into Arthur Crudup's "That's All Right." Phillips knew at once that he'd found his man. It took a while for the rest of America to catch on, but on April 21, 1956, Elvis's "Heartbreak Hotel" hit No. 1 on the charts published in *Billboard* magazine. A string of hits—"Hound Dog," "Love Me Tender," "All Shook Up"—followed, as did appearances on TV. East Coaster Steve Allen tried to make Elvis look foolish; his CBS rival Ed Sullivan, more attuned to Middle America, let him do his thing and broke all viewing records. Elvis began to make movies; *Jailhouse Rock* was a particular success, teaming him up with songwriters Jerry Leiber and Mike Stoller. Having taken the national media by storm, like Mary Pickford and Charlie Chaplin before him, Elvis proceeded to become a global star. Around the world, young people listened to his songs and felt a totally fresh passion and intensity. In Liverpool, England, a sixteen-year-old named John Lennon heard "Heartbreak Hotel," and it made his hair stand on end; for an even younger George Harrison, a few miles down the road, his first experience of the song was what he later described as an epiphany.

Along with rock 'n' roll music came new fashion. By 1956, the young girl on the 1948 stamp would have been wearing a knee-length polka-dot skirt and saddle shoes; the boy would have Brylcreemed his hair and put on a leather jacket and drainpipe jeans. He would drive, or aspire to drive, an automobile. The automobiles of the 1950s were as distinctive as the era's music—and are a natural for stamps. Issues celebrated them in 2005 and 2008, and no doubt brought a happy tear to the eye of some older collectors who had driven the vehicles when young. Kaisers, Studebakers, and Eldorados glinted with chrome; they sported rocketlike tailfins, wraparound windshields, or strange conical outgrowths on their bumpers; their V8 engines chortled with glee as they guzzled the era's cheap gas. If a young man was lucky enough to possess such a vehicle—most automobiles were owned by males in the 1950s—he would undoubtedly have gone on dates to a drive-in movie theater, of which there were 4,000 by 1955. There he might have tried to make it with his partner—many automobiles of the era had bench seats, front seating right across their width.

He would most likely have been unsuccessful: Rules were still rules. Compared to what was to come in the late 1960s, the 1950s generational split was quite narrow. The youngsters on the 1948 stamp probably went a bit wild, had a few spats with their parents, then found a partner and settled down. One assumes the last of these is what Jim and Judy did after the end of *Rebel Without a Cause*—a 1955 film supposedly about existential youthful rebellion but, it could be argued, more about the importance of family life and what goes wrong if parents are ineffective. Family and traditional conservative values were still essentially what the 1950s were about.

Part of that family life was now occupied by TV. By 1956, there were over 40 million sets in America—including one in the White House, where the man who had replaced Truman in 1953, Dwight Eisenhower, would often sit with the first lady, Mamie, eating dinners off trays on their laps while watching the new machine. One of the Eisenhowers' favorite shows was that of Lawrence Welk, who presented light musical entertainment "in the champagne style." They were also fans of Ed Sullivan (I don't know if they watched the Elvis broadcasts) and *I Love Lucy*, the most popular program of the era, starring Lucille Ball as a dippy but lovable showbiz wannabe. The main fare of 1950s TV, however, was westerns. *The Lone Ranger* first rode onto TV sets in 1952, accompanied by his Native American sidekick, Tonto, on his smaller, less impressive horse. The previously unrecognized role of dogs in the settlement of the West was celebrated in *Rin Tin Tin*. The year 1955 saw the Davy Crockett craze sweep the nation, showing the awesome power of the new medium for the first time. Three programs featuring the symbol of rugged settler bravery were aired in late 1954 and early 1955, and America went Crockett crazy. The theme song became a No. 1 hit. Kids sported Crockett caps in fake coonskin (girls could have worn Polly Crockett ones); publishers rushed to the presses with Crockett books; manufacturers produced Crockett lampshades, towels, schoolbags, mugs, figurines, toothbrushes, trading cards, jigsaw puzzles . . . It has been estimated that more than $100 million of Crockett merchandise was sold during 1955—after which the craze died out as quickly as it had arisen. The great frontiersman quietly reappeared on a 5¢ stamp in 1967.

I have concentrated on popular culture in this chapter, but supposing one or both of the youngsters in the 1948 stamp grew up to cast their aesthetic net wider? The era also introduced the artist Jackson Pollock's explosive, energetic "abstract expressionism": Pollock would lay the canvas on the floor and apply paint by any method that came to mind, dribbling it from the tube, throwing it, squirting it from a turkey baster, spreading it with palette knives or sticks. (Pollock was celebrated on a stamp in 1999, using a well-known photograph of him at work—minus his ever-present cigarette, a quintessentially cool item in 1948, which was airbrushed out to suit 1990s' sensibilities.) In literature, young "Beat" poets became ever more disaffected by what they perceived as the era's conformism and drabness—sophisticated jazz fans, they turned up their noses at the Moondog Coronation— culminating in Allen Ginsberg's reading of his protest poem *Howl* in 1955. Among the audience at this event, in a converted auto-repair workshop in San Francisco, was Jack Kerouac, whose novel *On the Road* followed in 1957. The book details journeys taken through bohemian America in search of vitality, authenticity, and spiritual fulfillment: Kerouac was a lapsed Catholic, and the hero of his novel is called Salvatore Paradise. Readers are still divided as to what he actually finds. Salvation and paradise? The dead end of psychological narcissism? Or, like Jim Stark, the Rebel Without a Cause, a simple longing for lost family?

For the Beats—if not for the couple at the drive-in—sexual morality was now becoming a matter of personal choice. Such an attitude did not go down well with many older Americans, including Eisenhower's postmaster general, Arthur E. Summerfield. Summerfield started as one of the great reforming postmasters but ended up doing the service few favors. In his first years, he cleared out a great deal of dead wood, modernizing the department's accounting system, renovating aging premises, and getting long-distance mail off slow, inefficient railroads and onto America's burgeoning domestic airlines. He refused to put political placemen in office, judging postmasters on merit. He also oversaw the introduction of a new set of definitive stamps to replace the 1930s Prexies, the Liberty issue, so named because the Statue of Liberty featured on the standard 3¢. Under Summerfield's aegis, the department was soon making a surplus, which should have been retained for investment in further modernization, but which he instead returned to the Treasury with a great fanfare to show off how much money he had saved. Summerfield also used the Post Office for a moral crusade. In 1959, he tried to have the novel *Lady Chatterley's Lover* banned from the mail. The courts refused to back him, and the case was much covered in the press. The novel, by a British literary writer unknown to the wider U.S. audience, D. H. Lawrence, became a bestseller. Summerfield then tried to make his point about the nation's morals by curating a show of pornography seized from the mails and insisting that the nation's opinion-formers and decision-makers visit it. This soon became a Washington joke, with people lining up to attend, but not for the reasons the curator intended.

It is, perhaps, easy to mock the Eisenhower administration, with the president enjoying his TV dinner in front of Lawrence Welk and Arthur Summerfield obsessing about pornography. But during the 1950s inflation stayed low, the economy boomed, and the fruits of that boom were reasonably spread out. The decade is sometimes called the one that "ended poverty." That's an overstatement: Poverty lingered on in the rural South and in parts of the big northern cities (especially, but not exclusively, among African and Latino Americans). But four-fifths of the population saw rising incomes and ever more things to spend that income on. The kids on the 1948 stamp were walking into a bright future, whatever kind of work they went into. Eisenhower can take much of the credit for this. He kept a light but firm hand on the national tiller, spending money when necessary—the interstate highway system was the product of his presidency—but always watching the budget. Viewed from our era, his presidency seems blissfully free of ideological grandstanding, on domestic matters at least.

Critics of Eisenhower say that 1953–61 were years of issues deferred, of difficulties postponed. Civil rights inched forward. How valid were the Beats' rants against the sterility of the emerging system of production and consumption? Most insidious of all, there was the ever-increasing threat of another war, this time featuring nuclear weapons aimed at America's own cities.

TWENTY-THREE

Smithsonian National Postal Museum

COLD WAR

NATO 4¢, 1959;
Scott catalog no. 1127

THIS STAMP IS THE WORK of Stevan Dohanos, an artist closely associated with the post for many years. We have already encountered his work at West Palm Beach, where he was responsible for the murals in honor of barefoot mailman James E. Hamilton. He also designed many covers for the *Saturday Evening Post*, a magazine that traces its origins back to Ben Franklin and had its heyday in the 1950s and 1960s. Several of these covers featured post offices, showing them to be hubs of rural American life, or showed mailmen, bags bulging with letters and parcels, battling inclement weather to do their duty and connect people. For Dohanos, the post is a metaphor for human interdependence and the need to actively sustain it. However, this stamp, in celebration of the tenth anniversary of the North Atlantic Treaty Organization, an alliance of Western nations opposed to Soviet expansionism, takes us to a much darker place: the Cold War.

We left the geopolitical narrative in 1950, with an Iron Curtain across Europe, with scientists on both sides of that curtain working on weapons of terrible destructiveness, and with hundreds of thousands of Communist Chinese troops surging into Korea.

In October 1950, U.S. forces had been stationed in the North Korean capital, Pyongyang; by January 1951, the South Korean capital, Seoul, was in Chinese hands. Harry Truman was advised to use the atom bomb but refused: The war would have to be won by conventional means. The right man to achieve this appeared, General Matthew Ridgway, and the Chinese advance was halted, then reversed. The war entered a new phase, with both sides entrenched along the 38th parallel where it had started nearly two years before. Peace talks began in July 1951, but progress was painfully slow. And the fact that the conflict was now static, more like World War I than World War II, did not mean fewer soldiers were dying.

Two events ended the stand-off, neither of them in Korea. In November 1952, Eisenhower was elected president with a promise to end the conflict. Then in March 1953, Stalin died. The dictator's successors did not want the war continued. Despite the best attempts of South Korea's president, Syngman Rhee, to sabotage peace, an armistice was signed on July 27. Eisenhower spoke to the nation on television, quoting Lincoln's Second Inaugural Address to show his desire for "lasting peace . . . with all nations."

He did not get his desire. The Soviet Union and China remained eager to spread their influence. At home, the pragmatic Eisenhower found himself outflanked by hawkish members of his own party, the most extreme of whom was

Joe McCarthy, a senator obsessed with Communism, who launched vicious attacks on public figures suspected of left-wing loyalties. At the same time, the old European colonial empires had collapsed, leaving power vacuums around the world, a factor not foreseen by Harry Truman when he had declared his universalist doctrine.

These forces began to play out. Vietnam had been a French colony before the war, then had been seized by the Japanese during World War II. After 1945, Paris sought to reclaim it, but the Vietnamese did not want to be reclaimed. Instead, resistance leader Ho Chi Minh asserted his nation's freedom in a speech that began by quoting the 1776 Declaration of Independence. He continued by alluding to the conference celebrated in FDR's "April 25" United Nations stamp:

> *We are convinced that the Allied nations, which at . . .*
> *San Francisco have acknowledged the principles of self-determination and equality of nations, will not refuse to acknowledge the independence of Vietnam.*

France did not acknowledge this independence and went to war. As this conflict ground on, Vietnamese nationalist forces became ever more closely aligned with the Communists. France appealed to the United States for help, and White House hawks urged Eisenhower to respond. The president, no lover of colonialism, found himself caught between his distaste for risking American lives to protect an old empire and the perceived need to combat Communism. He decided to stay out of the conflict, and the French were defeated at Dien Bien Phu, an isolated fortress at which Eisenhower had implored them not to make a stand.

In July 1954, Vietnam was partitioned. Stamps from the

two new nations tell us a lot about them. The first issue from Hanoi, capital of the North, showed Ho Chi Minh alongside Mao Tse-tung and Stalin's immediate successor, Georgi Malenkov—a clear sign of his ideological allegiance, though also a signal that the North saw itself as the equal of the two "big" Communist powers. The first major stamp issue from the South showed refugees from the North trying to escape the new regime on rafts. Arguably South Vietnam was already defining itself as "not being Communist" rather than anything positive.

Iran was another newly modernizing nation flexing its muscles against an old colonial power. Here, the issue was oil. Britain had been cashing in on the Iranian oil fields since 1933, when it had signed a very unequal deal with the shah. (Iran got 16 percent of the oil proceeds in theory, in practice much less once accountants had worked out what the "proceeds" were.) A new prime minister, Mohammad Mossadegh, was democratically elected in 1951 with a mandate to nationalize the oil wells. Relationships between Iran and Britain deteriorated quickly, and in late 1952 diplomatic relations were broken off. The White House hawks sensed a Communist threat and got to work on a plan to topple Mossadegh; Eisenhower did not approve but was worried about the disruption to the world's oil supplies, and in the end he was talked into it. Mossadegh was duly removed from power in a coup in August 1953. Peace was apparently restored, and the oil kept flowing, but America had lost its neutrality, ousting a democratic leader to preserve the interests of itself and a key ally.

A similar intervention followed in Guatemala. Back in 1944, an unsavory dictator had been replaced by a group inspired by FDR's New Deal. In 1952, President Jacobo Arbenz Guzmán began a program of nationalizing and redistributing land. Some of that land belonged to the U.S.-owned United Fruit Company. UFC lobbyists in Washington succeeded in spinning Arbenz's actions as Communist, and the Guatemalan leader suffered the same fate as Mossadegh, losing office via a coup. As with Iran, America was spooked by its fear of Communism into acting in ways that ran counter to its best traditions and deepest values.

More in line with those values, Eisenhower sought to trim military spending and to pursue a new policy of deterring wars rather than fighting them. Behind this thinking was the logic of the Cold War, that behind local wars lay global ideological forces. But the only way to put pressure on the source of the rival ideology, Russia, seemed to be with the threat of nuclear weapons—a Faustian pact that would surely lead to an arms race, and at worst to a holocaust.

This global tension lightened in 1955. A crisis over mainland Chinese shelling of Matsu and Quemoy, two small islands held by nationalist Taiwan, saw Eisenhower face down his internal opponents, resist escalation, and reestablish calm. In Europe, the four occupying powers in Austria agreed to hand over the reins to a democratic but neutral government. Germany proved more problematic but was at least clearly divided into the Soviet-occupied Democratic Republic (the source of thousands of "DDR" stamps in its forty-year lifetime) and a new West-facing Federal Republic. A summit meeting between the leaders of America, Russia, Britain, and France, held in Geneva in the summer of that year, was amicable: Eisenhower and Russia's Marshal Zhukov swapped war stories; differences of opinion were respected and rhetoric avoided. Back in the Soviet Union, its new leader, Nikita Khrushchev, even made a speech criticizing Stalin's excesses and promising a more gentle future.

However, the pressures against peace were so strong that the mood soon darkened again. As usual, Eisenhower did his best to avoid conflict. When Britain, France, and Israel went to war with Egypt over the Suez Canal in October 1956, he forced the aggressors to back down. But while that drama was unfolding, the Soviets heated up the Cold War by invading Hungary. Encouraged by Khrushchev's speech, the satellite nation had started to liberalize—too fast for its overlords, who sent in tanks. In the fighting, 3,500 Hungarians were killed; 35,000 people were arrested and several hundred executed, including the former prime minister, Imre Nagy. The goodwill of Geneva 1955 suddenly seemed an era away. Cold War was here to stay.

The Post Office Department did its bit in the propaganda effort in this war, issuing a series of Champions of Liberty stamps from 1957 to 1961, which featured individuals from around the world who had fought tyranny. The first of these was Ramon Magsaysay, the president of the Philippines and former anti-Japanese guerrilla fighter, recently killed in an airplane crash. The stamp's denomination was 8¢, the rate for an overseas letter—the Champions of Liberty issue was designed to send a global message. The series included Garibaldi, Simón Bolívar, and Mahatma Gandhi but also individuals with more obvious Cold War links. Ernst Reuter was an opponent of Nazism and mayor of Berlin during the 1948 airlift. Tomas G. Masaryk was the first president of Czechoslovakia—and, more pointedly, father of Jan Masaryk, a politician murdered by the Communists in 1948. (The Party line was that Masaryk had jumped from a window: Czechs at the time joked that Masaryk had been such a tidy man that when he'd jumped he'd shut the window after himself.)

The U.S. Post Office's opposite number in Moscow had

been churning out propaganda for some time—blatant in the Stalin years, more restrained by 1957. On October 4 it was given a truly remarkable national achievement to celebrate— and modestly issued a single 40-kopeck stamp. The event was the launch of *Sputnik*, the world's first satellite. *Sputnik* was a metal sphere about 60 cm in diameter—the size of a beach ball—and didn't do much apart from emit radio signals, but it was put in orbit by Soviet rocketry and stayed there, 200 miles above the Earth, bleeping defiance at a transfixed America for twenty-two days.

In the face of this, Eisenhower was his usual calm self—on TV he congratulated Russia on its achievement—but around him fear began to grow: If they could put this into space, how soon could warheads follow? On November 3, a much larger *Sputnik 2* was launched, with a canine passenger, Laika. Three weeks later, Eisenhower suffered a stroke. From then on he found himself more and more often outflanked by the hawks. Defense expenditure began to accelerate; public paranoia grew, which a weakened president was no longer able to calm. Sabers were rattled at old flashpoints: Berlin, Quemoy. In May 1960, an American U-2 spy plane was shot down over the Ural Mountains. The mercurial Khrushchev stormed out of a planned four-power summit in Paris, and in September lost his temper in a United Nations debate, banging his shoe on the podium in the middle of a discussion that had already descended into sloganeering. Eisenhower lamented, "I had longed to give the United States and the world a lasting peace; I was able only to contribute to a stalemate."

The old general was then at the end of his second term. I shall let another stamp tell the full story of the man who replaced him in 1961, John F. Kennedy; for this chapter it is sufficient to say that the Cold War hit new lows during JFK's term of office. Four months into that term, the CIA attempted to oust the Castro regime in Cuba by landing an underprepared force of exiles at the Bay of Pigs. It was a disastrous failure. In Europe, East Germany and its Soviet ally began building a wall around West Berlin to stem the ever-increasing tide of refugees fleeing the Democratic Republic. On August 24, Gunter Litfin, a twenty-four-year-old tailor from East Berlin, was shot trying to cross it. More attempted crossings and shootings followed. By October, armed Soviet and U.S. tanks were facing each other at its central crossing point, Checkpoint Charlie, with orders to fire back if fired upon. War was one nervous trigger finger away. More terrifying still, documents from the era reveal that both sides had plans that involved a quick escalation to massive use of nuclear weapons. America's Strategic Integrated Operations Plan—largely the work of the Strategic Air Command, a section of the USAF created by the ultrahawkish General Curtis LeMay—envisaged nuclear weapons being launched from bombers and missiles against nearly a thousand "military and urban-industrial targets" in Russia and China. Estimates of deaths ranged from 200 million to 600 million (the latter including the aftereffects of nuclear fallout). Less is known about Soviet intentions, but Khrushchev was certainly a believer in quick escalation, arguing the point with his more measured defense minister, Rodion Malinovsky.

Fortunately, Kennedy and Khrushchev communicated behind the scenes via a Soviet spy in Washington, and the situation at Checkpoint Charlie was defused, the tanks backing off five meters at a time. However, two days later, the Soviet Union detonated a hydrogen bomb. The Tsar Bomba (King of Bombs) was the most powerful weapon ever tested. The fireball from its 50-megaton explosion, nearly 2,500 times the strength of the blast that obliterated Hiroshima, was seen 600 miles away (and the sound heard forty-seven minutes later). Windows in Finland, a thousand miles away, were shattered. Maybe the day's orders fluttered slightly on the watchtowers along the Berlin Wall . . .

Stevan Dohanos's NATO stamp is ultimately deeply ironic. The work of a warm, humane, life-loving artist, it is a symbol of a conflict in which unspeakable disaster was imagined, planned for—and looked to be a distinct possibility.

TWENTY-FOUR

Smithsonian National Postal Museum

MURDER IN CAMELOT

Christmas 1963 5¢;
Scott catalog no. 1240

THE IDEA OF PRODUCING a Christmas stamp had been around for a long time; philatelist George W. Linn had led a lengthy campaign to persuade the Post Office Department to produce one. The battle was finally won in 1962, with a 4¢ featuring a door wreath and candles. The stamp that inspires this chapter is its successor. It is also the second U.S. commemorative stamp to be designed by a woman, following the work of Esther A. Richards on the 1930s National Parks issue. The 1963 Christmas stamp is by Lily Spandorf, an artist who specialized in scenes of the capital. It shows the National Christmas Tree, which, since 1923, is lit by the president in an annual ceremony. In the background stands the White House. Lights burn in two of the upstairs rooms: The first family is at home.

The stamp was issued on November 1. Twenty-two days later, the young head of that family was dead.

Like the other great reforming Democratic president of the twentieth century, FDR, John F. Kennedy came from a highly privileged background. His father was a self-made millionaire who was hugely ambitious for his sons. Part of this ambition came from Joe Kennedy's Catholicism; he was determined to beat the Protestant establishment at its own game. So the Kennedy sons grew up with a mixture of old-fashioned insider ambition and outsider status—a combination that fit the new era perfectly. The late 1950s and early 1960s saw the rise of a new American: smart, successful, and keen to succeed, but also eager to challenge orthodoxy. They read the liberal *New Republic* magazine and books like Vance Packard's critique of advertising, *The Hidden Persuaders* (1957), or J. K. Galbraith's *The Affluent Society* (1958). The men sneaked a peek at *Playboy*, which mixed sexy pinups with intelligent, freethinking articles; between the pictures there were earnest jazz reviews, classic short stories, and specially commissioned works by major writers like Ray Bradbury. These new Americans wanted politicians who were young, intelligent, daring, forward-looking, and glamorous.

Enter JFK . . . At the 1960 Democratic Convention, he talked of a "New Frontier," beyond which lay

> *uncharted areas of science and space, unsolved problems*
> *of peace and war, unconquered pockets of ignorance and*
> *prejudice, unanswered questions of poverty and surplus.*

The speech, cleverly referring to the Great Frontier theme we have seen mirrored in earlier stamp issues, won him the nomination, and he went on to beat Eisenhower's earnest, grumpy vice president, Richard Nixon, in the second-closest election so far. (The closest, ominously, was won by James Garfield in 1881.) There had seldom been a greater change in the White House. The familiar building you see in the background of Lily Spandorf's stamp was completely renovated inside; in April 1962, 80 million TV viewers were given a guided tour by the president's elegant wife, Jackie. A month later, the couple hosted a dinner for the French minister of culture, novelist André Malraux; Jackie wore her latest Christian Dior, and music came not courtesy of Lawrence Welk but from internationally famous violinist Isaac Stern, pianist Eugene Istomin, and cellist Leonard Rose. Welcome to Camelot, the gilded castle from which brave, cultured knights went out to do great deeds and right deep wrongs.

Kennedy quickly launched his assault on the four challenges beyond his New Frontier. The subject of space became a hot topic almost at once; in April 1961, the Russians put a man into orbit, Yuri Gagarin (prompting a flurry of stamp issues across Eastern Europe). America could only reply with suborbital flights (until 1962), but on May 25, Kennedy made a promise to Congress to place a man on the moon by the end of the decade. Many NASA employees were skeptical about this—it had not been long since Vanguard rockets were regularly exploding at Cape Canaveral. But the agency set to work to reach his goal.

More generally, there was a feeling that America's public services needed modernizing—including the Post Office. The Kennedy era saw the appearance of the jovial Mr. Zip, reminding correspondents to use the new Zoning Improvement Plan codes to facilitate mechanical sorting. (Another attempt at updating the system was less successful: missile mail. A rocket containing 3,000 letters was fired from a submarine to a naval base in Florida. It landed without causing any damage, but the idea didn't catch on.)

The president's lunar promise had as much to do with the second aspect of the New Frontier—"unsolved problems of peace and war"—as the first. Kennedy combined his liberal, *New Republic* approach to domestic issues with a combative attitude to foreign policy. The new "Space Race" was a continuation of the Cold War, both as propaganda—beating the Soviets to the moon—and as military technology: It was popular at the time to talk of a "missile gap" between the USA and Russia. This gap did not exist—or if it did, Russia was the nation with ground to make up—but it was clear that rocketry would be a key to future defense (though not postal delivery). Shortly after his moon promise, Kennedy met Khrushchev in Vienna, and after initial jollity, the mood turned sour. The Soviet leader took an aggressive tone and argued the younger man into a corner over Berlin. Kennedy had little option but to be aggressive back. Soon after, the tension in the divided former German capital, described in the previous chapter, began to rise. This part of the New Frontier was going to be hard to conquer.

The third aspect, ignorance and prejudice, was an area where historians now agree that Kennedy achieved little. He made some liberal-sounding appointments early in his presidency, such as making his brother Robert attorney general. In one way, this was a shameless piece of nepotism—Joe Kennedy had a hand in it—but in another an enlightened move: Robert was both a relentless opponent of organized crime and union corruption and a passionate advocate of civil rights. Eleanor Roosevelt was appointed to chair a Presidential Commission on the Status of Women. But few new laws were passed. Kennedy's defenders say that he did not have time—for example,

Eleanor Roosevelt's commission did not produce a report until October 1963—and argue that the substantial civil rights legislation of JFK's successor was built on his legacy.

The fourth aspect of the New Frontier, like the second and third, proved harder to conquer than Kennedy had hoped, and it was left to his successor, Lyndon Johnson, to make progress here as well. Johnson's "War on Poverty" was spearheaded by Sargent Shriver, a JFK appointee, and can be seen as the realization of a Kennedy policy.

If Kennedy was slow off the mark in domestic policy-making, it is because events forced his attention to remain on overseas matters. In 1961 there had been Berlin. In 1962 came Cuba.

On October 14, 1962, a U.S. spy plane flying over Cuba photographed large-scale building under way, which analysis revealed to be of missile launching sites—90 miles from the American coast. This brought to a head suspicions that had been forming for a while, that the Soviet Union was about to turn Cuba into a base from which almost all America could be attacked: Of major cities, only Seattle would be beyond the range of Russian SS-5 missiles. An action committee, Ex-Comm, was formed, and options discussed. To many in the military, such as General LeMay, the solution was obvious: launch a full invasion of the island at once, before the sites became active, which might be as soon as two weeks. Others took a more dovish line: blockade the island to prevent the missiles arriving and start negotiating for their return to Russia. The hawks argued back that stopping a ship on the high seas can itself be seen as an act of war—a blockade could bring all the consequences of invasion (escalation) with none of its benefits. As with Harry Truman and the bomb, the president alone had to decide.

On October 22, he did so. U.S. vessels began shadowing Soviet Bloc ships within 500 miles of Cuba. The navy had a clear set of procedures it hoped would avoid actual conflict. Signals were exchanged with the Russian tanker *Bucharest* before it was allowed to pass. (It did not appear to have any deck cargo, so was probably just carrying oil.) A neutral freighter, the *Marcula* from Lebanon, was stopped, boarded, and searched but found not to be carrying weapons and also allowed to proceed. Meanwhile, as the president had hoped, negotiations began: The KGB's station head in Washington, Aleksandr Feklisov, contacted an ABC journalist with a set of peace proposals.

On October 27, a U-2 spy plane was shot down over Cuba. ExComm argued that this was a provocation that could not be ignored: Cuba had to be invaded. The commander in chief resisted these calls. At sea, U.S. ships surrounded a Soviet submarine, *B-59*, and began dropping depth charges on it— not with the intention of destroying it but as an order to surface. Unbeknownst to them, *B-59* was armed with a nuclear torpedo, which it had approval to use if attacked. There was an argument between the submarine's senior officers: Was this an attack? Should they use the torpedo? Sanity prevailed, and the *B-59* surfaced.

On the very next day, negotiations with Moscow bore fruit. Khrushchev agreed to decommission the bases, in return for two U.S. promises: not to invade the island and to remove some of its own missiles in Turkey, close to the Russian border. Later, a "hotline" was set up between Washington and Moscow—a telegraph system, not the red phone of the popular imagination. Negotiations banning the testing of nuclear weapons began.

Sadly, this did not mean the end of the Cold War. We left

the small South Asian nation of Vietnam partitioned between North and South. But the Communist North retained its ambition for reunification—and the leadership in the South became ever more corrupt and unpopular. Dissent grew, which the North was happy to fuel. America sent advisers to Saigon to train the South Vietnamese army in counterinsurgency. By the end of 1961, there were 3,000 such people in the country; a year later, this number had tripled and included U.S. pilots flying combat missions. How much further would JFK escalate the conflict?

We will never know. On November 22, 1963, he visited Dallas, Texas. The plan was for him to fly in in the morning, travel by motorcade to a lunch with local dignitaries, then drive straight out to the airport again. Plans were announced in advance so the local populace could watch the president arrive. Air Force One duly touched down at 11:25 A.M.; Kennedy and Jackie got into an open-topped Lincoln with Governor John Connally and his wife, and they set off. At 12:29 P.M., the motorcade reached Dealey Plaza, where a crowd was applauding. Mrs. Connally turned to the president and said, "You can't say Dallas doesn't love you." A few moments later, three shots were fired. There is debate about the exact order of events, but the most widely accepted one is that the first missed, the second seriously wounded both Kennedy and Connally, and the third hit the president in the head and killed him outright.

A spectator reported seeing a man firing from the Texas Book Depository. Police immediately rushed into the building and found a discarded rifle with telescopic sights. A description of the suspect was circulated; half an hour later a Dallas patrolman pulled over a man fitting the description and was shot dead. The man was soon cornered, arrested, and charged. Forensic evidence linked him with the Depository: The police had caught the assassin, Lee Harvey Oswald. The question was immediately asked—did he act alone? It will probably never be answered to everyone's satisfaction. Two days later, Oswald himself was shot dead by a nightclub owner, Jack Ruby, who professed to have done it to spare Jackie Kennedy the anguish of appearing in court.

Since then, conspiracy theories have proliferated. Arguments for conspiracy are led by the suspicious silencing of Oswald but also point to a film that seems to show the president shot from the front. (Oswald fired from behind the president.) Standard security procedures were not followed: Agents should have been riding in the back of the car to protect the people inside but had been stood down at the last moment. The three shots were fired very quickly—too quickly for one man? Some witnesses claim to have heard shots from a "grassy knoll" in front of the presidential car. Against this, there is limited evidence to connect either Oswald or Ruby with groups likely to want to kill the president. Most assassinations are carried out by lone individuals. No fully convincing alternative scenario has yet been constructed. And Oswald was a trained marksman—if anyone could have fired three shots in five seconds, he could. (A recent, intriguing, and tragic third type of theory is that the president was shot by accident by a security guard trying to return Oswald's fire.) If you are over sixty, you probably remember the exact moment when you heard the news. The assassination of John F. Kennedy traumatized America, more even than that of Lincoln. In an age of expanding media, the story was hammered into everyone's consciousness by radio, newspapers, TV . . . And that Christmas, Americans had to use this stamp to send their cards.

TWENTY-FIVE

1863-1963 UNITED STATES 5 CENTS

EMANCIPATION PROCLAMATION

Smithsonian National Postal Museum

DREAMS AND NIGHTMARES

Emancipation Proclamation Centennial 5¢, 1963; Scott catalog no. 1233

IT IS FITTING THAT the first African American artist to design a U.S. stamp, Georg Olden, was responsible for the one commemorating the centennial of the Emancipation Proclamation. Olden had a distinguished career in design. He made his reputation in TV, creating the look of classic '50s shows—including the heart logo for *I Love Lucy*—then moved into advertising, where he became vice president of leading agency McCann-Erickson.

However, Olden's achievements were the exception rather than the rule at that time. Abraham Lincoln would not have been impressed by the progress toward racial equality made in the hundred years since his Proclamation. Stamps, as usual, mirror their era: In those hundred years only three African Americans had appeared on one. Booker T. Washington was one of the educators in the 1940 Famous Americans series. (In 1956, another stamp showed a log cabin "similar to the one in which he was born" to celebrate the centennial of his birth.) George Washington Carver, an agriculturalist who taught at Tuskegee, was honored in 1948. The trio is completed by Archer Alexander, a freed slave depicted on the controversial Freedman's Memorial, where he is getting to his feet in front of Lincoln.

We left the southern states at the end of the nineteenth century in the grip of Jim Crow. They stayed that way. Discrimination in the North was less official but still rife. The National Association for the Advancement of Colored People (NAACP) was founded in 1909—although much of its work between the wars concentrated not on advancement but simply on preventing lynching. After the Second World War, however, many black GIs came home no longer prepared to accept this state of affairs. The NAACP stepped up its campaign for full civil rights through lobbying politicians and initiating litigation. President Truman desegregated the armed forces in 1948. In 1954, the Supreme Court began a slow overturning of the *Plessy v. Ferguson* verdict, insisting on mixed-race schools. Outstanding individuals found themselves able to penetrate white institutions: Olden joined CBS in 1945 and was soon one of the network's senior designers. But for most black Americans, public life remained a round of petty reminders of their second-class status, with segregated restaurants, toilets, and drinking fountains—and poverty: The average income of black families in the 1950s was half that of whites, despite proportionally more black than white women going outside of the home to work.

A new form of protest began to evolve: mass, nonviolent civil disobedience. On Thursday, December 1, 1955, Rosa Parks was traveling on a bus in Montgomery, Alabama. Like all the city's buses, the vehicle had "colored" and "white" sections. The dividing line was flexible: If white passengers were standing, the driver could move the COLORED ONLY sign back a row and order the occupants of that row to stand. Parks was in such a row and was asked to move as the bus filled up. Three of her fellow travelers duly got to their feet; she didn't and was arrested. It was not the first incident of such a refusal and arrest, but this time people had had enough. Over the weekend, a city-wide bus boycott was organized—and lasted for more than a year, until the Supreme Court declared the segregation unconstitutional. The main medium through which this organization took place was that of the local churches, and a minister was put in charge of the protest—a young newcomer to the city named Martin Luther King Jr.

In February 1960, a small group of black students went to Woolworth's in Greensboro, North Carolina, bought some items, then sat down at the whites-only lunch counter, where they were refused service. They stayed for forty-five minutes, then left. The next day, a larger group repeated the process, and by the end of the week, the counter was clogged with protesters, including white sympathizers. Soon segregated facilities of all kinds were receiving this treatment—park benches, theaters, beaches, and even libraries. In 1961, "Freedom Riders" began traveling south on interstate buses. The vehicles were desegregated, but the terminals where they stopped were not (despite a Supreme Court ruling). At these terminals, white riders went into the black facilities and black riders into the white ones. The response was far from nonviolent. In Anniston, Alabama, a bus was firebombed. Many other riders were arrested, some ending up in Mississippi's notorious Parchman Farm penitentiary doing hard labor among the nation's toughest criminals—all for going into the "wrong" washroom.

The world was now watching: the Soviet Union eager to point out its rival's moral weaknesses, and the new, rising, nonaligned "third world," in the process of deciding which of the two big powers to follow. But progress remained slow. In 1963, Georg Olden's birthplace of Birmingham, Alabama, still had segregated public spaces. On May 3, a peaceful, dignified march of protest at this—the protesters included families—was set upon by police with pressure hoses and German shepherd dogs. In June, the state's governor, George Wallace, tried to invoke the doctrine of states' rights to ban two black students from entering a summer school at Alabama University. A furious President Kennedy went on TV to announce plans for civil rights legislation. However, many people felt this was too little, too late; in August, 250,000 demonstrators descended on Washington, calling for "Jobs and Freedom." A panicked capital prepared for the worst— troops were moved to the suburbs and hospitals emptied to admit casualties—but the event went off peacefully. It is now best known for King's "I have a dream" speech, but arguably an even bigger message came from the march as a whole: America saw a powerful, united, and peaceful movement, and many marchers felt a new optimism and communality of purpose.

The assassination of JFK threatened to destroy this optimism, especially since he was to be replaced by a tough Southern Democrat—not a political grouping noted for its support of civil rights. However, the new president, Lyndon Baines Johnson, was determined to continue his predecessor's work. In fact, LBJ was a more effective force for domestic change than Kennedy would have been, as he was a master of Capitol Hill dealmaking. In 1964, he steered the Civil Rights Act through a minefield of opposition that included fifty-four days of filibuster: interminable, rambling speeches designed to delay legislation. The act, signed into law on July 2, outlawed discrimination on grounds of "race, color, religion, sex, or national origin" at work or in public spaces such as restaurants, theaters, or transport. Federal funding would be cut off from any project guilty of discrimination. The act also attempted to tackle the old Jim Crow voting restrictions, but this was fiercely resisted at the state level. So the struggle continued: In 1965, a march in Selma, Alabama, was attacked by local police armed with clubs and tear gas. Johnson seized the moment and asked Congress for a Voting Rights Act. After the usual horse-trading, this act was passed on August 6, 1965.

Justice for all, at last? Five days later, rioting broke out in Watts, a poor black district of Los Angeles. For six days the area was ungovernable, and at the end of the fighting, thirty-four people were dead. To liberals, the Watts riots showed that LBJ's two acts did not go far enough; there were deeper, economic injustices to be addressed, without which the political changes meant little. (Johnson commented to an aide, "When you put your foot on a man's neck and hold him down for three hundred years, and then you let him up, what's he going to do? He's going to knock your block off.") Conservatives said that too much freedom had been given too quickly. America seemed to be polarizing fast—and to be expressing this polarization through violence. In 1966, Dr. King led a march through Chicago and encountered white hostility that shocked him; obscenities were shouted and bricks were thrown. King was a patriot, who felt deeply that the work he was doing was for all America, not just its colored inhabitants. By removing bigotry he was returning the entire nation to its moral, spiritual destiny as enshrined in the Declaration of Independence and the Constitution. Other, younger men began arguing a different view, that ancient chains could only be broken by separation, and separation could only be achieved by violence (which was "as American as cherry pie," to quote one radical, H. Rap Brown).

Summer 1966 saw a march to mark the first anniversary of Selma. At a rally for it, Stokely Carmichael, who had been sent to Parchman Farm for taking part in a freedom ride, called for "Black Power." He got a rapturous response from the crowd. In October of that year, the Black Panther Party was founded by Huey Newton and Bobby Seale. It issued a Ten Point Program based on socialist ideas and insisted on a uniform of black beret, leather jacket, and shotgun. Carrying weapons on California streets was legal at that time, but the Panthers' eager adoption of the gun sent a clear message: They saw themselves as victims of violence, especially from the largely white police, and believed they had a right to fight back. California's legislators suddenly decided there were too many guns on the streets. In May 1967, thirty armed Panthers marched into the California State Capitol in Sacramento to protest against attempted changes to the law. The summer of that year saw riots in many black neighborhoods, including central Detroit, where forty-three people lost their lives.

In March 1968, Dr. King led a march of sanitation workers in Memphis, Tennessee. The protest was intended to be peaceful but degenerated into disorder, now on the part of protesters, not state troopers. That evening, King said to his friend Ralph Abernathy, "We live in a sick nation." However, he remained in Memphis to organize a second march. As he sat on the balcony of his motel relaxing after a day of meetings, he was shot dead by James Earl Ray, an escaped convict and white supremacist.

Was this the end for nonviolence? It certainly looked that way: Riots followed Dr. King's assassination. Washington was particularly badly affected; at one point the fighting was only two blocks away from the White House, and the damage done blighted the capital's inner city for a generation. However, history never stays static. The year before, 1967, had already seen the appointment of the first black judge to the Supreme Court, Thurgood Marshall, and the election of black mayors in Cleveland and Gary, Indiana. The next year, 1969, saw further legislation to prevent white union "closed shops" on federal contracts. The concept of affirmative action, whereby set amounts of jobs had to be given to minority applicants, began to gain ground. The militant black separatist movement also began to suffer crises. Newton and Carmichael proved erratic leaders, and Seale disliked the limelight. The man who probably would have been the radicals' best front man, Malcolm X, a charismatic orator who had converted to the Nation of Islam in 1948, had been another victim of political assassination back in 1965.

In 1999, Malcolm X featured on a 33¢ stamp. Some figures in the media disapproved. Those on the right objected because of his radicalism; those on the left because it co-opted him into an establishment that he had never in real life belonged to. (Both arguments bear witness to the power of stamp issues to reshape the nation's perception of its own history.) The public, on the other hand, liked the issue—as did Malcom X's family, who attended the stamp's launch and accepted the honor with pride. But that was 1999. In 1969, it was not clear how this story would play out. Moderates argued that violence only heightened racial tension and that in the long run America's traditions of law, democracy, and meritocracy—the spirit of 1776—would deliver justice if given enough time. To this, radicals replied that these things had been given plenty of time. They could point to this stamp: How about one hundred (and, now, more) years since 1863?

TWENTY-SIX

Smithsonian National Postal Museum

THE LONGEST WAR

$1 Airlift stamp, 1968

THE COMMEMORATIVE STAMPS of 1968 project a calm message. One from May shows a fatherly cop helping a lost boy; some others celebrate historic flags, the frontiersman Daniel Boone, the 150th anniversary of Illinois statehood (a lovely design, evoking vast, abundant cornfields), a flying duck, and Walt Disney. The issues have a 1950s feel to them, as if Dwight and Mamie Eisenhower were still in the White House and all was well with the world. As the previous chapter has shown, this troubled year wasn't like that at all. Scratch the stamp above, for example, and a darker reality appears. The $1 Airlift, another of Stevan Dohanos's designs, was specially issued in April 1968 for families sending parcels to U.S. servicemen in Vietnam, a conflict that by that time had become hopelessly out of control and was dividing the nation as profoundly as the issue of race.

President Kennedy had not wanted full-scale involvement in Indochina. His hope was that, with U.S. military "advice," local anti-Communist forces would win. Lyndon Johnson initially believed the same. Johnson was also keen to institute his domestic reforms, creating a "Great Society" without poverty or prejudice, and didn't want to be distracted by overseas matters. But presidents can rarely choose where they direct their energies. During 1964, Vietnam forced itself onto his agenda—and stayed there. Despite the presence of 20,000 U.S. advisers, the South Vietnamese were losing their war against the northern Vietcong guerrillas. A third of the south was effectively under northern control. The Vietcong had even started issuing their own stamps for use in these areas; one from 1963 shows a U.S. helicopter being shot down during a skirmish at Ap Bac, a mere forty-five miles from Saigon. People began citing the "domino theory": that if South Vietnam fell, the rest of Southeast Asia, and maybe even India, would follow.

In August 1964, the destroyer USS *Maddox* was patrolling off the coast of North Vietnam. It was approached by three North Vietnamese torpedo boats. There is still debate about who shot first, but both sides fired weapons. There were no U.S. casualties, but the Gulf of Tonkin Incident sparked intense reaction in Washington, at least partially because an election was looming. The president asked Congress for, and was almost unanimously given, authorization to use nonnuclear forces in Southeast Asia without a formal declaration of war. The stage was set for escalation: The domino would not be allowed to fall.

In February 1965, after a Vietcong attack on a U.S. base at Pleiku in the central highlands of South Vietnam, America launched a series of limited air strikes on the North. The hope was that Hanoi would see that the United States meant business and back down. Instead, the North hunkered down for a long war. In March, 3,500 marines landed at Da Nang, eighty-five miles south of the border between the two Vietnams, to protect an airbase. In June, South Vietnamese forces were defeated by guerrillas at the Battle of Dong Xoai, deep in the south of the country. The U.S. commander, General William Westmoreland, realized that without active U.S. support, such defeats would become regular events, so he asked for a massive increase in American forces. The president gave Westmoreland what he wanted. Vietnam had become an American war.

One odd fact about the stamps of 1965 is that none celebrated the centennial of the end of the Civil War (or, for that matter, that of the death of Lincoln). The centennial of Sokol, a Czech émigré fitness association, and the Salvation Army were deemed deserving, however. Was the unpleasantness of war not something about which the authorities wanted to remind people? On August 5, CBS viewers watched in horror as they saw American soldiers set fire to Vietnamese peasant huts with Zippo lighters, watched by distraught old people and crying children. It was not the last such image they would see.

Over Christmas, Johnson tried to bring peace by announcing a pause in the bombing, but the North was not interested. (America's critics blame the United States for events in Vietnam, but it takes two sides to start and sustain a war.) At the end of January 1966, the bombing was resumed again. Ground forces launched major offensives. "This will divide America," warned Pulitzer Prize–winning journalist Walter Lippmann. But there seemed to be no way out without backing down—

which would, so many believed, set those dominoes tumbling, exactly at a time when Asian Communism was becoming increasingly sinister and psychotic. Chinese stamps of the era show the rise of Chairman Mao Tse-tung's cult of personality: By 1967, every issue was in praise of the Great Helmsman and his Great Proletarian Cultural Revolution. The escalation went on.

In April 1966, the first B-52 bombers were used. In September, the Pentagon admitted to using chemical defoliants to deny jungle coverage to the Vietcong. By the end of the year there were 389,000 U.S. troops in Vietnam—and the force had suffered more than 5,000 deaths. Fighting had begun to follow a dismally predictable pattern, with bombs raining down on preindustrial landscapes, and massive ground offensives seemingly clearing areas of Vietcong only for the enemy to filter back again the moment U.S. troops left. In response to the latter, the military called for more men and more weaponry, and the politicians grudgingly responded—while both desperately seeking talks with an unresponsive North and continuing to pump out the positive rhetoric to the American public. By December 31, 1967, the U.S. death toll had reached 16,000 and the number of U.S. troops 463,000. And then the Viet Cong launched the Tet Offensive.

This was a massive guerrilla attack in January 1968 on more than a hundred South Vietnamese towns and cities. One group of seventeen guerrillas even entered the U.S. embassy in Saigon. The invaders hoped to incite a South Vietnamese revolution. They failed, and were beaten back at great cost— but the propaganda effect of the offensive was immense. It yielded terrible images: the execution of a Vietcong suspect by a South Vietnamese general; a U.S. officer commenting on a small town bombed to rubble that "we had to destroy it in order to save it." But perhaps its biggest effect was to show the futility of the conflict. Tet had been a crushing defeat for the North, but one that the victors proved unable to build upon. Instead, the situation reverted to the way it had been before, as the defeated Vietcong melted back into the jungles and began to plan their next attacks.

On March 25, a group of "wise men," including General of the Army Omar Bradley met at the State Department to discuss the war, and their conclusions were subsequently reported to the president: America should get out. Shortly afterward, Johnson announced he would not run for reelection later that year and would instead devote his remaining time in the White House to finding an honorable end to the conflict.

It was a timely decision. The war had started to inject its poison into all areas of American life. Students had been objecting to the conflict since early 1965, and protests had grown ever louder and more widespread. In March 1967, Martin Luther King added his voice. (The issues of the war and race were intertwined, as a disproportionate number of young black men were fighting on the front line.) More generally, the war stoked an already febrile atmosphere of violence in the nation's streets; 1968 was the year Martin Luther King and Bobby Kennedy were gunned down and when militants seemed poised to take over the civil rights movement. It cheapened the politics that should have calmed this violence: The perpetual official statements that victory was just around the corner sounded ever more deceitful. It damaged America's image around the world, bringing global antiwar, anti-U.S. protests. (Nobody protested against the Viet Cong.) It was beginning to damage the economy; to prevent the war becoming even more unpopular, the government tried to finance it through borrowing rather than tax. (In the end it had to relent and impose a "temporary" 10 percent tax surcharge.) As a result, inflation began to rise. The price of a standard letter went up from 5¢ to 6¢ in 1968 and would leap to 8¢ in 1971, marking a 60 percent rise in two and a half years. (For ninety-five years, from 1863 to 1958, it had oscillated between 2¢ and 3¢.)

The nation needed leadership. It didn't get it. The 1968 election was fought between lackluster candidates, Hubert Humphrey and Richard Nixon, with George Wallace running as an independent. Nixon's call for "fresh ideas" won him a narrow victory. Peace talks began almost immediately after his inauguration in January 1969. The new president began to talk of U.S. withdrawal, of the "Vietnamization" of the war. A flag-waving 1969 South Vietnam stamp issue celebrated "mobilization," the call-up of every eligible male into the nation's army, the ARVN. However, at the same time, Nixon secretly escalated the bombing campaign, including extending it to a previously neutral Cambodia. Neither policy worked. Morale in U.S. ground forces was low to start with, and the announcement of their slow withdrawal made things worse. Drug taking among troops increased markedly, as did incidents of "fragging," in which unpopular officers were blown up by their own men. The bombing of Cambodia had little effect on the Vietcong but began the process of driving that nation into the hands of the Khmer Rouge, one of the nastiest regimes in world history.

In April 1970, President Nixon escalated the conflict in Cambodia by sending in ground forces. Even he couldn't conceal this from the public, and the response was furious. Students led the protests—which became so violent that armed troops had to be sent onto college campuses. Six protesters were killed, four at Kent State University in Ohio and two at Jackson State College in Mississippi. A huge range of people, previously quiet about the issue—including Vietnam veterans and serving GIs—joined in. Nixon pulled out of Cambodia and accelerated the bigger withdrawal from Vietnam itself.

The last U.S. ground combat troops left in April 1972, leaving bomber crews and advisers. The North then tried a major offensive, which the ARVN successfully beat back (with cover from U.S. bombers). The southern force could be proud of its achievement—special stamps were issued to celebrate this victory—but as America distanced itself ever more from its former ally, the Saigon government was doomed. A peace treaty signed in January 1973 allowed the Vietcong to retain areas of the South they had conquered. It also insisted the fate of the South be decided by democratic means—something the North had no intention of letting happen. In December 1974, a Vietcong incursion into Southern territory met with no American response. (President Gerald Ford asked Congress for funds to help the South and was refused.) On January 8, 1975, the North invaded. (A North Vietnam stamp from this time celebrates the second anniversary of the peace treaty that Hanoi was actually ripping to shreds. Stamps can tell deep truths, but also outrageous lies.) Vietcong battle plans assumed a two-year struggle, but the demoralized South collapsed in fifty-five days. On April 29, the last "Airlift" of the Vietnam War took place, from the grounds of the U.S. embassy in a Saigon whose streets were teeming with victorious Northern troops. The mission was successful, rescuing the last U.S. advisers and a thousand Vietnamese, but other southerners were less fortunate, having to escape by boat, ironically and tragically echoing the first South Vietnamese stamp issued back in 1955. Many "boat people" did not reach their destination—estimates of the death toll of this exodus vary wildly, but it definitely ran into tens of thousands.

In terms of U.S. lives, Vietnam was America's third-most-expensive foreign war, with 58,209 deaths (approximately 47,000 in combat, a figure not far behind World War I). But unlike the two wars that cost more lives, it did not end in victory. Unlike those wars, too, it split the nation. The jungles of Vietnam were for America what the trenches of the Somme and Passchendaele had been for Europe, a place of such horror that it led the country to question its own values, politics, and civilization.

The war remains controversial. Should it have been pursued with more vigor, launching a full-on invasion of the North despite the risk of bringing China into the conflict? Or should it never have been fought at all? Would the dominoes have fallen had it not been fought? Did it actually push dominoes over, by allowing America's enemies to present themselves as peace-loving victims of imperialist aggression? More generally, can such wars, so far from home, on such strange terrain and in such different cultures, be fought successfully? And even if they can, is it morally right to fight them? Being a "global policeman" sounds great if the cop is like the friendly one on that May 1968 stamp—but what do you do when law enforcement turns nasty? Few U.S. stamps have featured the Vietnam conflict since its conclusion, despite the many acts of heroism carried out in the war and the hundreds of thousands of lives affected by it.

TWENTY-SEVEN

Smithsonian National Postal Museum

THE DISCOVERY
OF EARTH

Apollo 8 6¢, 1969;
Scott catalog no. 1371

Time for something more cheerful! If Vietnam was a tragic failure, the American space program of the 1960s was a glorious triumph. America's Cold War enemies may have plastered their stamps with satellites and cosmonauts, but in the end, only one nation proved able to produce a stamp like the one above: the USA.

The ultimate success of the Apollo flights was, of course, getting a man onto the surface of the moon, as promised by JFK. A stamp was issued to celebrate this amazing achievement (a 10¢ Air Mail, the master printing die for which was actually taken to the moon on *Apollo 11*). However, I have chosen to show this stamp instead, which celebrates an earlier flight, *Apollo 8*. It's a personal choice: As an adolescent I was transfixed by this mission, the first time men had left Earth's orbit and voyaged the 250,000 miles to the moon. At one point, they were 69 miles from the lunar surface. At other points, they disappeared around the back of the moon, to a place no human eye had ever seen, twice to carry out maneuvers that, had they failed, would have meant death. They took stunning photographs of Earth as seen from space, as a small blue-green ball against a backdrop of utter, unending darkness, or—as in this stamp—a half-lit planet rising over bleak lunar craters.

NASA, the National Aeronautics and Space Administration, was created by President Eisenhower on October 1, 1958. Its first program for manned space flight, Project Mercury, was announced a few days later. This was proceeding at a reasonable pace—until Russia's Yuri Gagarin blasted off into Earth orbit on April 12, 1961. America's response was to send Alan Shepherd and Gus Grissom on parabolic flights that peaked in space (which is technically defined as more than 100 km above the Earth). Despite the talk at the time, the Soviet achievement was vastly superior. Gagarin's orbital flight was at 50 percent greater altitude and involved reaching speeds three and a half times that of the parabolic ones. America finally got John Glenn circling the Earth on February 20, 1962. A 4¢ stamp was prepared to celebrate this mission—in great secret, in case something went wrong (a reminder of the courage of space pioneers). Envelopes marked TOP SECRET were sent to 305 postmasters, who were instructed to open them only once Glenn had landed safely—which he did at 3:30 EST, after which the stamps went on sale.

Three more Mercury flights followed in the next fifteen months. The last one saw Gordon Cooper spending more than a day in space, but the Russians remained ahead. In August 1962, Andrian Nikolayev spent four days in orbit. On June 16, 1963, Valentina Tereshkova became the first woman in space. On October 12, 1964, *Voskhod 1* became the first vehicle to carry more than one person into orbit—three men, handpicked for political acceptability. (The original intended crew had included someone Jewish and the son of a man executed by Stalin.) On March 18, 1965, Alexey Leonov made the first spacewalk, from *Voskhod 2*.

However, Leonov's flight was beset by technical hitches, and the Voskhod capsule was abandoned. Work began on a new craft, Soyuz, and the Soviet program appeared to stall. Meanwhile, NASA was catching up. Many lessons had been learned from the Mercury flights, and a new program was launched. Project Gemini would send a series of two-man craft into orbit, to develop and test a range of technologies and skills needed for getting a man on the moon. These included rendezvous, docking, spacewalks, and support mechanisms for long flights. In December 1965, Frank Borman and Jim Lovell doubled the requirement for a lunar voyage by spending fifteen days in space with no ill aftereffects. They also made an unsuccessful attempt to dock with another Gemini spacecraft. The maneuver is harder than it sounds: Attempts to slow your craft down to dock successfully can send it into a lower orbit. The next year, a successful docking was made by *Gemini 8* and its captain, Neil Armstrong.

The third, and most expensive, U.S. space program was Apollo. Its aim was simple: to take men to the moon. Of all the technologies needed to achieve this, probably none was more stunning than the Saturn V launch rocket. With the two lunar craft on top (a "lunar module" for landing and a "command module" for takeoff and return to Earth), it was

363 feet tall—20 percent taller than the Statue of Liberty. It weighed 3,000 tons, but such was its power that two and a half minutes after takeoff the craft would be 40 miles above the Earth and traveling at 5,330 mph (and would have burned over 4 million pounds of propellant). At this point, its first stage would detach and fall into the sea, and a second stage would accelerate it to more than 15,000 mph. At 115 miles above the Earth, this second stage would be ditched, too. A third stage would add the extra 1,500 mph to get into orbit, which would be achieved twelve minutes after takeoff. The third stage would then be reignited to accelerate the vehicle to 24,500 mph—a speed that would get you from New York to London in 8.5 minutes, and also the velocity needed to escape Earth's gravitational pull.

The program got off to the worst possible start. On a prelaunch test on January 27, 1967, an electrical fire in their cabin killed the three astronauts of *Apollo 1:* Gus Grissom, Ed White, and Roger Chaffee. Subsequent inquiries showed that corners had been cut in the race to complete the command module. NASA underwent a brief period of introspection before settling down to the business of building a better craft. By October 1968, the project was ready to fly again: *Apollo 7* successfully tested the basic launch and reentry systems. It was time to go to the moon.

The Soviet lunar program had been experiencing difficulties, too, for various reasons including the death of its most inspirational scientist, Sergei Korolev, and rivalries between various government and military departments—there was no Soviet NASA in overall charge. However, the program had not halted, and there was still a chance that it could launch a last-minute manned flight to the moon and back, stealing the thunder of *Apollo 8*. A test flight bearing Russian tortoises made this journey in November but crashed on reentry. It was, however, announced by Moscow as a success. Until *Apollo 8* launched, nobody was totally sure a Soviet flight wouldn't get to the moon first.

Of course, nobody was totally sure anyone would get to the moon alive. The exact nature of the radiation to which the crew would be exposed was unknown. They would have to travel through two areas of high radiation called the Van Allen belts; even though the command module had been designed to deal with this, no one knew for certain that it would protect the astronauts. And what else waited out there? Bill Anders, one of the crew, reckoned they had a one-third chance of not coming back. At no time has the metaphor of space as a frontier been more appropriate: The three *Apollo 8* astronauts, Borman, Lovell, and Anders, were a modern Lewis and Clark.

The craft took off at 7:51 EST on December 21, 1968. It went, as planned, into orbit, and shortly before 11:00 accelerated away from the Earth, beginning its three-day journey to the moon. Much of this journey passed without incident, apart from the series of milestones: No human being had been 50,000 miles from Earth, or 100,000 . . . At 214,000 miles, *Apollo 8* crossed the "equilibrium point" where the gravitational pull of the moon becomes stronger than that of the Earth, after which the craft, which had been slowing ever since blasting out of orbit, began to accelerate. It passed within 70 miles of the lunar surface, then, hooked into its new center of gravitational attraction, began to swing around behind the moon—and out of contact. The astronauts could now see landscape never before seen by man, but they had other things to concentrate on; while on the dark side of the moon the engines had to be fired to put the craft into lunar orbit. If this went wrong, *Apollo 8* could have been hurled off into space or pulled down to the lunar surface. The world waited . . . Precisely on time, the craft reappeared. The "burn" had gone perfectly.

The famous "earthrise" pictures, one of which is used on this stamp, were taken by Bill Anders on the fourth orbit. On the ninth, penultimate, orbit, the crew made a TV broadcast featuring their reading of the first ten verses of the Book of Genesis, in the King James Version. On the tenth orbit, another crucial firing of the engines—behind the moon again—was necessary to get the craft on a trajectory back to Earth. A failure here would have meant *Apollo 8* would be trapped in lunar orbit forever. As with the first burn, the craft vanished from view . . . The world waited . . . Then *Apollo 8* appeared exactly on time, its path now set for home. Its journey back would take two days, nine hours (shorter than the way out, thanks to the stronger gravitational pull of Earth). When the command module finally splashed down, after traveling 504,006 nautical miles, it did so 4 miles from the ship waiting to pick it up.

The mission influenced many areas of American life. Environmentalism, for example: Bill Anders's photo of our planet as a single entity, richly fecund but alone in hostile space, was a vivid reminder of that entity's inhabitants' duty to look after it. (Anders himself commented that they had set out to discover the moon but instead discovered the Earth.) The peace movement got a boost: Human differences suddenly seemed trivial when seen from a quarter of a million miles away. The astronauts' readings from Genesis—and their repetition on this stamp—was part of a process whereby religion returned to the public arena. Back in 1925, the Scopes Monkey Trial had taken religion out of the realm of public debate; while it remained an admired trait for a leader to have a strong, quiet faith, that faith was not a card to be played in policy discussions. This mood began to change in the 1950s. As the threat of atheistic Communism grew, so did the public appeal of religious belief. The 1954 Liberty definitive was the first U.S. stamp ever to proclaim "In God we trust." (The phrase "under God" was inserted into the Pledge of Allegiance in the same year.) The *Apollo 8* commemorative stamp continued this trend.

President Kennedy's promise to put a man on the moon was finally fulfilled by Neil Armstrong on July 20, 1969—another amazing story, but one that has been told well elsewhere. Six other missions followed, one of which, *Apollo 13*, malfunctioned and had to be nursed back to Earth by its commander, Jim Lovell (who thus became the only person to leave Earth orbit twice but never actually step on the moon). The final Apollo mission, *Apollo 17*, featured drives in a lunar vehicle and a three-day stay on the surface. On December 13, 1972, its commander, Eugene Cernan, became the last man to step off the moon.

Since then, NASA has had to fight hard for its budgets, and the Space Race has given way to U.S./Soviet (later, Russian) cooperation. Other nations have ventured into space, and U.S. attention has refocused on space stations and reusable space shuttles. The Apollo project has become another piece of history. Since its termination, there have been more U.S. stamps celebrating Walt Disney characters than these amazing missions. Twenty-four men have left Earth's orbit and been to the moon. (Twelve have actually set foot on it.) The youngest of this group still living (at time of writing) is *Apollo 16*'s Charles Duke, now seventy-nine years old. Astronauts are made of tough stuff, but given the lack of current interest in lunar exploration, there will come a time in the not too distant future when there are no living men who have truly left the Earth and voyaged to another world. As a teenage boy who sat in front of the TV biting his nails while *Apollo 8* vanished behind the moon for the first time, I find that rather sad.

TWENTY-EIGHT

Smithsonian National Postal Museum

NEW REVOLUTIONS

Sidney Lanier 8¢, 1972;
Scott catalog no. 1446

THIS MIGHT AT FIRST SEEM a strange choice for a stamp to illustrate aspects of the late 1960s and early 1970s. Sidney Lanier was a relatively obscure nineteenth-century poet and musician from Macon, Georgia. He didn't have much influence on the era—unlike, say, Henry David Thoreau. But he looks the part, perfectly. With his vast beard, unkempt hair, and lost, soulful expression, Lanier could be a figure from a rock album cover of the early 1970s. John Lennon, perhaps? This is the face of a hippie. Stamps, even when trying to revisit history, can't help reflecting their own era.

The mid-1960s had seen the rise of a debate: accept the system or rise up against it violently. Later in the decade a third option began to emerge: reject the system, but do so gently. "Make love, not war." Politically, the new movement was rooted in opposition to the Vietnam War; culturally, it was driven by music. In 1966, young people in San Francisco could attend all-night gigs by Jefferson Airplane, Big Brother and the Holding Company, or, most iconic of all, the Grateful Dead, with their wild-haired, Lanier-bearded lead guitarist, Jerry Garcia. The music was based on the blues, with influences from country and folk—but it was loud, thanks to the new amplification technology. It was experimental, too, often featuring long improvisations, of which Garcia was a master. Floaty "psychedelic" light shows accompanied the performances, as did the opportunity to enhance the experience with LSD, a hallucinogenic substance developed in 1943 by Swiss chemist Albert Hoffman, initially used to simulate mental illness in psychological experiments. Like jazz and speakeasies in the 1920s, this was a radically new, all-embracing aesthetic experience. It was, to start with, an exclusive experience, but the music soon became mainstream, thanks to evolving broadcast and reproduction technologies. Three years after a few hundred hippies were getting high to the Dead in the Fillmore, half a million music fans descended on a small dairy farm in upstate New York for "Three Days of Peace and Music."

The Woodstock festival lived up to its slogan (if an event dominated by a 12,000-watt PA system can be called "Three Days of Peace"). For those days, 500,000 people shared a cramped—and soon very muddy—space with virtually no crime or violence. The music (except for Sha Na Na, a '50s rock 'n' roll tribute show) was of a kind that nobody would have imagined possible five years earlier. Though the two defining acts of the era, Bob Dylan and the Beatles, were absent, the crowd could enjoy the Who, Janis Joplin, Jefferson Airplane, Santana, Joe Cocker, Sly & the Family Stone, and

Jimi Hendrix, or, for those who preferred acoustic music, Richie Havens, Joan Baez, Arlo Guthrie, or Indian classical musician Ravi Shankar. Shankar's presence was particularly significant: The hippie movement turned its back on conventional Christianity and invited people to find their own path, and many people began to look to Eastern religion, seeing it as less structured and more mystical. The movement also rejected rationalism—at one point, the Woodstock audience started chanting at a rainstorm to go away—and conventional sexual morality (though, contrary to myth, most people at the festival kept their clothes on, despite those clothes being soaking wet). It was communal: On Saturday evening, John Morris, one of the announcers, asked everyone to light a match and hold it up to the sky; hundreds of thousands of people responded, and as they did so they felt part of something powerful and radically new.

An attempt to repeat Woodstock at Altamont, later in the year, ended in tragedy when a young man, probably on drugs, tried to rush the stage and was killed by security guards. Drugs were a central part of the hippie movement, and arguably its downfall. They certainly played a big part in the mental degeneration of Charles Manson, a psychopath whose "family" of hippie disciples carried out a series of murders, most notably that of five people, including actress Sharon Tate, at 10050 Cielo Drive in Los Angeles on August 8, 1969. If the new ideas had set free a great deal of light at Woodstock, at Altamont and 10050 Cielo Drive they showed their capacity to let loose darkness.

If the hippies had a grand vision, of an "alternative society" built on totally new cultural, social, and political—and chemical—foundations, other movements of this era sought to remedy more specific injustices. African American civil rights, illustrated by an earlier stamp, was probably the most visible, but there were many others.

Early feminism in the United States had been closely linked to abolitionism. Elizabeth Cady Stanton and Lucretia Mott first met at an antislavery convention in 1848—where they were barred from speaking because of their gender. Infuriated, they drew up a Declaration of Sentiments, echoing 1776: "We hold these truths to be self-evident, that all men *and women* are created equal." The Declaration also included eleven resolutions, including to struggle for the right to vote. This would be a long fight, culminating in the Nineteenth Amendment and its ratification in August 1920.

The 1960s saw the rise of a "second wave" of feminism concerned with discrimination in the workplace and, more insidiously, male dominance in other areas of life: home, family, politics, culture. Its seminal text, *The Feminine Mystique*, was published in February 1963. The book grew out of a survey carried out by journalist Betty Friedan of her former classmates, fifteen years out of college. She found many of these bright young women to be full-time housewives and deeply unhappy. Further research revealed many other women in the same boat. Friedan's book is about how this came about, the various ways in which women who sought fulfilling careers were put down and told instead that home (where they could exercise the "mystique" in the book's ironic title) and family should be satisfaction enough.

Soon after its publication, Eleanor Roosevelt's Commission on the Status of Women produced its report, and barriers to female participation in the workplace began to be dismantled. However, many people felt this did not go far enough. For example, of the forty special stamps issued in the two years after the commission's report, none was designed by a woman (though one did feature a painting by Mary Cassatt). By 1968, the movement had taken a more radical tone. That year, the Miss America contest was targeted by demonstrators, who interrupted the proceedings by unfurling a banner marked WOMEN'S LIBERATION, threw various beauty products into a "freedom trash can," and crowned a sheep as a rival winner. Some militants became convinced that men and women were irreconcilable enemies. The new movement, though, had many strands. Much of the new feminism was about new ways of enjoying life and finding self-expression, in "a fully equal partnership of the sexes," to quote the 1966 Statement of Purpose of the newly formed National Organization for Women. *Cosmopolitan* magazine, edited by Helen Gurley Brown, became the must-read for young career women eager for emotional and sexual fulfillment as well as a challenging public career.

Other groups were asserting their inalienable rights, too. Homosexuality had been taboo in postwar America (despite the 1948 Kinsey Report, which seemed to imply that 10 percent of the male population was gay and that a further 27 percent had dabbled in homosexual activity of some kind). Being gay could cost you your federal job. To associate, homosexual people had had to form obscure-sounding groups: Daughters of Bilitis for women, the Mattachine Society for men. (Bilitis was a supposed lover of the Greek poetess Sappho; "Mattachine" came from a troupe of Renaissance-era actors who always wore masks.) The Post Office played its part in the oppression, using a law from 1873 to prevent *ONE*, a gay magazine of astonishing mildness by modern standards, from being sent through the mail (a move later ruled unconstitutional by the Supreme Court). But times were changing. On June 28, 1969, New York police raided the Stonewall Inn, a venue for gay men in Greenwich Village. Such raids were commonplace, but that evening the club's patrons had had enough: A street riot ensued. In May 1970, activists interrupted a session of the American Psychiatric Association where electroshock methods of "curing" homosexuality were being demonstrated. The first anniversary of the Stonewall riot, June 28, 1970, saw the first Pride marches in New York, Chicago, and Los Angeles: The masks were off. Oddly, Austria, a country not generally known for its freewheeling liberalism, was the first nation to issue a Gay Pride stamp, in 2010.

At the same time these first Pride marches were held, one of America's bitterest and longest strikes was coming to an end. In the mid-nineteenth century, Mexican inhabitants of newly acquired American territories had been promised full U.S. citizenship. They did not get it; instead, Spanish-speaking landowners were hustled off their properties, and southwestern states brought in their own Jim Crow laws. Despite this, poverty continued to drive people north across the Rio Grande; by 1914, there were around a million Latino Americans ("Latino" is a broader term than "Hispanic," as it includes people who trace their origins back to Portuguese-speaking Brazil), and by 1940, this number had doubled. In the Southwest, many worked as transient labor with no employment rights. In the late 1940s, they began their own civil rights movement, which became closely intertwined with the fight for better pay and conditions on farms. On September 8, 1965, Filipino grape pickers went on strike. Other fruit pickers joined them—a new development, as the growers had traditionally played one nationality off against another. The United Farm Workers union was formed, led by Cesar Chavez, a man made from the same stuff as Martin Luther King: courageous, nonviolent, deeply religious, and a charismatic orator. The longer the strike lasted, the greater the temptation to resort to violence grew, but Chavez urged his followers to resist this, even going on a twenty-five-day fast to show the depth of his principles. In July 1970, the growers caved in, recognizing the union and granting the workers better pay and conditions. Chavez was honored on a stamp in 2003.

The year 1970 also saw the publication of Dee Brown's *Bury My Heart at Wounded Knee*, subtitled *An Indian History of the American West*. This book details the many injustices suffered by America's first inhabitants. At the same time, members of the American Indian Movement were occupying Alcatraz Island, which they claimed as theirs by right in compensation for land taken from them in breach of the Treaty of Fort Laramie. They did not get to keep the island, but a new sense of pride was kindled in Native Americans. The government began to reconsider its previous policy of "termination," whereby Indian nations lost their special legal status (and land) and their members became ordinary U.S. citizens. Native Americans and their culture have been featured on about seventy stamps since 1898, but almost all of these have been issued since 1977 (and before 2004, after which the attention of the USPS has gone elsewhere).

Another rising concern of these changing times transcended any group: environmentalism. Respect for, and the protection of, nature has a long history in the United States, which has been reflected in its stamps since FDR's 1934 National Parks issue. In 1956, three Wildlife Conservation stamps featured wild turkey, pronghorn antelope, and king salmon; the first two creatures had been rescued from near-extinction. From 1958, annual stamps celebrated the conservation of forests, soil (1959; a stamp issued the next day celebrated the petroleum industry), water (1960), and rangeland (1961). The year after this series ended saw the publication of the book now regarded as the instigator of the modern environmental movement, Rachel Carson's *Silent Spring*. This book illuminated the indiscriminate and dangerous use of pesticides, especially DDT, a chemical Carson claimed was killing not only wildlife but humans. The book remains controversial: Critics say that it hindered attempts to eradicate malaria; defenders say that the malarial mosquitoes had become resistant to DDT anyway and point to the connections between a large number of her critics and chemical companies. The postal authorities seemed to side with her defenders, honoring her with a stamp in 1981.

In 1971, change even came to the Post Office Department. Despite the best efforts of recent postmasters general (especially, in his best, earliest years, Eisenhower's Arthur Summerfield), the department still had too many political appointees in senior roles. By the late 1960s, this setup clearly wasn't working: The placemen did not have the skills to handle the ever-increasing volume of mail. In 1966, 75 billion items—mainly letters—were sent, but in the same year, Chicago's post office, then the largest in the world, ground to a halt, the building crammed with 10 million pieces of undelivered post. A commission was set up, which recommended the department become a "self-supporting government organization" with no political appointees, a faster-track promotion system, and power to set its own pay rates. After much wrangling, this came about on July 1, 1971, when the department became the U.S. Postal Service.

The radical movements of this era continue to generate heated debate. Much of their rhetoric now seems doctrinaire and melodramatic, and clearly some aspects of what was called the "counterculture" experiment failed: Massive drug use does not lead to personal or social liberation. However, in other ways, as Elizabeth Cady Stanton and Lucretia Mott understood, these movements can be seen as a continuation of the great project founded in 1776, of extending the rights of life, liberty, and the pursuit of happiness to all. Viewed from this long, historical perspective, choosing a nineteenth-century musician/poet to represent the era seems rather apt.

Smithsonian National Postal Museum

STUMBLING THROUGH THE '70s

Energy Conservation 10¢, 1974; Scott catalog no. 1547

ENERGY CONSERVATION? IN THE LAND of wildcatters, gushers, and gasoline at 20¢ a gallon?

Historians talk about the "long '60s." They disagree exactly where to begin that era. "Heartbreak Hotel"? JFK's election win in 1960? The end is crystal clear: October 17, 1973, the date on which the Organization of Petroleum Exporting Countries announced it would raise the world price of oil by 70 percent. Further price hikes were to follow: By early 1974 a barrel of the sticky black liquid would cost four times what it had in early October 1973.

The immediate cause of this was America's support for Israel in the Yom Kippur War (a failed attempt by Egypt and

Syria to launch a surprise attack on their neighbor). The longer-term causes were economic. The United States had stopped being self-sufficient in oil in 1950, when booming demand outstripped domestic production. Inflation, largely caused by the Vietnam War, had begun eating away at the global value of the dollar, the currency in which oil was traded. Non-U.S. oil producers had teamed up to form a cartel, determined to boost their real income from the sale of their product. On October 17, all these causes aligned.

By the last week of February 1974, 20 percent of American gasoline stations had no fuel. Others introduced rationing systems. The stock market, full of companies whose business models were based on cheap oil, was tumbling. It was the end of an industrial era, the death of the "great car economy." This stamp appeared in September 1974: a case, perhaps, of shutting the garage door after the Cadillac Eldorado 8.2-liter V8 has bolted.

The year 1974 was traumatic for another reason. While waiting in line to fill up with gas, you could turn on the radio and follow the latest developments in the Watergate scandal. Every day, murkier and murkier material seemed to be seeping out of the White House.

The Watergate scandal began with the arrest of five burglars at the headquarters of the Democratic Party National Committee in July 1972. It was discovered that they had been trying to bug the place. On whose orders? The finger soon pointed at the Committee for the Re-election of the President, gleefully named CREEP by its opponents. Who was in charge of this? The president, Richard Nixon, went on TV to deny any knowledge of the bugging. White House officials were then found to have been involved and were fired by Nixon.

It was then discovered that back in 1971 the president had set up voice-activated recorders to capture every conversation in the three main White House offices. A struggle began between the judiciary and the executive office for access to these tapes. A first set was grudgingly released and was found to have a mysterious 18½ minute gap—as well as revealing Nixon in an unflattering light: foul-mouthed (the tapes did the same job as Andrew Jackson's parrot) and paranoid about the press and the liberal intelligentsia. More tapes were requested; Nixon refused to hand them over; the Supreme Court insisted; the president had to obey. Among the next batch was a recording of Nixon, six days after the original 1972 arrests, asking his officials to prevent the CIA and FBI investigating the Watergate break-in. The tape proved that he had known all along the plans for the break-in. Three days after the contents of this tape were made public, he announced his resignation. The next day, he left the White House for the last time.

In a way, Watergate was a triumph for democracy. Nixon had lied and been found guilty—if not by the law, then by the jury of public opinion. But the whole affair seemed incredibly seedy. When it was all over, the sense was not one of celebration but more of relief that an unpleasant process was finally done with. Don't expect any Watergate stamps to be issued in the near future. (A set of unofficial stamps *was* issued at the time—by a Californian artist. Peter Martin, featuring satirical cartoons of key figures in the affair. Some were used on letters, much to the annoyance of the new USPS.)

The year 1975 got off to an even gloomier start, with the final days of the war in Vietnam. April brought helicopter evacuations from both Saigon and the Cambodian capital of Phnom Penh, the latter in the face of the psychopathic Khmer

Rouge—a regime that lasted three and a half years but issued no postage stamps, as nobody dared write letters: Being literate meant being sent to rural camps and worked to death. Supporters of the domino theory argued that Cambodia's fall proved their point; opponents responded that U.S. meddling in the country's affairs had brought about this cataclysm; everyone had to accept that America had failed dismally in Southeast Asia.

The United States wasn't hugely popular elsewhere, either. Countries in Africa were increasingly turning to the Soviet Union for inspiration and assistance. International terrorism was on the rise: Displaced Palestinians began resorting to terror tactics against Israel and its allies, the biggest of which was America. In September 1974, a TWA flight from Tel Aviv to JFK Airport was blown up, killing eighty-eight people. Home-grown terrorism was also on the rise in the United States, with Puerto Rican nationalists and the bizarre Symbionese Liberation Front, famous for the kidnapping of Patty Hearst, carrying out attacks on individuals. In December 1975, a bomb exploded at La Guardia Airport, killing eleven people; it is still not known who was behind this.

The next year, 1976, should have been one of celebration. The USPS kicked it off with three Spirit of '76 stamps; in February a set of fifty featured the flags of each state. Four handsome souvenir sheets, featuring classic paintings of key Revolutionary events (July 4, 1776; Washington crossing the Delaware; Valley Forge; Yorktown) followed in May, and a strip of four 13¢ stamps on July 4 itself. Elsewhere, a special "American Freedom Train," painted red, white, and blue, made its way across the country with a traveling exhibition that featured (among other things) George Washington's copy of the Constitution, Martin Luther King's pulpit, and a piece of moonrock. More than 7 million people visited, and many more stood by tracksides and waved cheerfully as it went by. On the night of July 4, fireworks lit up America's skies, especially in D.C., which hosted a massive display with a red, white, and blue theme and featuring one of the world's first laser shows, from the top of the Washington Monument.

The celebrations cheered many up, but somehow the mood didn't last. In Baltimore, a bicentennial cake was baked, the largest such confection ever, weighing 31 tons and using 120,000 eggs—but it was left out in a rainstorm (on a barge in Baltimore Harbor, not in MacArthur Park); the plan had been to sell slices to recoup the cost, but few people wanted to buy soggy cake, and it became a health hazard, attracting swarms of rats and causing bitter arguments about who should make good on the financial shortfall. Culturally, 1976 is probably best remembered for the pent-up rage of Robert de Niro as alienated Vietnam veteran Travis Bickle in the movie *Taxi Driver*. It was, perhaps, too soon after Watergate and Vietnam, and maybe even the violent polarizations of the late 1960s, to get into the party spirit.

The 1976 presidential election appeared to show a way forward. The two opponents, Gerald Ford and Jimmy Carter, were both individuals of decency and integrity. America had had enough of ruthless political bruisers. Carter won a close contest but soon ran into difficulties. Part of his attraction for voters was that he was a Washington outsider, free of the lingering stench of Watergate. Unfortunately, this virtue soon turned into a vice: Effective presidents have to be competent at the Capitol Hill game, but Carter wasn't, even ending up feuding with his own party. He tried to block initiatives that he felt were unnecessary "pork barrel" spending. (He was probably right, but previous presidents hadn't done this.) Congress replied by watering down his bills on consumer protection and health care. These battles led to partial government shutdowns on five occasions (though these were infinitely milder affairs than such shutdowns have become since 1996).

Another energy conservation stamp was issued in 1977—this time, in tandem with one promoting energy development. The president did his part for the latter, installing solar panels on the White House. More substantially, 1977 saw the opening of the Alaska Pipeline, bringing oil south from Prudhoe Bay deep in the Arctic. But America remained dependent on imported oil—which during Carter's term rocketed in price again. This sent another shot of inflation pumping through the U.S. economy. Traditional economists had no idea how to deal with this. Accepted models taught that inflation came with increased economic activity—"overheating"—which needed to be calmed down. But the new, oil-driven price rises came with economic stagnation. A new term entered the textbooks, "stagflation." However, none of the textbooks had a solution. Experts began to mutter darkly that the "American century" had come to an end. A bestselling business book of 1979, by Harvard professor Ezra Vogel, was called *Japan as Number One: Lessons for America.* Those lessons included central planning of industrial policy, more "group learning," and less individualism.

Miserable as stagflation was, even greater harm was done to the Carter presidency by political events in Iran. That country's former leader, Shah Mohammad Reza Pahlavi, had been a Westward-looking modernizer, friendly with the United States, but his reforms had been anathema to traditionally minded clerics and their followers. Opposition had grown and had been met with autocracy and repression, which further incensed Pahlavi's enemies. In late 1978 he was driven from power and replaced by the fundamentalist spiritual leader Ayatollah Khomeini. Khomeini was virulently anti-American, partially out of a general hatred of Western ways and partially because of the history of U.S. involvement in the region: People still remembered the CIA's toppling of Mossadegh back in 1953.

On November 4, 1979, a group of students broke into the American Embassy in Tehran. Their initial plan was to occupy the building for a short while to protest against Pahlavi's receiving medical treatment in Texas, but embassy guards fought back and the situation escalated. A mob surrounded the building; Khomeini put his weight behind the students, and a hostage crisis began.

If you'd sat in line for gas in 1974 listening to the latest on Watergate, you could now repeat the experience in 1979–80 with this crisis, which went from bad to worse. Fifty-three Americans were imprisoned in the embassy (fifty-two after one who suffered from multiple sclerosis was released half-dead). Diplomatic attempts to find a solution failed. Stories of mistreatment leaked out (accompanied by denials by the Iranian government). In April 1980, a group of Special Forces sent in to effect a rescue flew into a sandstorm and had to abort the mission. The whole fiasco seemed to sum up a decade of American loss: loss of status, loss of direction, loss of optimism.

Yet the late '70s weren't all gloom. People enjoyed themselves—as people always do. Hollywood rediscovered its mojo in 1977 with the first *Star Wars* movie. While *Taxi Driver* might have provided a deeper insight into the damaged psyche of post-Vietnam America, George Lucas's intergalactic epic was a lot more fun. Another hit of that year was *Saturday Night Fever*, which featured the new "disco" music. Lushly produced, exuberantly sexual, and often featuring superb musicians like Nile Rodgers and Bernard Edwards, disco was for dancing to. Stop worrying about stagflation; get out there and strut your stuff (preferably in your best white suit and purple shirt with a ridiculously large collar, as celebrated in a 1999 stamp). And if your rock-loving elder siblings disapprove, to hell with them.

The decade also brought quiet progress on civil rights. The number of black elected officials tripled, including Barbara Jordan from Texas, who gave the keynote address at the 1976 Democratic National Convention. From 1975, the sitcom *The Jeffersons*, a spin-off from *All in the Family*, entertained large audiences. Some critics complained that the program was not political enough, but that was the whole point—this was a show about an ordinary middle-class American family who just happened to be black. In 1978, the USPS began its Black Heritage series with a 13¢ featuring Harriet Tubman, who had been a key part of the "underground railroad," smuggling escaped slaves to Canada in the 1850s. Dr. King was the second person to appear, in January 1979. Since then there have been thirty-four more issues in the series, the most recent, at time of writing, featuring tennis player Althea Gibson.

The presidential campaign of 1980 was, for most of its duration, closely fought. The Republican candidate was Ronald Reagan, the former governor of California and star of *This Is the Army*, whom many people regarded as a lightweight. Democrats breathed a sigh of relief when he won the primaries, reckoning that a stronger candidate would have had the beleaguered President Carter on the ropes. However, in the one TV debate between Reagan and the incumbent president, the GOP's man revealed himself to be quick-witted and positive, in contrast to Carter, who was ponderous, worthy, and uptight. After that, a gap opened up between the two men, and Reagan won the election by a landslide. Some people argued that he'd just used his Hollywood skills to charm voters, and they feared for what he might do in the White House. Start a nuclear war? Turn stagflation into a new Great Depression?

America was about to find out.

THIRTY

Smithsonian National Postal Museum. © United States Postal Service

MR. REAGAN GOES TO WASHINGTON

Flag and Anthem issue 18¢, 1981; Scott catalog no. 1891

CHOOSING A STAMP to typify the Reagan era is not easy. In 1985, a $10.75 Express Mail featured a fierce-looking eagle—perfect, surely, for Reagan's aggressive foreign policy. It was also at the time the most expensive stamp issued in the United States, a symbol of the gap between rich and poor that began to increase at that time: a "yuppie stamp." Yet Reagan's foreign policy was not eagle-like all the time: A month before the $10.75 Express Mail stamp came out, Mikhail Gorbachev was elected general secretary of the Soviet Communist Party, and once the two men met, they established a rapport that soon led to White House hard-liners complaining that their leader was turning soft.

Another potential candidate to head this chapter comes from the 1986 AMERIPEX set, issued in honor of an international philatelic event in Chicago. This celebrated every nonliving president, however obscure. One of Reagan's first acts on taking office was to take down a portrait of Harry Truman in the Cabinet Room and replace it with one of a Republican president he said he wanted to emulate. Was it Lincoln? TR? No, his hero was Calvin Coolidge. Reagan pointed out that the thirtieth president had presided over an era of unprecedented prosperity (omitting to mention the fact that the Coolidge years had been followed by the Great Depression). However, despite Reagan's admiration for him, Coolidge was not the ideal metaphor for his years. "Silent Cal" had been notoriously taciturn, while Reagan was a superb communicator.

Opponents of Reagan—he was a controversial president—might opt for a third choice, a bizarre stamp that came out early in his first term and proclaimed "Alcoholism—you can beat it!" Recipients of envelopes bearing this stamp presumably weren't always pleased to be told they were alcoholics. However, there is no evidence that Ronald Reagan drove any more people to drink than any other politician.

So in the end, I opted for the one above, featuring Old Glory, a rather uninspired drawing of a piece of coast and a quote from "America the Beautiful." It's a very ordinary stamp but full of genuine patriotic intent. The nation's fortieth president was not dissimilar. Although his life had hardly been ordinary, Reagan had a simple, optimistic manner that resonated with ordinary voters. He was a patriot, and much of his success lay in reviving America's patriotism, which had taken a knock during the Vietnam/Watergate years.

Despite the ordinariness of his appeal, Reagan achieved

extraordinary things. His detractors argue that, in doing so, he was simply lucky. He certainly started lucky. Two days after his inauguration, Iran released the embassy hostages (though the new Islamic Republic kept producing anti-American propaganda stamps for years to come). Shortly after that, a lone gunman tried to assassinate him and failed; Reagan's gutsy reaction to his injuries made him even more popular with the electorate. Shortly after that, he was confronted with striking air traffic controllers and simply fired them, on the grounds that, as government servants, they had broken the law by withdrawing their labor. This was technically correct but arguably highly irresponsible. A replacement service was cobbled together and slowly brought up to speed; had an accident occurred during this process, the president would have been at least partially to blame. The Reagan luck held. No planes crashed.

The new president had two "big ideas." One was to take a much tougher stance against the Soviet Union; the other was to use a set of new economic policies to fight stagflation. How did they work out?

The Soviet Union had built on its successes of the early and middle 1970s, extending its influence and, more disturbingly, its military technology. Its new medium-range missile, known in the West as the SS-20, could be fired from a mobile platform, used solid fuel (so could be launched much more quickly than previous, liquid-fuel missiles), and could deliver a nuclear warhead up to 3,000 miles with an accuracy of 500 meters. During the late 1970s, it was deployed across Eastern Europe. Reagan felt it was time to confront this expansion and ordered an increase in military spending. The rhetoric expanded to match: On March 8, 1983, he gave a speech describing the Soviet Union as an "evil empire." Two weeks later, he announced plans for his Strategic Defense Initiative (SDI), which would create an antimissile shield around America directed from space and which soon became known as "Star Wars."

The dangers of this new tension quickly became apparent. On September 1, 1983, the Soviets shot down a civilian Korean airliner that had strayed into its airspace, killing all 269 passengers and crew. The very next day, Colonel Stanislav Petrov, duty officer on the Soviet early-warning system, received information that five U.S. missiles had been launched and were heading for his country. At that time, Soviet protocol was that in the event of such an attack, a massive counterstrike would be launched. Petrov's duty was to pass the information on to his superiors, who would then have two minutes to decide whether to initiate this response. However, Petrov suspected a malfunction—why would the U.S. launch just five missiles?—and did not pass the information on. His suspicions were correct: The phantom missiles were caused by a freak combination of weather conditions and satellites. (This story suggests an idea for a stamp issue: men who have prevented Armageddon. Colonel Petrov would be on it, as would the officers of submarine *B-59* at the time of the Cuban crisis. Two other candidates for inclusion are Russian president Boris Yeltsin, who decided to ignore an off-track meteorological research rocket in 1995, and British singer James Blunt, who, as a young army officer, disobeyed an order to attack Russian troops during the 1999 Kosovo crisis.)

The president was also uncompromising in standing up to what he saw as more insidious attempts at Soviet expansion. A far-left coup in Grenada led to a swift, successful invasion of the island (and a subsequent flood of Grenadian stamps celebrating him). Unfriendly regimes in other parts of the world proved more problematic, however, and Reagan soon found himself mired in struggles in Nicaragua and El Salvador. These battles were fought at arm's length, via U.S. support for anti-Communist guerrillas rather than Vietnam-style mobilization. Such wars tend to drag on, and these were no exception.

Confronting stagflation at home, Reagan was just as radical. He sought to conquer inflation using the "monetarist" economics of Milton Friedman, who said that the problem was caused by too much money in the system (and nothing else). The stagnation was attacked with "supply side" policies that sought to revive the productive economy. Cuts in income tax and (especially) capital gains tax were announced, which, it was hoped, would incentivize enterprise and free up money for investment. Business regulation that he saw as unnecessary was targeted. The initial effect of the new policies was to make things even worse. Cutting the amount of money in circulation created a recession; by November 1983, unemployment had hit 10.8 percent, its worst level since the Great Depression. However, his policies soon began to work. Inflation fell. and the economy picked up, driven by the new computing technology. Stagflation was replaced by a boom.

America found renewed confidence. As this stamp reminds us, patriotism became cool again. However, some of the older, more Puritan trappings of national identity were quietly dropped. In the 1980s, America wanted to party. Gay America, newly released from the old intolerance, took to the new atmosphere with particular relish—only to encounter a horrific new enemy. In 1981, doctors noticed an outbreak of rare types of pneumonia and cancer in young gay men, indicating failure of their immune systems. The same syndrome was then found in drug users and people who had received blood transfusions. In 1982, it was given the name AIDS, and in 1983, its cause was traced to a newly evolved virus. Research to find a cure began. The first anti-HIV drug, AZT, was tested in 1986. It was desperately needed: By the end of that year, 28,000 cases had been reported, of whom 25,000 had died, including Hollywood star Rock Hudson. Like the flu pandemic of 1918, AIDS struck the young. The world saw images of once-vibrant individuals suddenly wasting away. Unlike in the 1918 pandemic, the toll would keep rising. By the time an AIDS awareness stamp was produced in 1993, nearly 200,000 people in the United States alone had been killed by the disease.

In 1985, Ronald Reagan found himself with a new opposite number in Moscow. Mikhail Gorbachev initially sought to bolster the old Soviet system; his first action was to try to reduce the nation's vodka consumption. Over time, however, he became aware that more radical restructuring was needed (or, maybe, that a complete overhaul of the system would be an easier task). Reagan's first meeting with Gorbachev was in Geneva on November 21, 1985. After an initial coolness, the two leaders took a walk by the city's lake and found themselves getting along well. A second summit, in Reykjavik eleven months later, made little substantive progress—Reagan dug his heels in over SDI—but the chemistry between the two most powerful men in the world continued to develop. Gorbachev later said that it was at Reykjavik that he truly understood that America wasn't secretly planning to nuke Russia and really did want peace. The president developed a good relationship with Gorbachev because both men were, in their different ways, idealistic populists, outsiders to their respective establishments: Reagan to Washington's cerebral "think tanks" and Nixonian intrigues, Gorbachev to the old men in the Kremlin who had begun their careers in the shadow of Stalin.

The economic boom continued for the rest of Reagan's presidency. A sudden stock market crash in 1987 shocked everyone, but the market soon picked up and headed back upward. Relations with Russia continued to thaw slowly—much to the annoyance of some of Reagan's original supporters. The same year saw the signing of a treaty to remove the SS-20s from Eastern Europe, as well as America's Pershings from the west of that continent. At the same time, pressure was maintained on America's old Cold War adversary: Expenditure on SDI forced Moscow to keep up—or to try to; its creaky economic system was showing clear signs of being unable to deliver. On a visit to Berlin, Reagan challenged Gorbachev: "Tear down this wall!"

There were, of course, downsides. The country might have been making things—and money—again, but it was getting into debt. The annual budget deficit nearly quadrupled between 1980 and 1986, and the result of this was a ballooning long-term national debt. Supporters of Reagan say this was the cost of winning the Cold War and argue that Lincoln, Wilson, and FDR had incurred huge debts winning their wars, too. Critics say it was a cheap trick, mortgaging the future to buy the appearance of economic recovery. Not everyone got rich in the Reagan years, either. Welfare programs were cut; economists asserted that, instead, the new wealth would "trickle down" to the poorest in society. It didn't. The decade saw the continuation of the inner-city decline that had started with the late '60s riots and kept spiraling down in the 1970s. These once-desirable areas became centers of crime and drug addiction, with crack cocaine becoming the escape route of choice.

Reagan also got into trouble internationally with a scheme to finance "Contra" rebels in Nicaragua with money from sales of arms to Iran (which itself was a ruse to persuade the Iranians to release hostages in Lebanon). He claims not to have known about this skulduggery—which makes him a poor chief executive. Or was he lying? The American people chose to believe the former and to forgive him his poor management.

On the philatelic front, the era saw an increasing number of stamp issues: The 1980s USPS truly got the point, so misunderstood by Reagan's role model, Coolidge, that commemorative stamps are valuable sources of revenue. The Reagan years are often seen as politically extreme, but this is not evidenced on its stamps. Public service features regularly; for instance, 1985 issues celebrated public education and two New Deal fiftieth anniversaries, the Social Security and Rural Electrification acts. Nature and famous individuals from Horatio Alger to Eleanor Roosevelt continued to inspire most issues. The Love series was restarted in 1982, and an example appeared most years after 1984.

Ronald Reagan stayed popular throughout his time in office (with blips for the early recession and the Iran/Contra scandal), something that few presidents have achieved—since World War II, only Eisenhower, Reagan and Bill Clinton have managed it. His vice president, George H. W. Bush, won a comfortable victory in the 1988 election, and "the Gipper" (Reagan played George "the Gipper" Gipp, a Notre Dame football hero, in a 1940 movie) handed the office over to him in 1989.

Two stamp designs have featured Ronald Reagan since his death in 2004. Both try to convey his charm; neither quite achieves this. By contrast, another stamp issued around the same time as the first Reagan commemorative, celebrating Yip Harburg, lyricist of "Brother, Can You Spare a Dime?," succeeds at the same task perfectly. (It's one of my favorite portrait stamps.) Maybe that shows that the Reagan charm was affected: He was, by training, an actor. However, that charm worked on Mikhail Gorbachev, and it worked on the majority of the American people—at a time, after the uncertainty of the 1970s, when it was badly needed. In the end, like James K. Polk, Ronald Reagan did what he set out to do: in his case, reverse the Cold War and end stagflation. If he was a lucky president, he made the most of his luck.

THIRTY-ONE

Smithsonian National Postal Museum. © United States Postal Service

A NEW WORLD ORDER?

Desert Shield/Desert Storm commemorative 29¢, 1991; Scott catalog no. 2551

THE UNITED STATES DIDN'T ISSUE any stamps to mark the end of the Cold War, a forty-four-year conflict that had on several occasions threatened a nuclear holocaust and had cost trillions of dollars. Not until 2000, anyway, when the fall of the Berlin Wall was one of fifteen aspects of the 1980s celebrated in a millennium series, Celebrate the Century. (The set for that decade also included the Cabbage Patch Kids and figure skating.) But this extraordinary event can't be left out of this narrative.

In 1988, Bruce Springsteen crossed the Berlin Wall and played a free concert, which more than 300,000 young East Germans attended. The authorities hoped this would keep them happy, but it had the opposite effect; the event just made the audience want more freedom and fun. (Many flew homemade U.S. flags at the gig.) In August 1989, Hungary opened its borders with the West, and 13,000 East Germans immediately left by this route. October 7 was the fortieth anniversary of the DDR. A set of stamps was inevitably issued by that country, featuring the usual propaganda suspects (albeit less square-jawed than the old Stalinist versions): happy schoolchildren, workers, city planners, farmers. However, the real-life incarnations of these people had had enough. Rallies to celebrate the anniversary turned into protests; the country's aging dictator, Erich Honecker, ordered the use of force to silence this dissent, but party officials refused to obey, and Honecker was voted out of office by his own cabinet. On November 9, the DDR government announced it would let East Berliners visit the West. People were soon streaming across border crossings, watched by confused soldiers. People climbed onto the Berlin Wall, which had symbolized the division of the world since 1961, and started pulling it down.

If the domino theory had been a poor predictor of events in Southeast Asia, it proved a perfect model for Eastern Europe in 1989. The rest of the old Soviet European empire followed the DDR almost instantly: The old regimes in Czechoslovakia, Bulgaria, and Romania had all fallen by the end of the year, and rumblings had begun within the Soviet Union itself.

Instead of celebrating this extraordinary victory, U.S. stamps of this era chug pleasantly along, featuring beach umbrellas, ducks, classic movies, fish . . . Absurdly insular? Well, maybe—but they reflect the approach of George H. W. Bush. The president did not want to rub salt into the defeated enemy's wounds, eager not to stir up a reaction within Russia against the man who had allowed this to happen. Mikhail

Gorbachev might not have torn down the wall, but in refusing Soviet military assistance to the old East European Stalin-
ists, he had sealed its doom. Bush wisely felt that the least he
could do to reward this was to abstain from triumphalism.

Another foe imploded around this time, too: an economic
one. The authors of *Japan as Number One* and similar "declin-
ist" books generally spent the 1980s rubbing their hands with
glee: America might have turned a corner and started growing again, but their preferred candidate for global economic
leadership was doing even better. On December 29, 1989,
four days after the collapse of the last big Eastern European
Communist regime, Tokyo's Nikkei stock index hit an all-
time high of 38,957. At that point, the value of the companies
that it listed was greater than that of Wall Street and represented an astonishing 44 percent of the value of all the world's
stock markets. It then began to decline: The valuations represented a bubble, which duly popped. But unlike in America's
minicrash of 1987, prices did not recover, and instead kept
drifting down. The Japanese economy went into recession
and has struggled to grow since.

The final, unexpected triumph came in 1991. Like the fall
of East Germany, the collapse of the Soviet Union was essentially a victory for "people power." Once debate was allowed
in national media, it soon became apparent that people were
fed up with the corruption and cruelty of the old order. During 1990, elections were held in all the Union's fifteen republics. In Moldova, Georgia, Armenia, and the three Baltic
states, the Communist Party lost, while in others nationalists
gained substantial representation. Further elections in 1991
saw Boris Yeltsin defeat the official candidate for the title of
president of the Russian Republic. The Soviet Union was
breaking up. A coup launched on August 19 tried to halt this

process, but Muscovites took to the streets, Yeltsin climbed up onto a tank and denounced the plotters, and the coup failed. Former Soviet republics immediately began to secede, and on December 26, 1991, America's Cold War foe voted itself out of existence.

If U.S. stamps remain graciously silent about these events, Soviet ones show this sudden collapse. In 1989, there is still a fair smattering of red flags. As late as April 1991, an issue celebrates Lenin's birthday (it shows him hard at work on his crowd-pleaser, *Materialism and Empirio-Criticism*), but later that year, an issue celebrates the failure of the coup, showing three young men killed in the street fighting. In Russia's New Year issue for 1992, the letters CCCP (USSR) still feature, even though the Union no longer existed: The postal authorities didn't have time to remove them. From then on, however, they are gone.

By this time, America had also scored a decisive military victory that helped wipe away the shame of Vietnam. On August 2, 1990, Iraqi dictator Saddam Hussein invaded the small but wealthy oil-producing state of Kuwait. The international community was almost united in its condemnation of this—out of morality and out of a concern that Saddam now controlled 20 percent of the world's oil. The United States at once raced to protect its ally Saudi Arabia, which bordered Iraq (and which controlled even more oil): Operation Desert Shield. Diplomatic efforts continued to try to get Saddam to retreat from Kuwait, but in vain. On October 30, President Bush decided that if war was the only way of securing this result, it should be declared. However, he was aware of the need for legitimacy and support, both at home and around the world. On November 29, the UN Security Council passed a resolution telling Saddam to get out by January 15 or face the consequences.

A military buildup now began in earnest—as did a war of words. Three words in particular; this was an opportunity to replace the polarized global polity of the Cold War with what President Bush called a New World Order. In this Order, international law would be universally respected and enforced, not by a U.S. "global policeman" but by the United Nations. (America, now the lone superpower, would, of course, play its part.) Liberal democracy would flourish everywhere, springing up naturally as the last dictators withered away. This, one academic wrote, would be the end of history.

A coalition of thirty-four nations was quickly assembled, with nearly 800,000 troops (two-thirds from the USA), and when Saddam duly missed his deadline, it sprang into action. On January 17, Operation Desert Storm began, with the bombing of Iraqi infrastructure. The Iraqi air force was put out of action almost at once, and on February 24, fighting moved to the ground. Saddam had promised "the mother of all battles"; he provided a bedridden great-aunt, announcing a retreat from Kuwait two days later. One hundred hours after the first ground troops went into action, President Bush called a cease-fire to stop the slaughter.

It looked like a complete triumph for the New World Order, but the triumph brought problems of its own. Saddam was still in power. Ill-judged U.S. attempts to foment revolution in Iraq failed and led to vicious reprisals on minority groups such as the Kurds and the Marsh Arabs. These raised the question of how far the New World Order could or should go about preventing such internal barbarities. A new lack of clarity entered the debate.

Still, a fine victory had been won. The stamp at the head of this chapter was issued on July 2, 1991, to honor those who served in Desert Shield and Desert Storm. It features the Southwest Asia Service Medal, a special award designed by Nadine Russell of the Army's Institute of Heraldry. The medal was made official by the president in March 1991, but plans for it had begun in October 1990, and designs had been ready before the November UN resolution.

If Vietnam had been fought to the anguished strains of hard rock, Desert Storm was fought to a pulsating new music: hip-hop. Hip-hop emerged from dance parties in the South Bronx in the late 1970s. The music featured drum machines, snatches of old classics, "scratching" (an effect caused by manually reversing turntables), and rap: improvised, poetic lyrics chanted rather than sung. Like jazz, rock 'n' roll, and rock, it came with a cultural package: its own dances (breakdancing) requiring skill and youth, art (graffiti), and fashions. Like those musical forms, it soon spread from America around the world. By 1991, it had its own global superstars. Despite several of its practitioners having died early, violent deaths, none has made it onto a stamp yet, though an anonymous fan, complete with boombox and reversed baseball cap, was another aspect of the 1980s, along with the fate of the Berlin Wall, featured in the Celebrate the Century issue of 2000.

Despite his triumphs on the global stage, George H. W. Bush had problems back home. The economy went into recession, and his own party began to desert him. Bush was a Republican in the Eisenhower style. He signed into law liberal "big government" legislation like the Clean Air Act Amendments of 1990 and the Americans with Disabilities Act. He had not pursued Saddam to Baghdad, aware that his carefully assembled coalition (and with it, his New World Order) would have collapsed had he tried to. He made little effort to appeal to conservative religious groups, who were making their presence felt ever more strongly in the Republican Party. Many of these groups had been disappointed by Reagan; they felt they had helped him gain office, but his actions as president were often more pragmatic than his rhetoric promised. Bush they disliked even more. Abortion was still legal, as it had been since a 1973 Supreme Court decision. Prayers were still not part of official school assemblies (a ruling that went back to the First Amendment, which separated church and state). For many people there was a sense that moral relativism, especially in sexual matters, had gone too far. Bush didn't even speak publicly about these things, let alone take action.

When election time came in 1992, these factors told. An independent candidate, Texan software billionaire Ross Perot, began to eat away huge chunks of Bush support. (Another independent candidate, John Hagelin of the Natural Law Party, argued that social and global problems would be solved by the establishment of an elite corps of superenlightened Yogic Flyers. He did rather less harm to the Republican vote.)

After Desert Storm, the president had commanded an approval rating of 89 percent, but as the election approached, this plummeted, falling to below 40 percent before picking up a little bit. This late uptick was not enough: A younger, more dynamic man and his equally dynamic wife were knocking at the White House door.

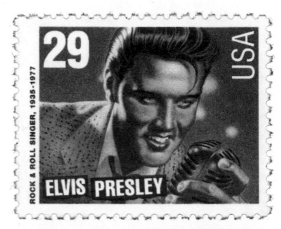

BOOM!

Legends of American Music, Elvis Presley 29¢, 1993; Scott catalog no. 2721

IN JUNE 1992, the largely young, hip audience of comedian Arsenio Hall's TV talk show were treated—or subjected, according to your political taste—to an instrumental version of Elvis Presley's "Heartbreak Hotel." The performer wore shades, swayed to the music, and filled in with some brief improvisatory licks. He was William Jefferson Clinton, and the following month he became the Democratic Party's candidate for president. Clinton was the child of the postwar baby boom who grew up in the rich popular culture created by rock 'n' roll—hence his love of the saxophone, which was genuine, not a gimmick. He'd been in the sax section of the Arkansas state band as a teenager and had briefly considered a career in music.

The Elvis tribute saxophonist duly won the primary and then took on the incumbent president, a man from a different generation. Twenty years older than Clinton, George H. W. Bush had been a navy aviator during the war and was a married family man by the time teenagers started checking into Heartbreak Hotel. Age hadn't made much difference between Ronald Reagan and his younger political opponents—Reagan even joked that he didn't consider their inexperience a disadvantage—but Clinton and Bush glared at each other across a cultural divide. It was as if the shock waves from Woodstock were only now reaching the top echelons of society. Clinton won the 1992 election, by a healthy though not massive margin.

As befits a baby boomer, the new president wanted to do things differently. This wasn't just because of Woodstock idealism: Clinton understood that the economic system had changed. The old cheap oil/automobile/heavy industry economy had died back in the 1970s. Bush, whose family had made its money in oil, belonged to that era. In the 1980s, a new system had arisen, and by the time Clinton moved into the White House its nature was clear. The Knowledge Economy would be driven by intelligence, not muscle. It would be global, not national. It would be innovative: Access to oilfields or big hunks of machinery would matter less than access to information and the ability to react quickly and imaginatively to it. This would be a more atomized world. The alert, agile individual (or small group) could dance circles around the lumbering old-style large organization. Clinton believed that these socioeconomic changes implied a new politics. The old left/right ideological gulf no longer made sense; the Knowledge Era leader had to pick from both, taking the social liberalism of the old left and the respect for the market of the old right. This was trumpeted as a radical new "third way," though it would hardly have surprised a traditional Victorian liberal.

Culture changed, too. The baby boomers didn't accept the old gap between high and popular art, between *Music Appreciation Hour* and the *Grand Ole Opry*. Arguably, they overturned it, with popular art seen as having more authenticity and relevance: Clinton, a highly intelligent man who had been a Rhodes Scholar at Oxford, didn't appear on Arsenio Hall's show to play Bach on a spinet. The stamps of the era show this—none more so than the Elvis issue above, which became the most collected U.S. stamp ever. It was the first in the long-running Legends of American Music series that spanned the entire Clinton presidency. Eighty artists were celebrated from various genres: country, jazz, blues (Robert Johnson became the first man to have both claimed to have sold his soul to the devil and appeared on a U.S. stamp), folk, Broadway, and Hollywood. Oh, and classical, represented by twelve opera singers, conductors, and composers (four of each). Popular cinema was celebrated in a 1994 issue featuring ten stars of the silent screen rendered into cartoons by Al Hirschfeld. Twenty Comic Strip Classics appeared in 1995 and five classic movie monsters in 1997.

Clinton inherited a foreign policy nightmare from his predecessor, a mission in Somalia that had originally been humanitarian but was fast becoming military. The country was mired in a complex civil war, and one faction started attacking UN peacekeepers. Attempts to fight back escalated to the October 1993 Battle of Mogadishu, subject of the 2001 movie *Black Hawk Down,* where eighteen U.S. soldiers and many Somalis were killed. The president pulled out, and public opinion hardened against foreign intervention. An unspeakable genocide in Rwanda in 1994 was allowed to proceed, and when inhabitants of the former Yugoslavia started slaughtering each other, U.S. response was initially muted. Only in mid-1995, after the discovery of the massacre of Srebrenica, was the full force of American power unleashed, which quickly brought the combatants to the negotiating table. The process was repeated in Kosovo in 1999.

Clinton can be criticized for his inconsistency, but he had inherited a mess. If there had been a philosophy to George H. W. Bush's New World Order, it had been "Intervene, but not in the internal affairs, however unspeakable, of nations." Nice and clear—but mission creep in Somalia had already undermined that clarity. What was Clinton's philosophy? In a 1999 speech he said of intervention around the world:

> *We cannot, indeed, we should not, do everything or be everywhere. But where our values and our interests are at stake, and where we can make a difference, America must be prepared to do so.*

It's pretty vague—what does "our values are at stake" really mean? When do you move from "being prepared to intervene" to actually bombing and shooting people? But it does, at least, include a lesson from Somalia (and, before it, Vietnam): "where we can make a difference." This is perhaps the thread of consistency through Clinton's foreign policy: He intervened where he thought he could be effective. This was certainly true in Northern Ireland, where both sides of a horrendous, seemingly endless conflict had a huge respect for the United States, so a U.S. president could make a difference. Clinton traveled to the province in 1995. His personal involvement in deescalating what was almost a civil war is still remembered with affection.

Clinton also understood that "nationhood" was a less fixed notion in the new, global era, so any doctrine that talked only about nations would be imprecise. We stamp lovers are at a disadvantage here: We're used to a world divided into clearly defined nations, issuing their own stamps, which we can then stick into equally neatly defined albums. In the 1990s, however, the biggest threat to America did not come from a stamp-issuing nation but from a loose confederation of terrorists, Al Qaeda.

Part of the Soviet Union's collapse had been brought about by its 1989 defeat in Afghanistan, which many people pointed out mirrored America's travails in Vietnam. Among the disparate groups fighting the Russians was a collection of Arab irregulars led by the son of a rich Saudi family, Osama bin Laden, a man with a virulent hatred of the West and all it stood for. Once Operation Desert Shield was under way, bin Laden began objecting to the presence of U.S. troops on the holy soil of Saudi Arabia. His objections were ignored by the Saudi government, which banished him; he fled to Sudan, where a fundamentalist regime had recently taken power, and began to plot his next moves.

On August 7, 1998, the eighth anniversary of the arrival of U.S. forces in Saudi, trucks full of explosives were driven up to American embassies in Nairobi and Dar es Salaam and detonated. The building in Nairobi was in a busy central part of town, and more than two hundred people were killed. In reply, Clinton ordered missile strikes on training camps in Afghanistan and a chemical factory in Sudan thought to be helping bin Laden. However, the camps were largely empty, and the evidence linking the factory and Al Qaeda was later found to be faulty. Unscathed, Bin Laden carried on plotting. Clinton worked on a follow-up plan to tackle Al Qaeda but did not act on it; he passed the plan to his successor, who didn't act on it either.

Clinton's greatest success was economic. The first baby boom president oversaw an economic boom of unparalleled magnitude. The last three years of his presidency saw unemployment below 5 percent, the level that most economists consider "full employment." Inflation stayed low. (In 1996, it never went above 2 percent.) He stemmed the financial hemorrhage of debt: The government actually had a surplus in 1998–2000, something that hadn't happened since 1947–49. Above all, the productive economy flourished, driven—exactly as Clinton had predicted—by entrepreneurship in the new information technology sector. Wall Street rose and rose, intoxicated with the prospects of the knowledge revolution . . .

At the same time, the era took a gentler tone, unlike the "me-first" '80s. It was, perhaps, still self-centered, but in a more reflective way. Nowhere was this more apparent than on Oprah Winfrey's TV program, which started in 1986 and became the most successful talk show of the 1990s. In 1993, 90 million Americans watched her help troubled singer Michael Jackson delve deep into his past, in a kind of televised therapy session. Therapy boomed in the '90s, not of the old Freudian kind, in which an expert deconstructed the patient's psyche, but one in which the client was placed at the center of things and the therapist listened and empathized. As the decade progressed, Winfrey's show moved from confessions to a wider focus on personal development and alternative spirituality. She was, in a sense, the fulfillment of the Woodstock ideal but in a smart, practical, media-savvy way that ordinary people could relate to; her fans didn't have to drop out or turn on to drugs in order to seek enlightenment. The rewards for her were spectacular, with great personal wealth and the award of the Presidential Medal of Freedom in 2013. The 1990s also saw social inclusiveness become ever more important, a theme reflected in stamps, with regular issues beginning for Chinese New Year (1992), Hanukkah (1996), and Kwanzaa, a celebration of African American heritage that had its first stamp issue in 1997. In 2001, a stamp was issued for the Islamic festival of Eid al-Fitr.

Not everyone joined in this new, open, optimistic mood, however. Radio hosts such as Rush Limbaugh regularly got in touch with their anger and became hugely popular. A government shutdown was forced by far-right Republicans in the House of Representatives, sending many government workers home without pay from November 14–19, 1995, and again from December 16, 1995–January 6, 1996: by far the most aggressive use of this tactic to date.

Bill Clinton read the political and economic changes of his era better than any other president since Kennedy and presided over a boom even more productive than those of the Eisenhower or Reagan years. However, to many people he is probably best known for his personal scandals. For all his virtues, Clinton had a Nixonian streak of deviousness and arrogance—did anyone seriously believe his claim that as a student he smoked marijuana but "did not inhale"? In 1998, rumors began to circulate that he had been having an affair with a White House intern, Monica Lewinsky. Clinton denied this, but it was later found out to be true—though the president still maintained he did not "have sexual relations with that woman." This, of course, led to endless debate about what exactly did go on. Clinton suffered the fate of Lincoln's inept successor, Andrew Johnson: impeachment (with a similar not-guilty verdict). Like Watergate, the whole affair ended up looking seedy from all angles. Several Republican politicians who were high-mindedly insisting Clinton's infidelity made him unfit for office turned out to have committed adultery themselves. Lewinsky, let down by both the president and the "friend" who snitched on her to the media, found solace in a new phenomenon, minor celebrity, trying to market handbags and appearing on reality TV shows before trying to quit the media spotlight—not an easy task. (The importance and the allure of media grew and grew in the 1990s, and for every Oprah, who mastered it, there were many more Monicas, who found themselves riding a tiger and ended up making themselves look foolish.)

As the decade came to its end, the stock market began to show classic signs of a bubble. As in 1929, a group of stocks took off from the rest and began to command ever more unrealistic prices. This time they were clustered around the Internet. If at the start of the decade people had been skeptical about the Knowledge Economy, by its end they had become wildly overoptimistic. "Dot-com" businesses had yet to make a cent of profit but were hyped by Wall Street analysts to the value of hundreds of millions of dollars. Part of the cause of this was easy money.

In 1999 a stamp was issued for Ayn Rand, the literary celebrant of unfettered capitalism. One of her greatest admirers was Alan Greenspan, chairman of the Federal Reserve Board, who could have curbed the market's "irrational exuberance" (a phrase he used back in 1996) with tighter monetary policies but preferred to just let it rip. Ayn Rand would have approved, heartily. The resulting bubble burst on March 10, 2000. Luckily, it did not have the same effect as in 1929: The market crash did not appear to affect the solidity of the banking system as it had back then, and, away from the virtual world of dot-coms, business continued as usual.

Despite the Lewinsky affair and the stock market bubble, Clinton's approval rating with the public remained constant. Most people had prospered during his presidency, and, like Ronald Reagan, the forty-second president had great charm. The Democrats should have won the 2000 election easily, but they fielded a well-meaning but uninspiring candidate, Al Gore. Even so, Gore won the popular vote by half a million, the third-closest election ever fought. However, this decision was not matched in the electoral college, and George W. Bush, the son of former president George H. W. Bush, was awarded victory instead. The ghost of Andrew Jackson, a Democrat deprived of the highest office by the Electoral College back in 1824 and replaced by a president's son, must have howled in protest.

THIRTY-THREE

Smithsonian National Postal Museum.
© United States Postal Service

THE VALLEY OF HEART'S DELIGHT

Computer Technology commemorative 32¢, 1996; Scott catalog no. 3106

TECHNOLOGY, AND ESPECIALLY INFORMATION TECHNOLOGY, was the big theme of the 1990s—and has arguably been the underlying theme of the entire period since 1973. This stamp, issued a few months before Bill Clinton secured reelection to his second term of office, allows us to tell its story in greater detail.

Ironically, back in 1973, the year the old oil/automobile economy hit the skids, a small series of stamps was issued celebrating "progress in electronics." Most of them featured rather ancient-looking gear—an old-fashioned phonograph horn from which you might expect to hear a scratchy recording of the Paul Whiteman Orchestra, and some of the equipment

Marconi had used to send the first radio message back in 1901. The 8¢ was more up-to-date, featuring a transistor, the basic building block of the new consumer electronics that had been changing people's lives since the 1950s: Most '50s teenagers first heard "Heartbreak Hotel" on a transistor radio. However, by 1973, even this was a little quaint. Electronics by then were about integrated circuits, or microchips.

Though it doesn't say so anywhere on it, the 1996 stamp at the head of this chapter was formally issued to celebrate the fiftieth anniversary of the U.S. Army's ENIAC (Electronic Numerical Integrator and Computer) machine—so let's start there. Precisely when the increasingly complex information processors that were being developed in the 1930s and 1940s qualify as "computers" is a matter of definition. (There have been lawsuits about it.) ENIAC certainly is a front-runner—though some historians give the honor of "first-ever computer" to the 1937 Atanasoff-Berry machine from Iowa State College, which represented all data in binary form and used electronics to process them, or to the 1941 Z3 of German inventor Konrad Zuse, which was the first electronic information processor to be programmable. The 1943 British Colossus code breaker, binary, electronic, and programmable, is also a contender but could only be used for one specific task. (For purists, a true computer has to be able to handle any kind of computational problem.)

First computer or not, the ENIAC was certainly groundbreaking. It was also massive. One hundred feet long, it contained more than 17,000 vacuum tubes and 5 million soldered joints, and used up so much power that (so legend has it) the lights in nearby Philadelphia dimmed whenever it was turned on. It weighed 30 tons—though in 1949, *Popular Mechanics* magazine made the daring prediction that computers in the

future would be much smaller and might, given enough technological progress, weigh as little as 1.5 tons. ENIAC's job
was to calculate optimum firing angles for artillery, but it was
also used for other tasks including the development of America's hydrogen bomb.

In the early 1950s, the first commercial computer, the
UNIVAC, went on sale. Remington Rand sold forty-six of
them, to government bodies or large corporations, for around
$1 million each (about $8 million in modern money). An early
UNIVAC correctly predicted the outcome of the 1952 presidential election, while professional pollsters called it wrong.

The transistor featured in the 1973 "progress" stamp series
was invented in 1947. This opened the door for all kinds of
lightweight, durable electronics—including those subversive
radios. They also found their way into computers, replacing the
old valves and radically increasing how much information could
be stored and how quickly information could be processed. In
1959, IBM launched its 1400 range. The company preferred
not to sell these valuable machines but to rent them out: You
could hire one for $2,500 a month. It received more than
5,000 orders almost at once, much more than it had expected.

A third generation of computers was launched by the integrated circuit, or microchip. This in essence printed a number
(ever increasing) of transistors onto a little piece of semicon-
ducting material, originally germanium but later silicon. The
first chip-based computers appeared in 1961, and the biggest
early client for them was, as for the ENIAC, the military,
who used them in the guidance system of the Minuteman
missile. As the decade continued, chips became smaller and
faster: In 1965, Gordon Moore, cofounder of chipmaker
Intel, noted that the number of transistors that could afford-
ably be put into an integrated circuit had doubled every two

years and suggested that this trend would continue. In the nearly forty years since then, Moore's prediction has proven uncannily accurate and has hardened into a "law."

In 1971, Intel produced the first microprocessor. This was effectively a computer on a chip: You input information and instructions (or the instructions are built in); it does the work and produces what you want. These printed minicomputers could be used to control all sorts of devices from cookers to satellites. Following Moore's Law, they became ever more sophisticated. One result of this was that computers themselves became smaller and cheaper. In January 1975, *Popular Electronics* advertised one you could build yourself from a kit. The Altair 8800 cost $397, took ages to assemble, was hard to program (you did so by flicking switches), and didn't do a lot when you did (a popular program enabled you to play a game predicting which of a row of lights would come on next). However, hobbyists, young males such as Steve Wozniak, Steve Jobs, Paul Allen, and William H. Gates III, loved it.

The Altair was just a box. By 1977, you could buy a more user-friendly machine with a screen, keyboard, memory, and ports to plug in peripherals such as printers. Several brands were on offer, including Wozniak and Jobs's Apple II. Useful software became available: WordStar for word processing, VisiCalc for spreadsheets. In 1980, Pac-Man began chomping his way across peoples' screens. In 1981, mainframe giant IBM shouldered into this market with its first PC, using Allen and Gates's DOS operating system and retailing at just over $1,500. It was a smash hit and created demand for more and better software. "Clones" of the PC then appeared, driving prices down . . . Soon more and more middle-class homes were sporting their own ENIAC in a corner.

The microchip made other consumer goods possible, too.

The CD appeared around 1983, making music reproduction perfect—though perhaps taking away the thrill of not knowing if your listen to your favorite cassette would be your last before the player chewed it up. Video recorders, once an expensive technology, became affordable in the middle of the '80s, as did camcorders and telephone answering machines. If you were next to an expensive automobile at a traffic light in 1986, you might see the occupant put a boxlike object to his or her ear and start talking into it: Mobile phones had arrived, though it took until the early '90s for them to be within most Americans' financial reach.

Nowhere was the economic effect of these changes more strongly felt than in California's Santa Clara Valley. In the early twentieth century, this had been the world's most productive fruit orchard, nicknamed by boosters "the Valley of Heart's Delight." But it was also home to a growing technology industry, largely thanks to Frederick Terman, a professor of electrical engineering at Stanford, who set up scholarships for bright students whom he then encouraged to start new businesses in the area (especially in the university's own industrial park). Like the movie pioneers of a previous generation, these young entrepreneurs found California's relaxed style more sympathetic than the East Coast. By 1980, there were about 3,000 electronics firms in the valley, 70 percent of them employing fewer than ten people. "Silicon Valley" (a term first used in 1971) became a global center for innovation, with its own ways of doing business: Deals between tech-savvy venture capitalists and prospective business owners could be done on the back of a napkin. (The lawyers would follow later.) The valley's delightful fruit trees were doomed.

The 1990s saw the rise of the Internet. Like much other development in this chapter, the story begins with government;

only once the basic technologies are in place and affordable can freewheeling private capital come in and start working its magic. The forerunner of the Internet was ARPAnet, a network connecting defense research at different universities. It was not, as is popularly believed, created to survive a nuclear attack but simply to connect academics. Launched on October 29, 1969—just over two months after Woodstock—the network grew slowly during the 1970s and 1980s. ARPAnet was superseded by other, bigger systems, on which, in 1989, Tim Berners-Lee proposed creating a "World Wide Web" of sites. (The terms "Web" and "Internet" are often used interchangeably, but the Internet is the infrastructure that is used by a number of systems, of which the Web is just one. E-mail is another.) Use then began to accelerate. In 1989, The World, the first public dial-up access service, was launched. America Online followed in 1991. By mid-1991, 10 million people could go online, three-quarters of them in America. By the time this stamp came out, in 1996, the figure was 45 million, with two-thirds in America. Of these 30 million U.S. citizens, half were connecting from home; 44 percent of households now owned a PC.

There was, of course, much more to come. 1996 also saw the beginning of serious e-commerce, with Amazon and eBay. The dot-com boom followed; the crash that came after did nothing to slow the continuing growth of the Internet. In 2002, there were 161 million Americans online, and more than 500 million people worldwide. The 2000s brought the development of "Web 2.0" technology; the "old" Web had been essentially a place you visited in search of views and information, but as the first decade of the new century unfolded, it became something in which everyone could participate: a true "global village."

And all thanks to the technology celebrated by this stamp. The chip was what economist Simon Kuznets called an "epochal innovation," a breakthrough, like the factory system, steam power, steel, electrification, or the internal combustion engine, that revolutionizes not only how things are made or how we get around but how people work, play, learn, think, communicate, fall in love, exercise power, and any and every other aspect of life. Such innovations create economic, political, and cultural eras. They also create lasting prosperity in the nations where they are first made, and which then foster them the most passionately. The microchip era began as an American one, and has essentially remained one, despite the globalization of the technology. During this time, the United States' GDP has increased tenfold—and that process is continuing, regardless of current economic turbulence. Moore's Law still seems to be in force, even given the almost unimaginably small size of modern chips, some of which are measured in atoms. The chip revolution continues.

Perhaps the USPS should have issued an entire series of stamps to celebrate it, not just one.

THIRTY-FOUR

Smithsonian National Postal Museum and
The Bergen Record © United States Postal Service

UNDER ATTACK

Heroes of 2001 First Class, 2002; Scott catalog no. B2

LIKE JOE ROSENTHAL's IWO JIMA stamp, this image captures an iconic moment of sudden pride amid chaos, heartbreak, and exhaustion. It was taken by photojournalist Thomas E. Franklin of the *Bergen Record* newspaper on September 11, 2001, about eight hours after American Airlines Flight 11 had smashed into the North Tower of the World Trade Center in Lower Manhattan. That dreadful event had occurred at 8:46 A.M.; at 9:03 a second plane hit the South Tower. Thirty-four minutes after that, a third struck the Pentagon. A fourth flight, United Airlines 93, crashed in a field in Pennsylvania half an hour later.

Firefighters and members of the New York City and Port Authority Police were called to the stricken towers. A control center was set up in the lobby of the North Tower and teams sent to both buildings with the initial task of getting everyone out. This was never going to be easy: The impact had twisted the frames of the buildings, so doors were jammed and passageways blocked. Nevertheless, the vast majority of individuals who had been in the towers below the points of impact were led to safety. (Even a few people from above the impact in the South Tower managed to escape down an undamaged stairwell, though many more went up the same stairwell, hoping in vain to be rescued from the roof.) At 9:59 A.M., the South Tower collapsed. Rescuers were immediately ordered to evacuate the North Tower, but due to poor radio reception, many did not receive this command and kept on working, including a group of Port Authority police officers who got twenty-eight people out of a cut-off suite of rooms, then returned to help others and were never seen again. This tower collapsed at 10:28 A.M., killing around 150 rescuers, including the Fire Department chief, Peter J. Ganci.

The once-magnificent World Trade Center was now a heap of red-hot rubble—in which people might still be alive. The heroism continued as searchers began braving toxic fumes and unstable footings to find survivors, of which, amazingly, there were several. Some of the rescuers, such as former marine Jason Thomas and retired fireman Bob Beckwith, were volunteers who had joined the operation out of a sense of public duty. The raising of the flag shown on this stamp took place at around 5:00 P.M., a spontaneous gesture by three firefighters, one of whom, Daniel McWilliams, had taken a flag from a boat moored nearby, then asked two colleagues to help him hoist it on a makeshift pole—after which they got back to work, unaware that they had been photographed.

America began to count the cost. The final death toll of the attacks was 2,996, of mostly people who had been working in the floors above the two impacts. The figure also includes 343 firefighters, 125 staff at the Pentagon, 246 passengers and crew on the four aircraft, and 60 police, 37 from the Port Authority and 23 from the NYPD. Subsequent deaths among workers, especially first responders, and among local residents and employers have also been attributed to inhalation of toxic smoke and dust.

The nation also began to piece together how this atrocity had happened: Terrorists had hijacked the planes, seized the controls, and flown into their targets. (On United Airlines 93, passengers had fought back; the hijackers had responded by crashing the plane.) Initial suspicion that the hijackers belonged to Al Qaeda was soon confirmed—though the exact details of who ordered what within that nebulous organization remain unknown.

Three days after the attack, President Bush came to the site of the Twin Towers and gave an impromptu speech through a bullhorn, expressing gratitude to the rescue workers and determination to capture and punish those responsible. It was interrupted by chants of "U-S-A": The nation's initial shock had turned to defiant anger. Less well remembered, three days after that, Bush visited a mosque in Washington and gave a speech reminding America that the fight was with terrorists, not Islam.

That fight was on, of course. Bin Laden had left Sudan in 1996 and gone to Afghanistan, then newly under the control of the Taliban. After 9/11, the United States asked for him to be extradited. The Taliban prevaricated, and an international consensus soon built up: Al Qaeda had to be defeated, out of considerations of justice and because it was not known what else they might have been planning. If that meant invading their obstructive hosts, then so be it. Bombing of selected targets began on October 7, and by November 12, Kabul was in the hands of the U.S.-led international force and its local allies, the Northern Alliance. Afghanistan being guerrilla country, bin Laden retreated to the mountains, where attempts to find him failed.

While this was taking place, the USPS became the vehicle for further terror attacks. On September 18, letters were mailed to various media organizations, containing anthrax-bearing spores and crude letters purporting to be from fanatical Islamists. On October 5, a photo editor for the *Sun*, a supermarket tabloid, died from the disease. A second set of letters, containing more virulent spores, was sent in early October to Democratic senators. On October 21, two workers at the Brentwood postal facility, which handles mail for Capitol Hill, were diagnosed with the disease. Thomas L. Morris and Joseph P. Curseen both died shortly afterward. A special medal, the Postmaster General's Medal of Freedom, bearing a picture of Ben Franklin, was created and awarded posthumously to the two men. Washington immediately tried to pin the blame for these letters on Al Qaeda, and when that looked unlikely, on Iraq. Only in 2008 did federal prosecutors finally accuse an American scientist, Bruce Ivins—but he never came to trial, as he had committed suicide shortly before the public accusations.

The official eagerness to blame Iraq for the anthrax letters was the sign of a new mood in the White House. Before 9/11, President Bush had been cautious about overseas interventions. After the attack, a new "Bush Doctrine" emerged, whereby America could and should launch unilateral, preemptive strikes on potential enemies. Gone was the international consensus-building that had been a part of both George H. W. Bush's and Bill Clinton's New World Order. Gone was the sense that an enemy would have to show its hand before American might was unleashed on it. It was enough for that country—or some people within it—to look ready to strike.

The fear was that a "rogue" state would develop nuclear or biological "weapons of mass destruction" (WMD), which would then, through policy or carelessness, fall into the hands of terrorists. Iraq, it was decided, was the most likely place this would happen—despite the fact that the nation had no links to Al Qaeda (which despised the Iraqi dictator as an apostate). Exactly how quickly the Bush administration decided to go to war with Iraq is not known, but the world soon seemed to be heading for inevitable conflict—certainly by the time this stamp appeared, on June 7, 2002. At the same time, America found itself drifting away from global opinion: Attempts to create a multinational coalition to prosecute the war failed; only Britain's Tony Blair offered substantial support. This was going to be a Bush Doctrine fight, preemptive and essentially unilateral.

As in the first Iraq conflict, military victory came quickly. The invasion began on March 20, 2003, and Baghdad fell on April 9. On May 1, the president announced victory from the flight deck of the aircraft carrier *Abraham Lincoln*. Though he talked in his speech about there being difficulties ahead, above him, a large banner trumpeted MISSION ACCOMPLISHED.

Things began to go wrong almost at once. The expected warm welcome from the Iraqi population did not materialize. Instead, the country tumbled into anarchy: A decision to dismantle the conquered nation's power structure left internal forces of law and order leaderless. Old Baathists (Saddam supporters) and religious extremists, both Sunni and Shia (Iraq is about two-thirds Shia and one-third Sunni), were soon fighting a vicious guerrilla war, often using suicide bombers, sometimes against each other, sometimes against the U.S./British forces. Despite extensive searches, none of the expected WMD were found. The capture of Saddam on December 13 did nothing to restore order. Then in March 2004, news began to trickle out that prisoner abuse was being committed in Abu Ghraib jail. Compared to the treatment meted out by the Saddam regime, the abuse was lightweight—but the images of prisoner humiliation by U.S. military spread around the world. Liberation was turning into occupation, and occupation into a propaganda tool for the very terrorists the war had been launched to thwart.

After two more years of increasing violence and anarchy, an increase in troop numbers (the "surge") and a new counterinsurgency strategy led by General David Petraeus began to work. Troops took to the streets and interacted more with ordinary Iraqi citizens. Middle-ranking former Baathists were allowed to return to positions of responsibility. On January 31, 2009, elections were held, and turnout was over 50 percent. (This may sound low, but many U.S. elections get only a slightly bigger percentage to the polls. That of 1996 only managed a turnout of 49 percent.) However, Iraq still has some way to go on the road to modern nationhood. The war proved hugely expensive. It did little to combat terrorism and arguably helped the extremists' recruitment drive.

Military justice was finally served to Osama bin Laden in 2011. Intelligence revealed that he had been hiding, not in a mountain dwelling but in a compound in Abbottabad, an outpost of the British Raj that had become the home of Pakistan's top military academy. On the night of May 1, two helicopters carrying U.S. Navy SEALs crossed the border from Afghanistan. CIA saboteurs blacked out the power to the bin Laden hideout. One helicopter landed within the compound but was damaged on landing; the other landed outside, and its occupants scaled the walls. Wearing night-vision gear, the SEALs fought their way past bodyguards into the house. On the third floor they found their quarry. Exactly what happened is not clear—did the terrorist leader reach for a weapon?—but the outcome is: He was shot dead. The SEALs spent twenty minutes searching for intelligence, then were airlifted out on a reserve helicopter, taking computers, phones, and bin Laden's body with them. He was buried at sea shortly afterward.

What President Bush called the "War on Terror" was not won, however. By 2011, the terrorists had already left Afghanistan for Yemen and the Horn of Africa, and new organizations were arising. The threat remains. September 11 was like the Battle of Shiloh, Poland 1939, or Hiroshima: a sign that the nature of war had radically changed. A conventional attack on a stamp-issuing state, Iraq, did nothing to dent terrorism. The conflict has instead developed its own tools and theaters: diplomacy, propaganda, suicide bombers, "surgical" strikes with drones or special forces, perpetual public vigilance, and, above all, intelligence. These in turn generate their own debates. How ethical are drone strikes? How much right do intelligence services have to pry on our lives? This new conflict involves us in all sorts of ways. Even stamps play a role in it. Every envelope that lands on a foreign doormat is a tiny piece of "soft power," or should be. Such power is an essential part of winning this new kind of war.

THIRTY-FIVE

Smithsonian National Postal Museum.
© United States Postal Service

THE CHINA SYNDROME

Beijing Olympics 42¢, 2008;
Scott catalog no. 4334

THE WAR ON TERROR MAY have become a part of our lives, but many people see it as essentially a sideshow, arguing that if there is a real struggle in the world it is economic. America held off the challenge of Japan in the 1990s, but a new claimant to the title of top nation has now arisen: China.

This stamp, the work of Hawaiian Clarence Lee, who designed the first Chinese lunar New Year stamp in 1992, was issued for the Beijing Olympics of 2008. The Chinese capital put on a magnificent show, with stunning stadiums and an even more stunning opening ceremony, which trumpeted both that nation's 5,000-year history and its bright future. The People's Republic went on to win 51 gold medals, 15 more than the United States: the first time it had been top of the medals table. True, the host country usually does well, but

America had been the No. 1 Olympic nation since 1996. (Before that date there had been an Olympic Cold War, with America and Russia battling for that honor.) Was this the sign of the emergence of the *real* New World Order? *China as Number One?*

On August 24, 2008, the games celebrated on this stamp closed with another magnificent ceremony. Three weeks later, on September 15, Lehman Brothers filed for bankruptcy, and the greatest financial crash to hit America and the West since the 1930s began.

The recipe for the crash had been bubbling away for a number of years. Arguably the first ingredient was put in the pot back in January 1965—a date when America had only recently started issuing stamps with more than two colors—when economics student Eugene Fama produced his Ph.D. thesis in which he argued that financial markets were "efficient": They represented a kind of perpetually self-updating summary of the knowledge of every expert on whatever that market dealt in. Despite events that appeared comprehensively to refute this thesis, such as the 1987 minicrash and the popping of the late 1990s tech bubble (in December 1999, the share price of Amazon.com reached $113; in October 2001, it fell as low as $5), this notion became fixed in the psyche of the people who operated and, more seriously, oversaw Wall Street.

The result was ever less regulation. The Glass-Steagall rules instituted after the 1929 crash were removed in 1999. These had prevented financial institutions from carrying out both speculative investment banking and "retail" banking (looking after our money, lending to home buyers and businesses), thereby protecting the latter from the riskiness of the former. Now banks could do both. In 2004, rules on leverage for the biggest banks were relaxed. They could borrow ever more money to support their investment banking activities. The financial instruments involved became ever more complex. Gone were the days of simple trading in stocks and shares. Wall Street in the 2000s traded derivatives, financial packages that, increasingly, nobody appeared to understand fully. Many of these derivatives contained mortgages, traditionally an investment "as safe as houses." But as the decade advanced, these became ever less safe, as new lenders entered the marketplace offering ever more attractive initial terms to an ever wider range of house buyers. This seemed like the American dream come true: Anyone, it seemed, could borrow to buy real estate and simply reap the rewards as house prices continued their inexorable rise in another "efficient" market.

Of course, the housing market did what all markets do when they become too full of speculators: bubble and then burst. Suddenly recent buyers were faced with losses on their properties and mortgage charges they could not afford. Foreclosures rose sharply. This meant that the mortgages in the complex financial instruments the big investment banks had leveraged themselves to buy suddenly became worthless. The even more complex instruments that had been sold to insure against such an eventuality became fathomless pits of debt.

The pressure for systemic collapse built up relentlessly but unseen. In March 2008, investment bank Bear Stearns had been rescued by JPMorgan Chase. Bear was generally regarded as the biggest risk-taker among the major investment banks, so its demise was not a total shock. In May, the government had to step in to bolster the finances of Freddie Mac and Fannie Mae, the nation's two biggest—and once upon a time, most respectable—mortgage lenders. Once again, this news was shrugged off; these organizations had never been at the heart

of Wall Street. However, over the summer it became apparent that the May support to the two lenders was a bandage
over a much deeper wound. On September 7, the government
had to take over both Freddie and Fannie to stop them collapsing. A financial avalanche began. A traditionally respectable big bank, Lehman Brothers, was now in trouble; it began
hunting around for a buyer, but nobody was interested. On
September 15 it filed for bankruptcy—the largest in U.S. corporate history. The next day, the insurer AIG had to be bailed
out by the government. Washington Mutual, another insurer,
soon followed. By October 3, the avalanche was over and the
extent of its destruction visible. The president asked Congress
for and, after much debate, secured a rescue package worth
$700 billion.

This bailout created great anger among ordinary Americans, who had endured years of lectures on the tough, necessary realism of an unregulated financial system. Some pointed
out that a 42¢ stamp issued just before the crash, in August
2008, provided a perfect metaphor for Wall Street's leaders
and regulators by showing a ship's wheel, and at the helm a
grinning Mickey Mouse. A deep recession followed. In 2009,
the U.S. economy shrank by 3.5 percent. China, by contrast,
had almost 9 percent growth that year.

By then America had a new president. Even before the
crash, the Republican Party had looked to be in trouble, thanks
to Iraq and the mishandling of Hurricane Katrina in 2005:
Many commentators viewed the Democratic presidential primaries as a kind of mini election. This soon became a two-
horse race, in which a win for either candidate would have
been a dramatic first for the United States: Barack Obama's
father was African, and Hillary Clinton would be the first
woman to run for the White House. In the end, Obama won.

His subsequent campaign had a whiff of Kennedy's Camelot about it. Young idealistic supporters turned out in force and used new technology to arouse and sustain interest; 2008 was the first Web 2.0 election. On November 4, Obama won nearly 10 million more votes than his rival, John McCain, in a turnout that was the highest since 1968. A wave of optimism—much needed after the crash and the subsequent slide into recession—greeted America's first black president, who responded with the slogan "Yes, we can!"

A second vast tranche of cash was issued to stimulate the economy. Whether because of this, or because of American resilience and entrepreneurism—or for both reasons—the U.S. economy returned to growth in 2010 and has kept growing, while most other developed economies are still stumbling along. Attempts were made to reregulate Wall Street and to tackle profligate use of energy. Overseas, Obama worked to repair America's soft power, which had been damaged by the previous administration's bullish unilateralism. In Cairo in 2009, he called for a "new beginning" in U.S. relations with the Muslim world, and in 2013, he gave a moving, idealistic speech at the funeral of Nelson Mandela.

However in other ways his administration has been unable to deliver on its promises. Congress has not "played ball," for which Obama's supporters blame it, but to which his opponents say he lacks the skill to operate the system. The issue of health reform has proven a particular difficulty. U.S. healthcare is excellent, but it is very expensive (most developed Western nations spend between 10 and 12 percent of their GDP on health care; the United States spends 17 percent), and many poorer citizens fall out of the net. But attempts to reform it hit intense opposition: In 2013, a splinter group in the Republican Party shut down the national government to make this point. When Capitol Hill finally got back to work, "Obamacare" encountered technical problems.

Inequality, which the president recently called "the defining challenge of our times," has continued to grow. This has been a trend since the 1970s, and its significance is hotly debated. Arguably, rising inequality does not matter as long as almost everyone is getting better off, albeit some faster than others: That's what happens in an energetic, freedom-loving, fast-changing society. But the current era seems to be one of rocketing wealth for a few and stagnation for the majority. Is such a pattern really compatible with James T. Adams's 1931 American dream of *a social order in which each man and each woman shall be able to attain to the fullest stature of which they are innately capable*? Is it good long-term practical economics? Consumer economies need consumers with money to spend. If the trend isn't desirable, can anything be done about it? Some people point to booming, low-wage, industrial China and say nothing can be done; welcome to globalization. One wonders if either Theodore or Franklin Delano Roosevelt would have accepted such fatalism, however.

And then there's the debt . . . The nation's indebtedness passed $10 trillon in the middle of the financial crisis in September 2008, at which point the National Debt Clock, a display counter installed by real estate developer Seymour Durst on the wall of his New York office, ran out of digits. At the time of writing, the figure is more than $17 trillion, and the numbers on a new, expanded clock continue to whirr past with shocking speed. Two-thirds of this money is owed within the USA's borders, to domestic savers, financial institutions, or government departments—but the rest is not. The Chinese government is a major stakeholder, owning 8 percent.

Despite the recent recovery, it is predicted that China will overtake America as the world's biggest economy. The disagreement is about when. The OECD says 2016, the U.S. National Intelligence Council 2027, the Hong Kong and Shanghai Bank (who, surely, ought to know) 2040. A few people say it will never actually happen and that China is like America in the 1920s, a bubble that will soon pop. The truth? History loves surprises and never moves in straight lines, so nobody can predict these big events with any certainty. The deciding question is probably what the next "epochal innovation" will be, and whether it will arise and be nourished in the United States or in China (or by some third power). Such things are by definition unknowable.

Even if China does surpass the United States, however, its wealth will have to be shared among four times as many people, so the average New Yorker will be far more prosperous than the average Beijinger. Western nations are better off in other ways, too: China's capital is cursed with some of the worst air pollution on the planet. The tone of life in the People's Republic is very different from that in the United States: Chinese stamp issues from 2012 included one to celebrate the seventieth anniversary of Chairman Mao's talk to the Yan'an Forum on Literature and Art, an occasion when the nation's leader told artists that they should serve the masses and that "anything at variance with [this] must be duly corrected." American artists may have to be wary of spiteful Internet commenters or fickle corporate sponsors, but they don't have to contend with a legacy like that.

And perhaps the battle for No. 1 is becoming less important anyway. Some economists argue that the most significant factor in the new century will be "the rise of the rest," a general increase in prosperity around the world, in many small countries and a few emerging regional powers, such as India, Brazil, Indonesia, South Korea, and South Africa. In such a world, the unilateralist Bush Doctrine will be unworkable: America will have to negotiate with others to get what it wants on the global stage. This would be more in keeping with the founding visions of George Washington and Thomas Jefferson, who were not concerned with world domination but instead with building a nation that was both prosperous and ethical. It would be more in keeping with most of America's history, too: Even the titanic struggles against Nazi Germany, Imperial Japan, and the Soviet Union were won with allies. And in such negotiations, America would still be arguing from a position of enormous strength: economic, military, and (especially) cultural. If the United States became one superpower among others, rather than the only such power, would that be so bad?

China may be booming and America may be facing difficulties with government shutdowns, inequality and debt, but a look through a U.S. stamp collection is a reminder that the nation has triumphed over external and internal challenges before. As Mark Twain might have said, "Reports of our decline have been greatly exaggerated."

THIRTY-SIX

Stamps.com

BOWLING ALONE

Self-designed stamp from
stamps.com, 2014

I REALLY DIDN'T WANT to include this item: It felt very wrong putting a picture of myself in a collection that has featured George Washington, Ben Franklin, Thomas Jefferson, and Abraham Lincoln, and the work of Raymond Ostrander Smith, Clair Aubrey Houston, Stevan Dohanos, and Georg Olden. But it is the mantra of this book that stamps speak of their eras, so welcome to the personalized twenty-first century! Such personalization is not new: Andy Warhol made his famous observation that in the future everyone would be "world-famous for fifteen minutes" in 1968, and the 1970s became known as the "me decade." Arguably the desire for "me" stamps has been around since then. What has finally made fulfilling that desire possible is technology. To create the masterpiece above, I simply went online, loaded up a photo from my computer, clicked a few icons to tinker with the design, entered some numbers to pay electronically, and a few days later "my" stamps arrived in the mail. I have to admit I'm still rather nervous about actually using them—what will people think?

However, "my" stamp is a neat way to end this story. It raises an issue that slipped through the net in the previous chapter, which dealt with big financial and political topics, and also provides a perspective on the future of the USPS and of stamp collecting itself.

The issue raised is that of self-obsession and loss of community. Americans, despite the talk about individualism, have actually always been great "joiners," eager to participate in group activities. But in 2000, Robert Putnam's book *Bowling Alone* highlighted and lamented the decline of this sociable, mutually supportive America. Putnam, a professor at Harvard, filled the book with graphs plotting levels of participation in community institutions, most of which begin to turn down in the 1960s and show the decline accelerating from the 1980s onward.

Critics of Putnam say that community has changed, not disappeared. Just as I created this stamp online, we now find our community there, in the world of social media.

Putnam's supporters reply that it's not the same. They cite the distinction between "bonding" and "bridging." Bonding is with other people like ourselves; bridging connects us with people in many respects totally unlike ourselves—for example, a meeting to protest the planned building of a nuclear power station next to a small town, which will involve rich, poor, old, young, black, white, male, and female alike. It is this bridging that electronic communities fail to effect. Instead, online groupings simply bond, shrinking society not to disconnected individuals but to little pods of people similar to each other who have little understanding of what different types of person are like. (To this, Putnam's critics say, "So what? It's nicer to be surrounded by people like us.")

It is, of course, dangerous to assume that just because a trend has been spotted it will last forever. Putnam himself points out that a similar destruction of what he calls "social capital" took place in the Gilded Age, but the Progressive Era that followed was a golden time for the formation of civic groups. History has a delightful habit of surprising everyone, especially "experts."

"My" stamp also raises questions about the future of the USPS. If technology made this stamp possible, financial necessity made it actually happen. The USPS needs to raise more money, and this issue is seen as one way of doing it. In 2012, the agency announced a staggering loss of $15.9 billion—not quite in the same league as Wall Street, but still a large hole that will ultimately have to be filled by the taxpayer if the USPS does not return to profitability. Closer examination of the figures showed that around two-thirds of the "loss" was a paper one, inflicted on the USPS by a requirement—made of no other public body—that it pay over $10 billion into a fund to cover the health benefits of future retirees. Political wrangling over this requirement continues. However, even when this is taken into consideration, the loss runs into billions of dollars. Can the USPS survive?

The obvious reason for the shortfall is the decline in the number of letters sent. Interestingly, the year Putnam's book came out saw the peak volume: In 2000, the USPS delivered over 103 billion pieces of First Class Mail (essentially, letters). In 2012, that figure fell below 70 billion—still a lot of mail, but a return to a level last seen in 1984. The most obvious culprit for this is the Internet, but the 2008 crash appears to be as much to blame: As late as 2006, the USPS was making a decent operating profit. If the Internet is at least partly responsible, it also creates great opportunities, as ever more people are ordering products online, which then need to be delivered to their homes. In this market, the USPS faces competition from UPS and FedEx, but it still has a unique delivery network. (Competition in this market isn't straight-forward: FedEx uses the USPS for a fifth of its deliveries.) While the agency is clearly in trouble, it is not the hopeless basket case some critics make it out to be.

There is also a debate about the extent to which the USPS has to emulate a public corporation and make profits, and how much it is a social service, repaying society in other ways apart from returning dollars to the Treasury. Back in 1829, Andrew Jackson said in his first State of the Union speech that the post was

> *to the body politic what the veins and arteries are to the natural—conveying rapidly and regularly to the remotest parts of the system correct information of the operations of the Government, and bringing back to it the wishes and feelings of the people.*

Clearly the post no longer has a monopoly on this function—and hasn't since the telegraph and the telephone—but it still plays a connective role. As Stevan Dohanos under-stood, mail carriers are joiners in communities, bearers of communication, but also communicators themselves, famil-iar, reassuring figures in the roughest or remotest neighbor-hoods. This network and this role are probably the USPS's greatest assets, and it would be a shame if they were trimmed out of existence in the name of efficiency. Can they be leveraged (to use suitable business jargon) in new ways? The greatest postmasters general—Franklin, Blair, Wanamaker—understood the need for balance between the perpetual need to avoid waste and a deep sense of the postal service's public value. They brought imagination and vision to sustaining—or rather, as this is an active, creative process, reinventing—this balance.

Even if the USPS survives and flourishes, what will happen to stamps and stamp collecting? Stamp use is falling even faster than levels of mail—for example, the booming parcels market seems not to bother with them at all—while at the same time "collectable" issues flood off the presses, often in special sheets that almost defy you to actually use one of the stamps to post a letter. The "me" stamp is only a logical extension of this flurry of new issues. But let's be positive. Unlike most of these other issues, my stamp is actively intended for postal use not just for putting straight into a collection. Personalized stamps could even lead to a new branch of philately. People could collect stamps featuring their own family or individuals or groups they admire. There is no reason why a personalized stamp issued by someone famous couldn't become a prized rarity. Imagine if Jack Kerouac had once, and only once, made a set of stamps featuring himself.

What would be missing from such items is an obvious political overtone, which would seem to be a loss for the stamp lover who is also a historian. We've seen many stamps in this book sending out deliberate political messages, from the cold official gravity of Edwin Stanton to the tragic drama of Iwo Jima. However in a broader sense, a personalized stamp also sends out a clear political message, that not everyone can become president but we can all feature on a stamp. There is something Jeffersonian about this, an echo of the Declarations of Independence and of Sentiments—if it is a self-evident truth that all men and women are created equal, then why shouldn't we all appear on a stamp?

Personalized stamps are surely best seen as just another snapshot of the continuing story of America. That narrative remains as exciting and unpredictable as ever, and I see no reason why the nation's stamps, in whatever form they take, shouldn't go on telling it. Collecting these items and enjoying the stories they tell will continue to be a delightful pastime.

APPENDIX

1. George III of Great Britain Revenue Stamp, 1765

Only thirty-two copies of the original 1765 dark red proof impressions still exist. Twenty-six of them are in one sheet, which is owned by the British Library in London as part of its Philatelic Collection. Three singles and a pair are in private hands, and one is part of the Smithsonian National Postal Museum's permanent collection. So there's not much point in trying to collect these.

Another way of owning a little bit of the Stamp Act would be to collect memorabilia from this era.

Teapots were made with NO STAMP ACT or STAMP ACT REPEAL'D written on them. Ironically, they were made in Britain, for the American market. These can be costly, however. (There's one in the Smithsonian.)

Prints both protested the Stamp Act and celebrated its repeal. Most famous is Benjamin Wilson's *The Repeal; or, The*

Funeral of Miss Ame-Stamp made in 1766, which shows a funeral procession bearing the ill-fated act to a vault. The vault, interestingly, is intended for the burial of various tyrannical acts, many dating from the lead-up to the British Civil War of 120 years earlier, such as the Star Chamber Act and the Ship Money Act—and any other "which tended to alienate the Affections of Englishmen to their Country." The rebels—or many of them, anyhow—still thought of themselves as Englishmen, fighting a traditional English yeoman's battle against tyrannical power. Back in 1766, 2,000 of these prints were sold, for a shilling each. (The issue sold out in four days.)

2. George Washington 10¢, 1847
Scott catalog no. 2

Designer: Unknown. The engraving was done by Asher Brown Durand and is based on a picture of Washington by Gilbert Stuart.
Printer: Rawdon, Wright, Hatch & Edson
First date of issue: July 1, 1847
Number issued: Just over a million were issued, but 159,000 were destroyed when the stamps were taken out of circulation in 1851.

For beginners: Even poor examples—philatelists call them spacefillers—can cost several hundred dollars, and good examples over $1,000. Start saving.

For experts: Mint examples of the stamp are very rare and worth over $5,000.

For philatelists who think they have died and gone to heaven: The 5¢ New York postmaster's provisional, which appeared two years before this official, national stamp, is also black and features the nation's first president, though facing to the viewer's left rather than right.

3. Ben Franklin 1¢, 1851
Scott catalog no. 5

Designer: The frame and lettering were designed by Henry Earle. The picture of Franklin is based on a bust by Parisian sculptor Jean-Antoine Houdon.

Printer: Toppan, Carpenter, Casilear and Co.

First date of issue: July 1, 1851

Number issued: 35,000 (of this exact design). Various other 1¢ Franklins with slight variations were produced in the next ten years. Around 12 million appeared between 1851 and 1857, the year when perforations were introduced. Between 1857 and 1861, 50 million perforated examples were made.

For beginners: The perforated, post-1857 examples (Scott catalog no. 24) are a better bet, cataloging at around $50.

For experts: Mint examples of genuine 1851 printings go for tens of thousands of dollars.

For philatelists who think they have died and gone to heaven: Forget this issue and pick up a 1¢ Franklin from a later set: the one issued in 1868 with a Z grill. Grills were sets of indentations in the paper, designed to make ink soak in so that the stamps could not be reused. They were only applied to U.S. stamps in the late 1860s and early 1870s, after which the experiment was discontinued. (The idea didn't catch on internationally, either. Peru is the only other nation to treat its stamps this way.) Z grills are not shaped like a Z; they just happen to be in a series that starts with type A. Only two examples of this stamp are known to exist. One belongs to the New York Public Library, as part of the Benjamin K. Miller Collection; the other belongs to financier William Gross, who funded the (superb) redevelopment of the Smithsonian National Postal Museum.

4. THOMAS JEFFERSON 5¢, 1856
Scott catalog no. 12

DESIGNER: The lettering was by Henry Earle and the intricate frame by Cyrus Durand, using a geometric lathe of his own invention. The portrait was engraved by Joseph I. Pease based on a portrait by Gilbert Stuart.

PRINTER: Toppan, Carpenter, and Co. (John W. Casilear had left the business in 1854, to concentrate on painting romantic landscapes in the Hudson River School style.)

FIRST DATE OF ISSUE: March 15, 1856

NUMBER ISSUED: Around 150,000 of the original printing, with no perforations. Around 2,500,000 perforated examples between 1857 and 1861.

FOR BEGINNERS: Another expensive stamp, I fear. The original, imperforate ones cost over $500; post-1857, perforated examples about half this.

FOR EXPERTS: Different shades of this stamp have remarkably different values.

FOR PHILATELISTS WHO THINK THEY HAVE DIED AND GONE TO HEAVEN: The deepest red printing is called "Indian Red." It has its own Scott catalog number, 28A, and is worth $175,000 in mint condition.

5. ANDREW JACKSON "BLACK JACK" 2¢, 1863
Scott catalog no. 73

DESIGNER: James Macdonough, based on miniature of Jackson by John Wood Dodge
 PRINTER: National Bank Note Company
 FIRST DATE OF ISSUE: July 1, 1863
 NUMBER ISSUED: 256,000,000

FOR BEGINNERS: Phew! A stamp one can easily afford!

FOR EXPERTS: The Confederacy also issued stamps featuring Jackson—and actually got there first. A 2¢ green came out in March 1862, and the "Red Jack," which looks quite like the Black Jack (no "U.S." at the top, of course) but in bright red, was issued in May 1863.

FOR PHILATELISTS WHO THINK THEY HAVE DIED AND GONE TO HEAVEN: The stamps can be found on envelopes as "bisects," where they have been cut in half to represent 1¢ worth of postage.

6. James K. Polk 32¢, 1995
Scott catalog no. 2587

First date of issue: November 2, 1995
Number issued: 105,000,000

For beginners: Though it was not massively popular—critics at the time described it as "drab"—the stamp is easy to collect.

For everyone else: Not much to do here. Sit back and listen to "James K. Polk" by the band They Might Be Giants, which features an instrumental break in the middle on musical saw. The songwriters don't share my view of Polk, by the way.

7. Confederate 5¢, Jefferson Davis, 1862 (London Printing)
Scott catalog no. CS7

Designer: Jean Ferdinand Joubert de la Ferté
  Printer: Thomas de la Rue and Co. Ltd., London
  First date of issue: April 16, 1862
  Number issued: 12,000,000. A further 36,000,000 were printed in Richmond, Virginia.

For beginners: Despite its unusual historical interest, this stamp is not expensive.

For experts: The 1¢ Calhoun, which never came into use, was also printed in London. The stamp was orange, with frame and lettering both similar to that of the 5¢ Davis; 400,000 examples were made. This stamp can be bought for about $100.

FOR PHILATELISTS WHO THINK THEY HAVE DIED AND GONE TO HEAVEN: Confederate postmasters' provisionals are more interesting than the rebels' officially issued stamps. But most interesting of all, surely, is a stamp on envelope, inside which is a letter to or from the theater of war.

8. ABRAHAM LINCOLN 15¢, 1866
Scott catalog no. 77

DESIGNER: James Macdonough
    PRINTER: National Bank Note Company
    FIRST DATE OF ISSUE: April 15, 1866
    NUMBER ISSUED: 2,139,000

FOR BEGINNERS: Decent used copies of the stamp sell for about $40.

FOR EXPERTS: The stamp was issued with grills of type E and F. The former is quite rare, the latter less so.

FOR PHILATELISTS WHO THINK THEY HAVE DIED AND GONE TO HEAVEN: The 15¢ Lincoln was also issued with the Z grill. Only two examples exist—which makes them as rare as the 1¢ Franklin Z grill. Somehow the Franklin has become better known.

This may be because another Lincoln stamp exists in an even rarer form: There is only one known example of the 1869

90¢ Lincoln actually still on an envelope. Addressed to Mr. Bancroft at the Ice House, Calcutta, India, the unique envelope was stolen from a collector in 1977, then turned up in a Chicago stamp shop in 2006.

9. LOCOMOTIVE 3¢, 1869
Scott catalog no. 114

DESIGNER: James Macdonough
PRINTER: National Bank Note Company
FIRST DATE OF ISSUE: March 27, 1869
NUMBER ISSUED: 335,534,850

FOR BEGINNERS: Another nice, easy stamp to collect. The colors vary. It's worth paying a bit extra for a strong, clear printing rather than a washed-out one.

FOR EXPERTS: In 1875, the stamp was reissued, in much smaller quantities, to be shown at the 1876 World's Fair in Philadelphia. The 1875 reissues have no grills (almost all the 1869 originals have grills) and were printed on hard white paper, so the design stands out. Used copies of this are particularly rare.

FOR PHILATELISTS WHO THINK THEY HAVE DIED AND GONE TO HEAVEN: Full unused sheets of these stamps, issued to postmasters but never sold, still exist. There are 150 stamps on each sheet.

10. EDWIN M. STANTON 7¢, 1871
Scott catalog no. 138

DESIGNER: Butler Packard
 PRINTER: National Bank Note Company
 FIRST DATE OF ISSUE: March 6, 1871
 NUMBER ISSUED: 3,000,000. Two-thirds have grills, one-third do not.

FOR BEGINNERS: A decent used example should cost around $25.

FOR EXPERTS: A second printing of this stamp was carried out in 1873, by a new supplier, the Continental Bank Note Company. The 1870s were a time of fierce competition in the security printing industry; a third supplier, the American Bank Note Company, was also in the market. Continental printed about 2,500,000 7¢ Stantons.

FOR PHILATELISTS WHO THINK THEY HAVE DIED AND GONE TO HEAVEN: This series was also reprinted in 1875. For some reason, the reprints of this series were often cut apart with scissors, so an 1875 reprint that has been well cut, with four proper margins, is particularly valuable.

11. COLUMBUS 400TH ANNIVERSARY $5, 1893
Scott catalog no. 245

DESIGNER: Based on medal by Charles E. Barber
 PRINTER: American Bank Note Company. This company ended up winning the 1870s "war of the printers," taking over

its rivals and printing all U.S. stamps for over a decade. By 1893, however, its monopoly was being challenged again—this was the last issue it would print.

FIRST DATE OF ISSUE: January 2, 1893

NUMBER ISSUED: 27,350 printed; 21,844 sold

FOR BEGINNERS: Collecting a full set of Columbians can get expensive. The last three ($3, $4, and this $5) were all printed in very low quantities (around 20,000). The $1 and $2 weren't a lot better, with around 50,000 being printed of each. You can fill any spaces with the reissue from 1992, as long as you don't mind the lack of authenticity.

FOR THE EXPERT: Letters sent from the fair bore a special postmark, which read "World's Fair Station 1893," plus date and time of posting.

FOR PHILATELISTS WHO THINK THEY HAVE DIED AND GONE TO HEAVEN: The biggest block of $5 Columbus is of fourteen stamps. (It was verified as genuine in 1991, the 250,000th verification by the Philatelic Foundation.)

12. TRANS-MISSISSIPPI EXPOSITION COMMEMORATIVE $1, "WESTERN CATTLE IN STORM," 1898
Scott catalog no. 292

DESIGNER: Raymond Ostrander Smith, based on *The Vanguard*, a painting done in 1878 by Scottish artist John Mac-Whirter

PRINTER: Bureau of Engraving and Printing, Washington,

D.C. In 1894, the government bureau undercut private rivals in a bidding war and became the sole printer of America's stamps. It would hold a monopoly on this function for many years.

FIRST DATE OF ISSUE: June 17, 1898
NUMBER ISSUED: 56,900

FOR BEGINNERS: Another expensive stamp, with used examples costing around $400. As with the Columbians, one can cheat by filling spaces with the reissue of a hundred years later. The 1998 reissue is bicolored (as the 1898 issue was originally intended to be, but the Bureau was too busy printing bonds to finance the Spanish-American War, so ended up printing the series monochrome).

FOR PHILATELISTS WHO THINK THEY HAVE DIED AND GONE TO HEAVEN: First day covers exist for all the stamps in this series except the $2. FDCs of the $1 are extremely rare: An example recently sold for $150,000.

13. PAN-AMERICAN EXPOSITION 10¢, 1901
Scott catalog no. 299

DESIGNER: Raymond Ostrander Smith
FIRST DATE OF ISSUE: May 1, 1901
NUMBER ISSUED: 5,043,700

FOR BEGINNERS: At last, an affordable commemorative stamp and series!

FOR EXPERTS: First day covers exist for the 1¢, 2¢, and 5¢.

For philatelists who think they have died and gone to heaven: Being bicolored, these stamps have the potential for the frame and the vignette (the design in the middle) to be printed different ways up. Welcome to the surreal world of "inverts," a world of upside-down steamboats, railways, automobiles, and (later) aeroplanes. Welcome, also, to a world of extremely expensive bits of paper! Three of the pan-American series were misprinted in this way, the 1¢, 2¢, and 4¢. A recent sale of a set featuring one of each netted nearly $200,000.

14. Panama-Pacific Exposition
Commemorative 2¢, 1913
Scott catalog no. 398

Designer: Clair Aubrey Houston
First date of issue: January 18, 1913
Number issued: 503,713,086

For beginners: A nice, easy stamp to collect.

For experts: This stamp was printed in different shades. A darker "carmine lake" shade is rare—only forty examples are known to exist.

For the philatelist who thinks they have died and gone to heaven: This stamp was originally printed with "Gatun Lock" written where it now says "Panama Canal." However, the picture on the stamp is not of this lock but another one, the Pedro Miguel Locks. The error was spotted in time, and all the stamps printed with the mistake destroyed. Or were they . . . ?

15. 3¢ Victory stamp, 1919
Scott catalog no. 537

First date of issue: March 3, 1919
Number issued: 99,585,200

For beginners: Many poor examples of this stamp exist. Spend a few dollars more for a decent one.

For experts: As with the Canal stamp, this exists in various shades. Scott 537a, "deep red violet," is the rarest—but should not be bought without certification.

For philatelists who think they have died and gone to heaven: Few first day covers of this issue exist.

As we enter the 1920s, arguably the start of the "modern" age, the volume of stamp production increases. Techniques improve, too—though errors can still creep in. Once FDR gets into the White House, more commemoratives are issued. As a result of these changes, stamps from now on become cheaper to collect and more standard, and there are fewer by-ways for philatelists to journey down. I shall describe the stamps in less detail from here on—though the occasional quirk has to be mentioned.

16. Golden Gate definitive 20¢, 1923
Scott catalog no. 567

Designer: Clair Aubrey Houston, based on a painting by William A. Coulter.
   First date of issue: May 1, 1923
   Number issued: 1,077,488,777 between 1923 and 1931. From 1931, the stamp was issued with slightly bigger perforations: 672,906,900 of these were printed.

17. Lindbergh commemorative 3¢, 1927
Scott catalog no. C10

Designers: Clair Aubrey Houston and A. R. Meissner (an artist employed by the Bureau)
   First date of issue: June 18, 1927—less than a month after Lindbergh landed in Paris
   Number issued: 20,379,179

For philatelists who think they have died and gone to heaven: Forget this issue, and dream of owning an "Inverted Jenny" instead.

18. Kansas Overprint 8¢, 1929–30
Scott catalog no. 666

Original stamp designer: Clair Aubrey Houston
   First date of overprint issue: May 1, 1929
   Number issued: Records not kept

19. NATIONAL PARKS ISSUE 10¢, FARLEY SERIES, 1935 (IMPERFORATE, UNGUMMED)
Scott catalog no. 765

DESIGNER: Esther A. Richards
   FIRST DATE OF ISSUE: (Original stamp) October 8, 1935; (Farley reprint) March 15, 1935
   NUMBER ISSUED: (Original stamp) 18,874,300; (Farley reprint) 1,644,900

20. IWO JIMA ISSUE 3¢, 1945
Scott catalog no. 929

DESIGNER: Victor S. McCloskey Jr., based on a photograph by Joe Rosenthal
   FIRST DATE OF ISSUE: July 11, 1945
   NUMBER ISSUED: 137,321,000

21. UN PEACE CONFERENCE COMMEMORATIVE 5¢, 1945
Scott catalog no. 928

DESIGNER: Victor S. McCloskey Jr.
   FIRST DATE OF ISSUE: April 25, 1945
   NUMBER ISSUED: 75,500,000

22. SALUTING YOUNG AMERICA 3¢, 1948
Scott catalog no. 963

DESIGNER: Victor S. McCloskey Jr.
  FIRST DATE OF ISSUE: August 11, 1948
  NUMBER ISSUED: 77,800,500

23. NATO 4¢, 1959
Scott catalog no. 1127

DESIGNER: Stevan Dohanos
  FIRST DATE OF ISSUE: April 1, 1959
  NUMBER ISSUED: 122,493,280

24. CHRISTMAS 1963 5¢
Scott catalog no. 1240

DESIGNER: Lily Spandorf
  FIRST DATE OF ISSUE: November 1, 1963
  NUMBER ISSUED: 1,291,250,000

25. EMANCIPATION PROCLAMATION CENTENNIAL 5¢, 1963
Scott catalog no. 1233

DESIGNER: Georg Olden
  FIRST DATE OF ISSUE: August 16, 1963
  NUMBER ISSUED: 132,435,000

26. $1 Airlift stamp, 1968
Scott catalog no. 1341

Designer: Stevan Dohanos
  First date of issue: April 4, 1968
  Number issued: Not known

27. *Apollo 8* 6¢, 1969
Scott catalog no. 1371

Designer: Leonard E. Buckley, based on a photograph by Bill Anders
  First date of issue: May 5, 1969
  Number issued: 187,165,000

28. Sidney Lanier 8¢, 1972
Scott catalog no. 1446

Designer: William A. Smith
  First date of issue: February 3, 1972
  Number issued: 137,355,000

29. Energy Conservation 10¢, 1974
Scott catalog no. 1547

Designer: Robert W. Bode
  First date of issue: September 23, 1974
  Number issued: 148,850,000

30. Flag and Anthem Issue, 18¢, 1981
Scott catalog no. 1891

Designer: Peter Cocci
    First date of issue: April 24, 1981
    Number issued: Not known

31. Desert Shield/Desert Storm commemorative 29¢, 1991
Scott catalog no. 2551

Designer: Jack Williams, based on medal by Nadine Russell
    Printer: J. W. Fergusson Co., for Stamp Ventures Inc.
Toward the end of the twentieth century, the printing of some commemoratives was tendered out to private companies.
    First date of issue: July 2, 1991
    Number issued: 200,003,000

32. Legends of American Music, Elvis Presley 29¢, 1993
Scott catalog no. 2721

Designer: Mark Stutzman
    Printer: Bureau of Engraving and Printing
    First date of issue: January 8, 1993
    Number issued: 517,000,000
In 1992, ballots were put out in U.S. post offices, asking the public to vote whether they wanted a young or an older Elvis on a forthcoming stamp. More than 1.2 million people replied, and the vote was over 75 percent for the younger image.

In 2006, the USPS did a survey of households to find out which stamps had been most kept by the public as collectables. The 1993 Elvis won by a huge margin, with an estimated 124 million. (Second was a then-recent series, Wonders of America, of which 87 million stamps were kept.)

33. COMPUTER TECHNOLOGY COMMEMORATIVE 32¢, 1996
Scott catalog no. 3106

DESIGNERS: Nancy Skolos and Tom Wedell
   PRINTER: Ashton Potter (USA) Ltd.
   FIRST DATE OF ISSUE: October 8, 1996
   NUMBER ISSUED: 93,512,000

34. HEROES OF 2001 FIRST CLASS, 2002
Scott catalog no. B2

DESIGNER: Derry Noyes, using a photograph by Thomas E. Franklin
   PRINTER: Ashton Potter (USA) Ltd.
   FIRST DATE OF ISSUE: June 7, 2002
   NUMBER ISSUED: 204,000,000

35. BEIJING OLYMPICS 42¢, 2008
Scott catalog no. 4334

DESIGNER: Clarence Lee
   FIRST DATE OF ISSUE: June 19, 2008
   NUMBER ISSUED: Not known

INDEX